D1369943

Theory and Research in Administration

THEORY AND
RESEARCH IN
Administration

/

ANDREW W. HALPIN

Washington University

THE MACMILLAN COMPANY / NEW YORK

COLLIER–MACMILLAN LIMITED / LONDON

To Roald F. Campbell, Educational Statesman

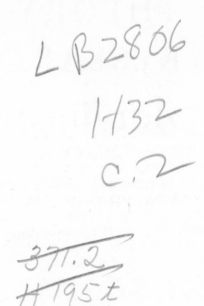

© Copyright, Andrew W. Halpin, 1966

First Printing

Library of Congress catalog card number: 66-11578

THE MACMILLAN COMPANY, NEW YORK
COLLIER–MACMILLAN CANADA, LTD., TORONTO, ONTARIO

Printed in the United States of America

FOREWORD

It is a personal and a professional privilege to be invited to write the foreword to this book. Andrew W. Halpin was a colleague of mine, first at Ohio State University and later at the University of Chicago. We shared a number of teaching and writing endeavors. In these many relationships I found Andrew Halpin to be a hard-headed empiricist and a tender-hearted friend. He is not an easy man to live with. Almost each day he commands time to share his reading, to explore an idea, to penetrate a facade, to resist opportunism, to recognize intellectual integrity.

As his colleague I saw not only his finished writing, much of which appears in this volume, but I saw also the gestation period, the quick insights, the careful reading of others, the design of investigation, the meticulous gathering of data, the honing of each word, the deliberate stretching of his audience.

To the new movement in administration Halpin is a major contributor. His work has contributed to the extension of knowledge about organization behavior. In Parsonian terms he has dealt chiefly with the managerial level of organizations, and to this aspect of administration he has applied his social-psychological insights. He would disavow the development of a theory of administration, but Part One of this volume is conceptual in nature and will stimulate anyone interested in theoretical formulations. In Part Two he reveals himself as the empirical researcher seeking to describe the world of administration as it is "out there."

But the material in this book suggests that Halpin is more than a social scientist. His "Eloquence of Behavior" and his "Ways of Knowing" reveal that he is also a humanist who would heed the poet, the playwright, and the novelist as they describe man "in the round." Both as a humanist and as a social scientist Halpin has

v

found the world wanting and some of its actors less than genuine. These perceptions have led him into the realm of social criticism. Perhaps as part of this same concern he has sensed that some administrators and some scholars of administration are not authentic. I, for one, hope he will pursue the idea of authenticity so brilliantly introduced at the conclusion of his study of organizational climate.

It is my pleasure to commend this book to students of administration. It is red meat, not pablum. One's own preconceptions may be attacked, but new vistas will also be opened. Educational administration will be seen not only as a field of practice but also as a field of study intimately related to the broader world of scholarship.

Roald F. Campbell

PREFACE

During the past decade, graduate training for educational administrators has been marked by a dramatic change in emphasis. The "new movement," which began in about 1954, has stressed the importance of administrative theory, has drawn heavily upon research from the social sciences, has recognized that educational administration is not an entity distinct from other forms of administration, and has eschewed research of a "nakedly empirical" type in favor, instead, of hypothetico-deductive research that is rooted in theory. As is always the case with any innovation or with any social change, this change has not taken place on an even front. Even today there are professors of educational administration at many universities who teach their courses with blithe innocence of the ideas introduced by the "new movement." At the other extreme is the University of Chicago, which has been strongly identified with the new approach for at least a decade. Other programs that are guided by the points of view presented in this book can be found at such centers as the Claremont Graduate School, Cornell University, Washington University (St. Louis), and the University of Wisconsin.

Because of a set of fortuitous circumstances, I have had the opportunity of being closely associated with the "new movement" since its outset. The material in the chapters that comprise the present book has all been published elsewhere. These chapters were written at different points during an eight-year period; they reflect my views and interests in the field of educational administration. Colleagues in various parts of the country have urged me to collect this material between the covers of a single book. This is that book.

The order of the chapters is not chronological in respect to the dates at which the respective chapters were first published. Nor do the contents of the book deal with but a single theme. When I examined my interests during the past decade, I found that they could be grouped into four categories.

I—The nature of theory and how it should be applied to research on administration.

II—Substantive research on administration.

III—The study of the relationship between verbal and non-verbal behavior, with a focus upon what happens when a "receiver" of a message discerns dissonance between the verbal and nonverbal outputs of a "sender."

IV—Reflections upon the nature of scientific inquiry and the pertinence of these ideas for the training of research workers in education and in the behavioral sciences.

The four parts of the book deal respectively with these four categories.

Because each chapter was written originally for a specific audience, and because these audiences differed markedly from each other, I have necessarily modified my writing style accordingly. Thus, Part Two (Chapters 3 and 4) represents straightforward reports of research. Chapter 5 was presented initially as a lecture to a university-wide audience. The points I make in this chapter are highly pertinent for the training of administrators, but they also have significance for human beings as human beings. Hence, the style of this chapter is far lighter than the style I have used in Chapter 2. Likewise, Part Four is composed of what can be construed best as three essays that contrapuntally pursue a single theme.

I deliberately have not revised the papers presented here. To take such unfair advantage of the omniscience of retrospect is tempting, but to submit to this temptation is to become guilty of creating pseudo-events that violate the integrity (or truth, if you wish) of those events that did happen. The actual historical development of the ideas that appear within any discipline can be traced through the reports and publications of those men who, in the very act of writing, *invent* the course of that development. Each invention of this kind is usually derived from primary sources, or from primary observations. Or, at least it should be. But, for a variety

of reasons, there are other men—themselves not the "inventors"—
who purport to trace the development of ideas within a discipline,
but who, instead, tend to *reconstruct* what actually happened. This
reconstruction is done subtly, and perhaps even unwittingly, by
omitting a reference here and there, by magnifying the significance
of certain contributions, and by slanting material so that no member of an editorial advisory committee and no member of a "power
network" (i.e., somebody who *may* at some future date be "useful"
to the writer) can possibly take offense. The result of such "history" is usually a bland, homogenized caricature of what actually
has happened. Even as I prefer not to distort what other investigators have said, in order to serve a present purpose for myself,
so too have I refused to "doctor" what I have said in the past in
order to make those past remarks more consonant with my present
beliefs. Thus, for example, in Chapter 4 I have noted that the
concept of *Consideration,* as presented originally in Chapter 3,
has certain distinct shortcomings. But I have not taken advantage
of the benefit of hindsight by rewriting the section on *Consideration*
(in Chapter 3) in such fashion as to suggest that I understood the
limitations of this concept in 1956, when, indeed, the specific
limitation discussed in Chapter 4 did not occur to me until 1962.
In brief, I have allowed each chapter to stand "on the record" as
it was written originally.

The chapters of this book were written with a focus on educational administration, but the research findings and observations
are generalizable to other areas of administration as well. I have
consistently maintained that the "g-factor" in all forms of administration is sufficiently large to justify the study of administration
qua administration. For example, the leadership studies described
in Chapter 3 were begun as part of an Air Force research project
on crew composition. Several techniques developed by this project
were later applied in industrial, educational, and public administration settings. Similarly, the research technique described in
Chapter 4 has been applied to a hospital setting. Furthermore, I
believe that the findings reported in Chapter 4 have sufficient generalizability to warrant replications of this research within industrial and corporation settings. The material in Chapter 5 has been
used in executive training programs in industry, in education, and

in public administration. Finally, in Part Four I am not speaking restrictively to educational administrators. Here I raise questions that are pertinent to all areas of educational research, but questions that should be equally provocative for many social scientists. Accordingly, although the material in this book has been derived within the context of educational administration, it applies to other areas of administration as well.

My professional discipline is psychology. My earlier experience was in clinical psychology, but I currently identify myself as a social psychologist. How, then, did I get interested in educational administration? And how did I get the opportunity to participate, from the outset, in the exciting changes that have accompanied the growth of the "new movement" in educational administration? The answer is simple: in 1953 I had the good fortune of meeting Dr. Roald F. Campbell, now Dean of the School of Education at the University of Chicago. He, of course, has been one of the most prominent leaders of the "new movement," and he was one of the very first professors of educational administration to welcome suggestions from social scientists. He sponsored my first research in the area of educational administration, and in one way or another, directly or indirectly, it is he who has made it possible for me to participate in this "new movement." To Dean Roald F. Campbell I owe my single, greatest professional debt. By dedicating this book to him, I can express only a token of my deep gratitude for all that he has done for me, both as a colleague and as a friend.

A. W. H.

CONTENTS

FIGURES

TABLES

Theory and Research in Administration

Generalizations, one is told, are dangerous. So is life, for that matter, and it is built up on generalizations—from the earliest effort of the adventurer who dared to eat a second berry because the first had not killed him. So I will stick to my generalizing. . . .

Freya Stark

FROM *The Lycian Shore* (New York: Harcourt, Brace & World, Inc., 1956), p. 103.

PART ONE

Theory in Administration

1

The Development of Theory in Educational Administration[1]

Our purpose is to communicate with each other to try to develop useful theory in educational administration. A seminar in which professors of educational administration and social scientists work together is salutary; it illustrates the progress made in the past decade—progress characterized by a marked change of emphasis in the training of administrators. Traditionally, our training programs have stressed the "practical" and have concerned themselves more with techniques than with understanding. During the postwar period, however, administrators have become increasingly aware of the role of theory and have come to recognize the contributions that social scientists can make to our understanding of educational administration. The superintendent's job and the jobs of principals and supervisors have been viewed afresh in the light of recent human-relations research. Those of us responsible for training administrators have welcomed research findings on leadership and group behavior, and we have found ourselves drawing heavily upon insights into administration derived from other disciplines. But at the same time we are appalled by the poverty of theory within our own field and dismayed by the extent to which our own research has been anchored to "naked empiricism." Out of this realization has grown our present attempt to develop theory in educational administration.

RECENT CHANGES IN VIEWS ON ADMINISTRATION

Several influences during the postwar period have contributed to this realization. Three in particular deserve mention. The first was the establishment of the National Conference for Professors of Educational Administration (NCPEA) in 1947. This group, through its annual meetings and other activities, has facilitated communication among those who train administrators and has fostered higher and higher standards of training.

The second influence—one is tempted to say "revolution"— came about through the Kellogg Foundation's support of the Cooperative Program in Educational Administration (CPEA). This program, begun in 1950, provided much-needed support for research and development. Among other things, it opened new avenues of communication between educational administrators and the members of other disciplines. Professors of educational administration and social scientists began to talk to each other. This did not come easily, for each group was wary of the other. As members of these two groups discovered that they were not speaking the same language and found that their orientations were strangely different, their initial wariness gave way to varying shades of frustration, rejection, and hostility. It took time to overcome these negative attitudes, to develop ways of communicating with each other, and to develop the mutual respect necessary for efficient cooperation. Some of the original eight CPEA centers have made substantial progress in this regard.

The third influence is that of the University Council for Educational Administration (UCEA), established in 1956. Even during its first year, the UCEA, along with the Educational Testing Service and Teachers College, sponsored a large research project designed to develop measures of the performance of school administrators.[2] The financial support for this project comes primarily from the United States Office of Education, but also there will be contributions from Educational Testing Service, Teachers College, and others. The UCEA is also cooperating with the University of Chicago in sponsoring this seminar. Several other UCEA projects are contemplated.

As in any form of social change, progress has been slow and along an uneven front. Three recent books reflect the present state of affairs.[3] First is the signal book by Coladarci and Getzels, *The Use of Theory in Educational Administration*,[4] published in 1955 and stimulated—at least, in part—by the authors' participation as consultants at the 1954 NCPEA meeting in Denver. Coladarci and Getzels call attention to the dearth of theory in educational administration, emphasize the integrity of theory and practice, and propose one approach to a theory of educational administration. This important monograph has not yet had much time to "take"; it will require a few years for its full impact to be appreciated. The second book, sponsored by the American Association of School Administrators, is Moore's *Studies in School Administration: A Report on the CPEA*.[5] Moore, in reviewing the publications that have appeared thus far from the eight CPEA centers, observes that few of the investigations are theory-oriented. The bulk of the studies reviewed are exhortations, how-to-do-it prescriptions, catalogues of opinion, or normative "status" investigations which do not permit us to generalize beyond the immediate data. The third book, sponsored by the NCPEA and edited by Campbell and Gregg, is *Administrative Behavior in Education*.[6] Here again, the contributing authors found a lack of theory-oriented research. However, Griffiths[7] in his chapter has taken steps in working toward a theory of educational administration. The current gloomy side of the theory picture that these three books reflect is of less importance than what they herald for future, more constructive efforts to develop better theory. Note that all three books appeared within the space of two years. The significant point is that they appeared at all; they examine issues that would not have come within the purview of educational administration prior to the end of World War II.

This brief historical perspective has bearing upon our task in this seminar because our progress may be impeded by the same issues that have cropped up from time to time in the NCPEA, CPEA, and UCEA. Several of these issues were epitomized in the communication problem that beset the authors who produced the NCPEA book. A few of the contributors sought to employ the social scientists' point of view and stressed the importance of theory; other contributors held to a more "practical" orientation. The writers found that they often were talking past each other. A demonstration of good will among the participants and superb tact on the part of the editors helped to achieve constructive communication between the adherents of these two groups. The development of better communication and understanding among the members of that writers' group is a story in itself and one that would be well worth examining as a guide for other groups engaged in cooperative enterprises of this kind.

We are faced with a similar problem. Our seminar group is composed of people from two major backgrounds: educational administration and social science. What can we learn from the experience of the NCPEA writers' group that will help us accomplish our present task? Perhaps by identifying the issues that have baffled others we can place ourselves in a position to approach these problems with greater rationality.

Our problems appear to arise from three major sources which we may classify roughly as substantive, communicative, and motivational. These sources of difficulty are not distinct; they overlap in subtle and intricate ways, and in a sense all revolve around problems of communication. However, let us pretend that there are no interaction effects among them.

THE SUBSTANTIVE PROBLEMS

In our efforts to develop theory in educational administration, we have been impeded by three substantive problems: (1) We have not been clear about the meaning of theory. (2) We have tended to be preoccupied with taxonomies and have confused these with theories. (3) We have not been sure of the precise domain of the theory we are seeking to devise. Let us examine each of these in turn.

The construction of a theory demands an act of creative imagination. This is a tough assignment that many of us are not equal to, nor can we get help from a how-to-do-it manual. Theories cannot be produced on demand; they evolve, and they evolve in many shapes and in many different degrees of precision. The building blocks of which they are composed—the constructs, the postulates, the assumptions—may be molar or molecular. Thus, Parsons' "input" and "output" of social organizations[8] and Hemphill's leadership acts[9] are concepts of different orders. A theory may be broad and eclectic in its range, or narrow and specific. Shartle,[10] for example, in formulating his theoretical framework for the studies of behavior in organizations, has deliberately sought constructs from a variety of disciplines and has sketched his ideas on a broad canvas. The components of a theory may also differ in the ease with which testable hypotheses can be adduced from the postulated model. Thus Getzels and Guba[11] have tested empirically several specific hypotheses about role-conflict derived from their model. On the other hand, the tridimensional concept of the *job*, the *man*, and the *social setting*, to which Griffiths[12] refers, is essentially a taxonomy rather than a theoretical model in the strict sense of the term. For this reason, it does not lend itself to the derivation of specific, testable hypotheses.

Consequently, it is not surprising that we may sometimes wonder about the meaning of theory. Theories do not come in a standard brand; we find them in packages of different size and shape, wrapped in different ways, and labeled differently. One must respect these differences and must recognize that theories, like the human beings who create them, follow different courses of development and grow at different rates. We must avoid rejecting a theoretical proposal simply because it still has a few rough edges. *But it is one thing to respect these differences; it is another to deny them.* The crux of the problem is that the term "theory" carries the burden of too many different meanings. Fiegl has stated the problem well:

> A set of propositions may be called a "theory" for various reasons. It may be because these propositions are highly inferential —either because of the sweep of their generalizations or because of the remoteness of the concepts from those of direct observation. That is, we tend to regard assumptions as theoretical if they are only very incompletely or very indirectly confirmed. This customary terminology does not altogether recommend itself for the simple reason that a well-confirmed set of propositions could then not be called a theory. Yet, such is the ambiguity

of our terms, that by a "theory" in the empirical sciences we may mean anything from a style or jargon of mere descriptions, from a mere classification, inventory, or typology to a full fledged hypothetico-deductive system; from a bold guess or a suggestive working hypothesis, a program of research, to an elaborate model in either analogical or purely abstract mathematical terms.[13]

In educational administration this issue is complicated even further by the fact that some writers have used this term in the sense of "value theory," to refer not to how administrators *do* behave but to how they *ought* to behave. This confoundment between the "is's" and the "ought's" of behavior is responsible for a greater failure in communication between educators and social scientists than any other issue. No one will deny that we need normative standards—in the ethical meaning of the term— for how administrators *ought* to behave, but these prescriptions do not constitute a theory. These standards cannot be secured through the methods that we must use for constructing a theoretical model in science. In this model we must confine our attention to how administrators *do* behave. In short, the description of events and their evaluation must be kept distinct. To state the issue in other terms: the immediate purpose of research is to enable us to make more accurate predictions of events, not to prescribe preferential courses of human action.

Miller[14] has noted our problems of communication in educational administration and has urged us to use words with greater precision. One place at which we might start is with the concept of "theory." Specifically, we may want to examine the advantages and the disadvantages of restricting this term to the meaning assigned to it by Feigl:

> In order to provide for a terminology which will not constantly involve us in a tangle of confusions, I propose to define a "theory" as a set of assumptions from which can be derived by purely logico-mathematical procedures, a larger set of empirical laws. The theory thereby furnishes an explanation of these empirical laws and unifies the originally relatively heterogeneous areas of subject matter characterized by those empirical laws. Even though it must be admitted that there is no sharp line of demarcation (except a purely arbitrary one) between theoretical

assumptions and empirical laws, the distinction, at least in the sense of a gradation, is illuminating from a methodological point of view.

One more terminological suggestion may help: Let us speak of scientific explanation wherever more specific or more descriptive statements are derived from more general or more hypothetical assumptions.[15]

Our first major problem, then, in developing theory in educational administration is that we do not share a common understanding of the meaning of theory.

Note that according to Feigl's definition, a taxonomy, or classificatory scheme, is not a theory. To say that a proposal is only a taxonomy is not to disparage it, for even in the physical and biological sciences we find taxonomies that have served as useful precursors to theory. The difficulty is that taxonomies can become alluring in their own right and that sometimes we are tempted into offering them as "genuine" theories.

There are three related snares that we must watch out for in establishing taxonomies. First, the number of classifications we establish is limited only by the size of our vocabulary. The cogent question is whether the verbal categories we posit correspond to events in the "real" world, whether the events assigned to these categories are in fact mutually exclusive. It requires no great imagination to produce new sets of verbal categories—lists of skills and competencies, and various tabulations to describe the components of the administrative process. But for research purposes we must still demonstrate that one set of categories permits us to make a better prediction of events than another. The merit of our rubrics must be determined not by their Trendex ratings but by the quality of hypotheses that can be generated from them, by the extent to which they improve the accuracy of our predictions.

The second snare in using taxonomies is that we run the risk, say, of mixing oranges and battleships. We seldom are sure that the rubrics we have established are at a similar level of ordinality. There is the further danger that we may mix phenotypic and genotypic categories quite indiscriminately. The essential snag, of course, is that the taxonomic method—as we have ordinarily used it in education—is based upon the Aristotelian as opposed to the Galilean mode of thought.[16] The taxonomic approach therefore fails to take advantage of the very shift in emphasis which has brought about such great progress in the physical and biological sciences.

The third snare in using taxonomies is the fallacy of assuming that, if we juxtapose two or more taxonomic schemata, we can somehow or other produce a theory. We discover, however, that even when we force two taxonomies into mating position, nothing happens: the conception of theory demands greater fertility than taxonomies possess. Why? Because the classification of similarities and differences does not in itself permit us to specify the *order* of the phenomena we study or to define the relationships that obtain among them. This must be accomplished by a creative act of a different kind. Taxonomies have their place, but they do not automatically grow into theories. Nor do all taxonomies have good potentials for being developed into theories. Much depends upon the type of events that are classified and the exclusiveness of the categories into which the events are sorted. But even the best of taxonomies, or the best two or more taxonomies taken in conjunction, will not yield a hypothetico-deductive theory.

Much research energy in educational administration has been dissipated through the failure to recognize the snares of the taxonomic method. One need only examine the bulk of the studies conducted through the CPEA. We can charge off our early mistakes as "good learning experience," but it is difficult to condone dogged persistence in repeating these same mistakes.

In sum, then, our second major problem in developing a theory of educational administration is that we have tended to be too preoccupied with taxonomic methods.

Finally, we have not been sure of the precise domain of the theory we are seeking. Administration is a practical art, pursued by men in a world of action. Yet a theory of administration can be practical only in a limited sense: it can permit us to declare that if you do *x*, consequence *a* will result; if you do *y*, consequence *b* will result. However, the theory itself cannot give us information on whether consequence *a* or consequence *b* is more *desirable* for a given organization at a given time. Accordingly, when we say that we want to develop theory in educational administration, it is important for us to find answers to certain questions. What is the domain of the theory that we are trying to forge? What kinds of predictions are we seeking to make? To make these predictions with sufficient accuracy to warrant our efforts, how molar can we afford to make the components of the theory? How molecular? It is not enough to say that we intend to make better predictions of behavior and of other events; we must also specify the level of events and the kinds of behavior with which we propose to deal.

This is the place, too, where we must be sure to keep our "is's" and "ought's" straight, where we must be prepared to take all our hidden value assumptions out into the open and make them explicit.

Hence, there are three major questions about theory that we must examine. The first is: What is the minimum number of value assumptions we must invoke in order to construct a satisfactory theory of educational administration? And the corollary: Can we agree on these assumptions? The second question concerns the molar-molecular issue. Should we seek to articulate molar theories, such as Parsons' and Shartle's, with theories of a more molecular type, such as Hemphill's and Getzels'? If we agree that this is desirable, then how do we achieve articulation? The third question relates to possible differences between *administration* and the special province of educational administration. Obviously, business administration, hospital administration, public administration, and educational administration have many characteristics in common. To the extent that we can, indeed, identify a *g* (or general) factor, a theory of administration is meaningful. But there are *s* (or specific) factors, too, that distinguish educational administration from other forms of administration. These *g* and *s* factors require examination.

These, then, are the major substantive problems that impede the development of theory in educational administration. It will not be enough to "solve" these problems; they will have to be "resolved." And resolved means re-solved—solved again and again. Now, let us turn to the major communicative issues.

THE PROBLEMS OF COMMUNICATION

Even in this brief attempt to discuss the problem of developing theory in administration, questions about the use of language arise. Practitioners and theorists must work together in developing theory and must be able to communicate with each other. Unfortunately, because of differences in their training, background, and day-to-day sphere of operations, the members of these two groups tend to think about events in different ways—and with different time-perspectives. The way they think, the concepts and ideas they use, and the conceptual frameworks within which they organize their ideas are different. This does not mean that one way is right and the other wrong. Each can be right for its own purpose. Nor does it necessarily mean that the two approaches are irreconcilable.

We must guard against castigating the practitioner as being purely empirical. The general run of practitioner is no more purely empirical than many social scientists. There are scientists so utterly empirical that their research never gets off the ground. On the other hand, there are scientists and administrators, too, who consistently soar in the clouds. They forget that every theory must be rooted in the actual world of experience. In cloud soaring, the scientist has an advantage: he can get away with flights into space for a longer time than the administrator; he is not as promptly called to account. But he, too, must eventually relate his theory to the "real" world.

The scientist has no monopoly on theory: effective administrators have invariably based their decisions upon some kind of theory of administration. The administrator, however, does not usually state this theory explicitly; he may not even recognize it as such. The explicitness with which a theory is stated contributes to the ease with which we can examine it, subject it to criticism, and modify it. But let us not make the mistake of assuming that explicitness, in itself, guarantees a better theory. A good theory can suffer through lack of explicitness, but a poor theory, no matter how explicit, will remain sterile.

When the practicing administrator and the social scientist encounter each other, several intriguing reactions occur. The scientist is quick to see shortcomings in how administrators perceive their problems. He notes especially the lack of "operationally defined" terms and the intermingling of facts and value judgments. Consequently, the probing character of the scientist's questions can help the administrator better understand his own problems. The administrator, however, does not always detect shortcomings in how social scientists formulate problems. He often allows himself to be too impressed by the scientist's technical jargon; he is afraid that by asking questions he may expose his naïveté. This is unfortunate, for hokum can suffuse the scientist's language just as easily as it can bog down the language of the practical man. Yet because science is a sacred cow in our culture, the pronouncements of scientists have been sanctified. Nor has this situation been relieved by scientists who trade upon the obscurity of their own jargon. What we forget is that no change in the wording can make a trivial idea profound; we sometimes mistake complexity for profundity.

The administrator's hesitance in questioning the scientist results in a loss for both groups. The social scientist loses the wealth of ideas that practical men can contribute; he loses an important feedback on his own theorizing. Similarly, the administrator loses either by contenting himself with a superficial acceptance of what the scientist has to say or by categorically rejecting as impractical all that the scientist has to offer. In either event, the schism between the two groups is made more pronounced. Despite pious protests on both sides that theory and practice are an integrity, these adjurations become an empty catechism, while each group, *de facto*, continues to play its own game by itself.

Each set of players has its own defense mechanism. The scientist becomes increasingly disdainful in casting his pearls of wisdom—and I have chosen this metaphor deliberately because of the attitudes of many social scientists. The scientist concludes that it is not his responsibility to communicate his ideas clearly to the ultimate consumer. On the other hand, the practitioner consoles himself with the knowledge that he is on the *real* firing line, that what he contributes to his school system is more important than any misty theory.

To circumvent these language difficulties, we must be sure that we understand the referents of the concepts we use. This understanding can be achieved only through patient and respectful questioning and cross-questioning. We shall have to learn to be tolerant with each other, and we must be willing to ask questions that appear naïve. Naïve questions are disarming; they puncture the balloon of hokum that gives our jargon a false impression of substance. In addition to patience and respect, it would be well for us to bring to our task a good sense of humor. In many ways administrators and scientists take themselves too seriously. What we need most, perhaps, is the freshness of approach that marked the little boy in *The Emperor's New Clothes.*

We already agree on the interdependence of practice and theory. Incantations on this score need not be repeated; we must, however, vivify this point through a rich supply of concrete examples, so that administrators will be better able to relate their day-to-day experiences to appropriate theoretical frameworks. We need to build bridges between our theories and live, concrete case material. Sargent and Belisle[17] and Griffiths[18] have made a start in this direction.

THE PROBLEMS OF MOTIVATION

The third source of problems in developing a theory of educational administration is motivational: what are our personal motives in working on this problem? This is a delicate issue, but it demands examination.

Administrators and social scientists alike must guard against personal motives that are less than lofty. We are part of our culture, and there are values in our society that can lead us astray in our effort to develop a theory. The present comments will be confined to only three of these values. First, as we noted earlier, is the high value our society places on Science, with a capital S. The second and third values have been identified by Shartle in his list of value dimensions.[19] The second is newness—that new ideas and things are better than older ones. The third is change—that frequent changes are better than infrequent ones.

People in the advertising business know how to capitalize upon all three of these values. By putting a TV pitchman into a white coat they give a greater credence to their claim for THE BIG CHANGE: Wheezies, with their NEW scientific filter, with 20,972.68 separate filter traps, will not produce lung cancer. Observe the shrewd touch of including the .68 filters; this "accuracy" makes the statement more scientific.

In the world of everyday affairs we are all barraged by appeals to change to something new, appeals often bolstered by the argument that the new is more scientific. This applies to detergents, automobiles, and movements in education. For example, there is a tendency in education to join new movements not so much because of their intrinsic soundness, but simply because they are new. "Progressive" education, the look-and-say method of reading, and group dynamics have each, in turn, been embraced with greater enthusiasm than understanding. Fads and styles in education, like the length of women's skirts, have had their ups and downs and have been pursued accordingly. We would like to hope that our pursuit of theory in educational administration is based upon appeals of less transitory revelation. Our task deserves a stronger commitment than this.

However, one must be wary of succumbing to such temptation. For example—and with no intention of presumption—John Dewey and Kurt Lewin were less dogmatic and less zealous about their own ideas than were their disciples. Consequently, our progress in developing useful theory in administration may depend, at least in part, upon our ability to keep this endeavor from being viewed as a new *movement*. Progress will be steadier and more constructive if we can discourage as prospective co-workers those eager individuals who, in perceiving the effort as a new bandwagon, aspire to increased status by being among the first to jump on it.

To repeat, our purpose is to enrich our understanding of administration. The fact that our effort to devise theory is new, that it reflects change, and that it wears the white cloak of science guarantees neither the achievement nor the intrinsic merit of our objective. Although the values of science, newness, and change have a positive side, they can also become meritricious. Consequently, our effort should not be construed simply as a new gimmick for educational administration, nor should it be proffered as a panacea.

Likewise, we must not let our ideas degenerate into slogans.

Expressions such as "research design," "action research," "group dynamics," and "the whole child" have been used so loosely and with such abandon that they have been debauched of meaning. "Administrative theory" will become another empty slogan if we use it as a rallying cry and proselytize in its name.

Some of us will need to examine our motives rather carefully. Are we seeking a better *understanding* of theory, or are we trying to *promote* the idea of theory? These motives are starkly different. In seeking a better understanding of theory, and through patient application to the development of better theory, we shall gain greater acceptance for this approach. But this acceptance will come about through the merit of what we actually accomplish, not through claims of what we intend to accomplish. Neither a particular theory nor the *idea of theory* are things to be sold, to be marketed as an advertiser might market a new breakfast cereal.

Most administrators develop skillful techniques to secure support for the programs they initiate. This often is necessary in education, and for this reason some promotional ability on the part of the administrator is useful. But because these promotional skills have proven effective in other areas, a few of us may be tempted to apply them to the present endeavor. This would be a mistake, since it would reflect motives alien to our purpose. Our gains must be measured by the integrity of the ideas we generate, not by the number of supporters we enlist. In education we have paid so much obeisance to the dogmas of democratic method that we have failed to stipulate those areas where the method does not apply; we have failed to observe, for example, that the merit of a theory cannot be assayed by majority vote.

Social scientists, too, are not innocent of contaminated motives. Few are as crass as one former colleague who declared, "A theory is better than money in the bank. You can't get ahead in this field unless you publish a theory—*any* theory." The promotion system in American universities, with its premium upon the length of a professor's publication list, does little to discourage this attitude. Furthermore, Professor Zilch likes to be able to refer to Zilch's theory even if it consists of nothing more than two fugitive ideas held together with Scotch tape. As Zilch, or one of his brethren, once declaimed, "I don't care whether they understand me, damn me, or praise me, just as long as they quote me." These premises lead to a preoccupation with theory for the sake of theory. The theorist becomes concerned chiefly about the elegance of his creation and is motivated by the admiration he expects from other theorists who are playing this same narcissistic game.

The theory, of course, is only a model, and it has no more reality than its creator endows upon it. Bross's observation on this point is pertinent:

> There is another very grave danger in the use of models. After a scientist plays for a long time with a given model he may become attached to it, just as a child may become, in the course of time, very attached to a doll (which is also a model). A child may become so devoted to the doll that she insists that her doll is a real baby, and some scientists become so devoted to their model (especially if it is a brain child) that they will insist that this model *is* the real world.[20]

When social scientists and administrators come together there is a danger that the negative aspects of their motives will be accentuated. The scientists, not quite prepared to answer the questions of practical administrators, may tend to regress to the "theory for the sake of theory" position. The administrators, on the other hand, following the line of least action, may be inclined to support the *idea* of theory without fully comprehending its meaning. The interplay of these defense mechanisms can create for both groups an illusion of greater agreement than actually exists.

One purpose of administrators and scientists working together is to provide better reality-testing for their ideas; without this, the scientific method sacrifices its most important self-corrective feature. Thus, continuing the quotation from Bross, we find:

> Now things are not this bad at the scientific level largely because of the self-corrective features of the sequential process of model-making which provide a periodic return to the real world after each excursion into the symbolic world. The test of the model acknowledges, as it were, the supremacy of the real world. If the model fails to predict what will happen in the real world, it is the model that must give way. This is the standard of scientific sanity.[21]

This standard will guard us against a search for *the* theory of educational administration and will help us recognize the possibility of alternative explanations. The scientist's predicament in this regard has been nicely stated by Einstein:

> In our endeavor to understand reality we are somewhat like a man trying to understand the mechanism of a closed watch. He sees the face and the moving hands, even hears it ticking, but he has no way of opening the case. If he is ingenious he may form some picture of a mechanism which could be responsible for all the things he observes, but he may never be quite sure his picture is the only one which could explain his observations. He will never be able to compare his picture with the real mechanism and he cannot even imagine the possibility or the meaning of such a comparison. But he certainly believes that, as his knowledge increases, his picture of reality will become simpler and simpler and will explain a wider and wider range of his sensuous impressions.[22]

Thus, as various theories of administration are presented to us, we need not ask, which is right? Each may help us make better predictions of events, and for this reason may appear "good" or "right." But note, as Einstein observes, that the scientist can never be quite sure his picture is the only one which could explain his observations. The fact is that we can never open the case to find out what really makes the watch tick.

This should teach all of us concerned with theory development some sense of humility, a sense less conspicuous among social scientists than among physicists and biologists. Specifically, we may do well to examine the principle of complementarity that Niels Bohr has enunciated in the field of atomic theory.[23] This principle, in slightly paraphrased form, states: The use of certain concepts in the description of nature automatically excludes the use of other concepts, which, however, in another connection are equally necessary for a description of the phenomenon.[24] From this perspective, the dilemma of free will versus causality is resolved; both "explanations" are needed, and in their own right both are tenable. The application of Bohr's principle to the social sciences has not been examined—let alone spelled out. But if we view various theories of administration in the spirit of Bohr's principle of complementarity rather than construe these theories as *competing* explanations of the truth, our progress will be healthier. This attitude may also alleviate some of the obnoxious symptoms of young investigators freshly pregnant with theory.

There is no intention to paint as a villain every scientist who devises a new theory, to imply that his motives are solely those of self-aggrandizement. Nor need we denounce categorically administrators who conscientiously seek to promote the idea of theory. Both scientists and administrators may operate with perfectly decent motives; the ends they avow may be perfectly laudable. But the means most readily available to them within their respective milieux may contaminate these ends and may, in fact, subvert their personal motives. Consequently, we must all be alert to the devious ways in which our motives can be corrupted by the social pressures under which we operate. This awareness will not guarantee the elimination of such corruption but may reduce its likelihood.

To recapitulate, our problems in developing a theory of educational administration may be classified under three general headings: substantive, communicative, and motivational. For purposes of presentation, these three sources of difficulty have been discussed in order, in the knowledge that the problems we encounter within a specific context can never be attributed to a single source of difficulty apart from the other two. Most of our difficulties stem from problems of communication, from the fact that we do not always make our concepts clear. Unfortunately, even when a writer defines his concepts with startling precision, there is no assurance that his readers will receive his concepts in this way. Their own predilections may prevent them from incorporating into their own thinking the writer's ideas. This is why repeated feedback is needed between communicator and recipient.

What are the implications of these remarks? We must listen to each other with respect. We must feel free to raise critical—even damning—questions, but without malice or antagonism, and stand ready to answer such searching questions, but without defensiveness. We must all recognize that we are engaged in solving what Hemphill refers to as a "mutual problem."[25] To accomplish this, each of our cooperating disciplines must forego any claim to a monopoly on wisdom.

If the lessons we have learned for NCPEA, CPEA, and UCEA

mean anything, then the successes of the future will depend upon liberal portions of two ingredients. The first, of course, is complete respect for each other's intellectual integrity. The second is patience—the patience to listen and to explore each other's ideas through questioning and cross-questioning in an effort to comprehend what we are saying to each other. More than mere verbal acceptance is necessary; we must form a basic understanding as well. This kind of listening is tough work, but there is no alternative.

NOTES FOR CHAPTER 1

1. Reprinted, by permission of the publisher, from Andrew W. Halpin (ed.), *Administrative Theory in Education* (Chicago: Midwest Administration Center, University of Chicago, 1958), pp. 1-19. Delivered to the first seminar of the University Council for Educational Administration, sponsored by the Midwest Administration Center, University of Chicago, in November 1957.

2. Subsequently reported by John K. Hemphill, Daniel E. Griffiths, and Norman Fredericksen, *Administrative Performance and Personality* (New York: Bureau of Publications, Teachers College, Columbia University, 1962).

3. That is, November 1957.

4. Arthur P. Coladarci and Jacob W. Getzels, *The Use of Theory in Educational Administration* (Stanford, Calif.: Stanford University Press, 1955).

5. Hollis A. Moore, Jr., *Studies in School Administration: A Report on the CPEA* (Washington, D.C.: American Association of School Administrators, 1957).

6. Roald F. Campbell and Russell T. Gregg (eds.), *Administrative Behavior in Education* (New York: Harper & Brothers, 1957).

7. Daniel E. Griffiths, "Toward a Theory of Administrative Behavior," *ibid.,* pp. 354-390.

8. Talcott Parsons, "Some Ingredients of a General Theory of Formal Organization," in Halpin (ed.), *Administrative Theory in Education,* pp. 40-72.

9. John K. Hemphill, "Administration as Problem-solving," *ibid.*, pp. 89-118.

10. Carroll L. Shartle, "A Theoretical Framework for the Study of Behavior in Organizations," *ibid.*, pp. 73-88.

11. Jacob W. Getzels and Egon G. Guba, "Social Behavior and the Administrative Process," *School Review*, 45 (1957), pp. 423-441.

12. Daniel E. Griffiths, *Human Relations in School Administration* (New York: Appleton-Century-Crofts, 1956), p. 4.

13. Herbert Feigl, "Principles and Problems of Theory Construction in Psychology," in Wayne Dennis (ed.), *Current Trends in Psychological Theory* (Pittsburgh: University of Pittsburgh Press, 1951), p. 181.

14. Van Miller, "Assessment and Projection," in Campbell and Gregg (eds.), *Administrative Behavior in Education*, pp. 513-527.

15. Feigl, "Principles and Problems of Theory Construction in Psychology," in Dennis (ed.), *Current Trends in Psychological Theory*.

16. For a discussion of phenotypic versus genotypic categories, see Kurt Lewin, "The Conflict Between Aristotelian and Galileian Modes of Thought in Contemporary Psychology," *Journal of Genetic Psychology*, 5 (1931), pp. 141-177.

17. Cyril G. Sargent and Eugene L. Belisle, *Educational Administration: Cases and Concepts* (Boston: Houghton Mifflin Co., 1955).

18. Griffiths, "Toward a Theory of Administrative Behavior," in Campbell and Gregg (eds.), *Administrative Behavior in Education*.

19. Shartle, "A Theoretical Framework for the Study of Behavior in Organizations," in Halpin (ed.), *Administrative Theory in Education*.

20. Irwin D.J. Bross, *Design for Decision* (New York: The Macmillan Company, 1953), pp. 171-172.

21. *Ibid.*, p. 172.

22. Albert Einstein and Leopold Infeld, *The Evolution of Physics* (New York: Simon & Schuster, 1938), p. 33.

23. Niels Bohr, "The Quantum Postulate and the Recent Development of Atomic Theory," *Nature*, 121 (April 14, 1928), pp. 530-590.

24. Diagrams of a mechanical model designed to illustrate the complementarity principle can be found in John A. Wheeler, "A Septet of Sybils: Aids in the Search of Truth," *American Scientist*, 44 (October 1956), pp. 360-377.

25. Hemphill, "Administration as Problem-Solving," in Halpin (ed.), *Administrative Theory in Education*.

2

A Paradigm for Research
on Administrator Behavior[1]

The paradigm, or model,[2] proposed in this chapter offers one approach to the study of administrator behavior in education. It provides the basis for a systematic classification and critique of existent and ongoing research on administrator behavior, and is designed to suggest fruitful lines of inquiry for new research. Its function is analogous to that of the table of atomic numbers in chemistry. Chemists have used the atomic table to locate missing elements and to predict their relationship to known elements. Similarly, this model may help us to spot missing elements in our research knowledge about administration and to achieve a closer integration between empirical findings and theoretical analysis. Our ultimate purpose, of course, is to promote the development of a theory of administration.

THE PURPOSE OF THE PARADIGM

Several investigators have noted the need for such a theory. Barnard,[3] Leighton,[4] and Simon[5] stressed this point a decade or more ago; but its cogency for educational administration has been recognized only within the past few years, especially by Coladarci and Getzels,[6] Cornell,[7] Griffiths,[8] and Walton.[9] These men have deplored the fact that educational research has relied too heavily upon naïve empiricism and has failed to pay sufficient heed to the role of theory. Coladarci and Getzels, in particular, have made an important contribution in identifying the principle obstacles to theory development in educational administration. But this current resurgent interest in developing theory is not confined to *educational* administration; it pervades the entire field of administration, and is exemplified by the *Administrative Science Quarterly*,[10] a new journal "dedicated to advancing basic understanding of administrative processes through empirical investigation and theoretical analysis." Litchfield[11] and Thompson,[12] in their keynote articles in the first issue (June 1956), plead for a general theory of administration and delineate the critical issues that must be taken into account if this goal is to be reached.

"Theory" in this context refers to theory as defined in science, a hypothetico-deductive type of theory to be distinguished from value-theory as the latter is conceived in philosophy.[13] Even in science the term "theory" is used in various ways and with differing degrees of generality. But here it will be used not merely as a euphemistic synonym for any speculation about administrator behavior—no matter how vaguely formulated—but in the restrictive sense employed by the social scientist.[14] To do this, every concept which is used in thinking about administrator behavior must be defined, and operational definitions[15] must be employed wherever possible. In this usage, theory entails more than mere classification, for scientific concepts are not of the same order as those that give synthetic unity to the common-sense world. Cassirer has pinpointed this difference:

> Man lived in an objective world long before he lived in a scientific world. Even before he had found his approach to science his experience was not a mere amorphous mass of sense expressions. It was an organized and articulated experience. It possessed a definite structure. *But the concepts that give to this world its synthetic unity are not of the same type nor are they on the same level as our scientific concepts.* They are mythical or linguistic concepts. If we analyze these concepts we find that they are by no means simple or "primitive." The first classifications of the phenomena which we find in language or myth are in a sense much more complicated and sophisticated than our scientific classifications. Science begins with a quest for simplicity. *Simplex sigillum veri* seems to be one of its fundamental devices. This logical simplicity is, however, a *terminus ad quem,* not a *terminus*

a quo. It is an end, not a beginning. Human culture begins with a much more complex and involved state of mind. Nearly all our sciences of nature had to pass through a mythical stage. In the history of scientific thought, alchemy precedes chemistry, astrology precedes astronomy. Science could advance beyond these first steps only by introducing a new measure, a different logical standard of truth. *Truth, it declares, is not to be attained so long as man confines himself within the narrow circle of his immediate experience of observable facts.* Instead of describing detached and isolated facts science strives to give us a comprehensive view. *But this view cannot be attained by a mere extension, an enlargement and enrichment of our ordinary experience. It demands a new principle of order, a new form of intellectual interpretation. . . .*

But what science seeks in phenomena is much more than similarity; it is order. The first classifications that we find in human speech have no strictly theoretical aim. The names of the objects fulfill their task if they enable us to communicate our thoughts and to coordinate our practical activities. They have a teleological function, which slowly develops into a more objective, a "representative" function. Every apparent similarity between different phenomena is enough to designate them by a common name. In some languages a butterfly is described as a bird or a whale is described as a fish. When science began its first classifications, it had to correct and to overcome these superficial similarities. *Scientific terms are not made at random; they follow a definite principle of classification. The creation of a coherent systematic terminology is by no means a mere accessory feature of science; it is one of its inherent and indispensable elements.*[16]

For this reason we will develop a systematic terminology, and will emphasize basic as opposed to applied research. Brown's statement of the case for pure research in science is endorsed:

> As the survival of our remote ancestors was dependent upon their ability to capture game, our own survival is dependent upon our ability to generate and to capture ideas. The constant search for the practical application and for the obvious result with the consequent exclusion of other intellectual pursuits can only lead to the nourishment of mediocrity and eventually to our downfall.[17]

This respect for basic research accounts for the many recent dramatic advances in social science research. Without a similar orientation in education, we can scarcely hope to engage in successful long-range programmatic research.[18] Brownell, for example, has noted the need in education for programmatic research of this character and has based his plans for a broad and rapid expansion in the research operations of the United States Office of Education upon this premise.[19] In subscribing to a *program* of research, individual investigators are not obliged to commit themselves exclusively to large-scale projects; they must, however, be prepared to show how the smaller, specific studies they propose will fit into the mosaic of a more comprehensive research endeavor. The paradigm described here is a rough design for such a mosaic. Single research studies or groups of studies may be fitted into this mosaic with equal ease. The criterion for inclusion is not the size or scope of a study, but the consistency of its essential concepts with those that compose the paradigm. The practical objective of programmatic research is, of course, to reduce the incidence of episodic, disconnected studies and to stimulate the systematic cumulation of research findings.

This paradigm should help us move toward a theory of administration and will encourage research of a more programmatic character. However, as it stands now, the paradigm is *not* a theory. It is offered as one way of thinking about research on administration that may accelerate the development of a useful theory. In science, no single theory holds a monopoly on wisdom, and one test of the merit of a theory is whether it leads to "bigger and better theories" from which can be adduced relevant, testable hypotheses. In short, how seminal is it? Although the paradigm does not purport to be a theory, it nevertheless should be judged by these same criteria. Does it, for example, permit one to conceptualize administrator behavior in a more constructive fashion? Will it stimulate programmatic research? This, then, is the spirit in which the paradigm is proposed—solely for heuristic purposes.

The paradigm is predicated upon two strategic assumptions:

1. That apart from educational administration, hospital administration, business administration, public administration, and so on, there exists a discipline of administration *qua* administration; this is a domain worthy of study.

2. That greater strides will be made at this juncture if research efforts are focused upon the behavior of administrators rather than upon either administrative behavior or the totality referred to as "administration."

According to the first assumption, observations will not be confined to administrator behavior *in education*, for it is believed that the characteristic ways in which administrators behave are essentially the same whether the administrator operates in industry, government, the military, or public education. Litchfield has stated this issue well:

> The most serious indictment which must be made of present thought is that it has failed to achieve a level of generalization enabling it to systematize and explain administrative phenomena which occur in related fields. Indeed, so far are we from broad generalizations about administration that we appear to maintain that there is not a generic administrative process but only a series of isolated types of administration. We seem to be saying that there is business administration and hospital administration and public administration; that there is military administration, hotel administration, and school administration. But there is no administration. We buttress this conclusion and make a general theory more difficult of attainment by developing separate schools in these fields in our universities. We organize ourselves into separate professional societies, and we have developed separate bodies of literature which speak to one another infrequently. . . .
>
> Actually our practice is years ahead of our thought. There is abundant evidence to demonstrate our unexpressed conviction that there is much that is common in administration. Here are a few illustrations of the point. The emerging concepts of human relations, communications, or operations research are as applicable to a hospital as they are to a bank. The constant movement of executive personnel from business to government, from the military forces into large business, from both government and business into education, is emphatic testimony supporting our conviction that knowledges and skills are transferable from field to field because of an essential universality in the administrative process itself. Again, it is a commonplace to observe that management consulting firms find their knowledges and skills applicable in the department store, on the one hand, and in the

government bureau or the university, on the other. We are thus faced with the curious dichotomy of a practice which acknowledges common ground among applied fields of administration and of a body of thought which makes no effort to delineate areas of common interest. As theorists we have not yet established generalized concepts which keep pace with the facts of contemporary administration.[20]

When the public school is compared with another institution it may be found that the organizations' tasks differ and that the situational conditions which influence the behavior of work groups differ, but the major dimensions of administrator behavior are the same. Obviously, nothing is to be gained by minimizing the differences between education, industry, and government, but it would also be a mistake to gloss over the similarities among these institutions. The field of educational administration is not so rich in knowledge that findings from other institutional settings can be disregarded. To the extent that two institutional settings are alike, knowledge gained about the behavior of administrators in one setting is equally applicable in the other. Consequently, in this chapter we will report relevant findings on administrator behavior without regard to whether they have been drawn from education, industry, or government.

According to the second assumption, the paradigm has been designed for the study of administra*tor* rather than administra*tive* behavior. This is a deliberate distinction, for our research interest centers upon the behavior of the officially designated administrators of formal organizations. In these terms all school superintendents and school principals are administrators and, *ipso facto,* leaders. Shartle chose this same definition of a leader in formulating the approach that he and his colleagues have used in the ten-year program of the Ohio State Leadership Studies:

> Naturally, in selecting persons for study one must apply a definition or have specific criteria. We may define a leader in several ways, such as the following:
> 1. An individual who exercises positive influence acts upon others.
> 2. An individual who exercises more important positive influence

acts than any other member of the group or organization he
is in.

3. An individual who exercises most influence in goal-setting or
   goal-achievement of the group or organization.
4. An individual elected by a group as a leader.
5. An individual in a given office or position of apparently
   high influence potential.

Since we are studying organizations in business, industry, education, and government, we have chosen initially to select on
the basis of the last definition, namely persons in high office.
Later on we may select persons on the basis of other definitions.[21]

By taking this stand, we avoid disputes about who the leaders
in a given situation *really* are, and we can agree to postpone the
study of leadership acts initiated by group members, other than
the formal leader. This is a strategic decision to facilitate research.
Because this approach has produced an important body of research literature, we shall capitalize upon these gains by using a
similar approach in constructing the paradigm.

In referring to leadership behavior there is no restriction to
overt behavior nor a commitment to a strictly behavioristic point
of view. The term "behavior" is used in a broad sense to include
an individual's perceptions, feelings, attitudes, thoughts, and
verbalizations as well as his overt actions. Some of these experiences are more difficult to observe than others; some lend themselves to reliable measurement, and others do not. But differences
in their accessibility to observation by an outside observer and
differences in the reliability of measurement do not alter the fact
that these phenomena are all significant facets of the individual's
behavior.

FOUR COMPONENTS OF ADMINISTRATION

Having stated the purpose of the paradigm and having identified
the two major strategic assumptions upon which it is predicated,
we can now examine a few of its key concepts.

Administration, whether in education, industry, or government,
refers to a human activity that involves a minimum of four components:

1. The Task
2. The Formal Organization
3. The Work Group (or Work Groups)
4. The Leader (or Leaders)

At this juncture, we shall define these components and incorporate them into a static model. In the next section we shall place them into the paradigm itself and show their interrelationships.

The Task

Without a task or mission the organization to be administered has no reason for being. Formal organizations such as businesses, armies, or school systems are established to serve economic and social purposes. The task of Industry X, for example, is to design, manufacture and sell product lines k, l, and m; to stay in business; and to build capital reserves as a bulwark against untoward contingencies. The task of the Air Force's Strategic Air Command is to be continually alert so that its aircraft can immediately counter any act of war by obliterating the enemy's strategic targets. The task of the public schools of Community Y is to "educate" the children, and perhaps the adults, of that community. The connotation of "educate" may be spelled out differently in various communities, and the task objectives may thus differ from community to community. Nonetheless, a common core of objectives is shared by most American schools.

The task of the organization should be carefully specified, for many dilemmas in administration arise simply because the organization's task has been formulated too loosely to permit efficient operation. Then, too, the organization's task may change during the course of time, or different aspects may require emphasis at different periods in the life of the organization. For example, a rapid inundation of new families into a community may force a school superintendent to place higher priority upon new buildings and the recruitment of teachers than upon curriculum modifications and special services. The survival of the organization may depend upon the leader's (and/or the group members') capacity to recognize that the organization's task either has changed or had better be changed. Accordingly, the task must be subjected to continuous redefinition.

It is necessary to distinguish between the task and the problem. The task is the purpose or mission of the organization as defined, whether formally or informally, by "observers" of the organization proper. Thus the task of Public School X is defined by public consensus, by regulations of the State Department of Education, and by the policies of the local Board of Education. The problem is defined as the perception of the task held *at a given time* by significant members of the organization. The most significant organization member, of course, is the administrator, or formally designated leader.

The task and the problem are not necessarily identical.[22] Conceptually, a distinction must be made between the problem as specified by the actor, and the task as specified by the experimenter or another person observing the actor. As viewed by an observer, the task can be defined as *the confronting of an actor with a designated stimulus situation in which the actor is proffered a stated reward for following specified rules of procedure in responding to the situation and for satisfying specified criteria by which his acts are judged to be successful (that is, warrant the actor's receiving the reward)*. In what might seem to be a similar set of circumstances for observer and actor, however, it must be recognized that the two may have very different views of what is taking place. To keep this distinction clear, the term "problem" is used to represent the actor's conception of the response to the situation and of his stake in it. The problem of the actor can be defined as *a perceived stimulus situation which the actor feels impelled to modify in order to realize some desired outcome*.

Statements of the task in terms of lofty, pious, but vague objectives are little more than exercises in rhetoric. For maximum organizational effectiveness the task must be spelled out in respect to changes that the organization is seeking to induce either in behaviors or behavioral products. Without specifications of this kind, the members of an organization find themselves at a loss to know whether the organization is achieving its presumed objectives. Perhaps the most significant contribution that the top administrator can make to his organization is to translate the objectives of the organization from the vague, exhortative language of the politician and propagandist into a language by which the effectiveness of ongoing operations can be measured.

The Formal Organization

An organization may be defined as a special kind of group—a social group whose members are differentiated as to their responsibility for accomplishing the group's task. One writer states:

> A group may or may not have leaders. If it does have leaders, it is an organization, for at least some of the members are thereby differentiated from the others as to responsibility or role expectation in relation to some common purpose.[23]

Most organizations in contemporary society describe job positions, allocate functions, delegate responsibilities, and establish some form of organizational hierarchy. Most dramatically, the famous Western Electric studies[24] indicate that informal organizations develop within the formal framework, and that the informal and formal networks do not always coincide. Stogdill has summarized the variables which define formal and informal organizations:

> It would appear then that there are two fundamental sets of variables which define the operations of an organized group. These are:
>
> 1. *Variables which define formal organization.* These are:
>   (a) Responsibility variables (the work one is expected to do).
>   (b) Formal interaction variables (the persons with whom one is expected to work).
> 2. *Variables which define informal organization.* These are:
>   (a) Work performance variables (the tasks one actually performs).
>   (b) Informal interaction variables (the persons with whom one actually works).[25]

It is important to recognize the informal organization as well as the formal, and to take these informal organizations into account. *But it is equally important that the formal organization not be forgotten.* Yet discussions of "democratic leadership" and "group leadership" in education often overlook both the formal organization of the school and the responsibility that the administrator—and he alone—must discharge.

The Work Group

The work group is composed of individuals chosen to fill positions specified by the formal organization. An organization may contain one or more work groups, and differential status is usually ascribed to the various groups. Similarly, within a given work group, job assignments carry with them differential status in the organization.

In a small school the work group is composed of the principal and the teachers. A school custodian and a bus driver may be members of this same work group, but their job assignments ascribe to them a status in the organization different from that of the principal and teachers. In a larger city school system the teachers of School *A* may constitute one work group and those of School *B* another. The staff of supervisors may compose another work group directly responsible to the superintendent through serving him in a staff relationship.

In studying administrator behavior there is an advantage in focusing attention upon the relationship between the administrator's behavior and the productiveness of his "face-to-face" work group. This is the locus at which most problems of administration may be studied in microcosm. By starting with this face-to-face group, we do not deny the necessity of studying administration at a more macrocosmic level as well, for the type, range, and frequency of administrative problems are obviously related to the size and structure of the organization. Nonetheless, for strategic reasons we direct the initial research efforts to the immediate work group, because this is a manageable unit within which one can directly observe the behavior and interactions of group members.

An administrator is properly pleased when the members of his immediate work group get along well together as individuals and seem to enjoy being members of the group. But note that their ease in getting along well together is not the primary criterion by which these individuals have been chosen as members of the organization. Presumably they have been selected in terms of professional competencies pertinent to the task of the organization. High group "morale" is a desirable by-product, and administrators will naturally seek to establish good morale; but high morale among group members is not the primary task of the organization. This task is defined in entirely different terms, and usually by agents external to the work group itself.

The term "morale" requires comment. This is an emotionally charged term that means different things to different people. Haire describes this dilemma nicely:

> MORALE. There is probably no other field in the general area of social psychological problems in industry in which there are so many publications as there are under the general heading of morale. The number of independent measurements of the state of morale in different situations and with different instruments is legion, and it has become necessary to fall back on a biennial bibliography simply to keep abreast of those reported in professional journals. . . . In spite of all this material it is still difficult to say what is meant by morale, what its springs are in the human organization of a factory, or what its results are. . . . There is no question but what morale—however the concept should be defined—is a real phenomenon. Indeed, there is little question that it is an important variable. However, this field, representing a triangular meeting of difficult grounds in motivational theory, the theory of social organization, and the techniques of interviewing, is still largely unrewarding. It remains as a technical problem, both from the point of view of the investigator who does not know quite how to tackle it, and from the point of view of the industrial executive or consultant social scientist, who does not know quite how to handle it, but who feels that it is there and that it must be important.[26]

Two points in particular should be made about the concept of morale. First, whatever it is, it is not a unidimensional concept. It has more than a single component, and each component can be defined best only in respect to the operations by which it is measured. High morale in respect to one component does not guarantee high morale in respect to another. Secondly, there is no necessary relationship between high morale and high productivity. An increase in morale may or may not be accompanied by an increase in productivity, and even where both rise together it is extremely difficult to establish a causal relationship. Does higher productivity, for example, increase morale; or is it improved morale that makes higher productivity possible?

Although it would be desirable to discard this term, its loss might at this time make communication awkward. Accordingly, we will use it in the present context, but we must emphasize that it is a "loaded" term which has not been properly defined.

The Leader

One member of the organization is formally charged with responsibility for the organization's accomplishment. This individual—the formal leader or administrator—may in turn select other subgroup leaders or administrators charged with responsibility for the task accomplishment of these subgroups within the larger organization. Each subgroup contributes to accomplishing the organization's task. To avoid duplication of effort and to minimize jurisdictional disputes, the administrator of the larger organization may specify for each subgroup leader the task of his subgroup. Moreover, the top administrator ordinarily sets the conditions for communication channels within the organization and stipulates the limits of authority and responsibility of each subgroup leader.

Each subgroup leader is placed at the nexus of those formal communication lines along which information pertinent to the efficiency of his subgroup is transmitted. The top administrator is situated at the nexus of communication lines between the organization and all other groups and organizations external to his own.

Each leader is confronted by a dual set of duties: (1) as a problem solver or decision maker; and (2) as a group leader vis-à-vis his own work group—that is, the members of his immediate staff. Subleaders are confronted with these same sets of duties but must also perform (3) the duties prescribed by their roles as group members responsible to their own supraordinate leader. We will consider here only the first two sets of duties.

The Leader as a Decision Maker. As a problem solver or decision maker, the leader is confronted first, last, and always by the task of the organization. The statement of the organization's task—and the specificity, or more commonly the lack of specificity, with which this is stated—seldom includes details on how the task is to be accomplished. In fact, the task statement may contain contradictory and irreconcilable elements. The task may be conceived as a broad stimulus object or "field" presented to the leader and his group. Within this stimulus field, the leader perceives or identifies certain problems. At this stage of the game the leader's interpretation of the task (that is, which interpretation is the problem) and his interpretation of the current stage of development of the organization (that is, how far the organization has progressed toward solving this problem) play an important part. Not every problem can be identified, let alone solved. So the leader *selects* those aspects of the task that he identifies as the problem. The problem as he perceives it may reflect his own predilections and personal value system rather than its relevance— as might be determined by a jury of outside observers—to the task. There also is evidence to suggest that executives carry their own personal "leadership styles" from one organization to another,[27] and that this predilection for a particular leadership style influences the leader's perception of the organization's problem(s). Undoubtedly, the *Zeitgeist*, too, influences an executive's perception of the chief problems that confront the organization.

The *ordering* of problems (as perceived by the leader) and the extent to which authority for their solution is delegated to sub-leaders or group members constitute an important area of problem solving and decision making for the administrator. In ordering problems the administrator may feel that the highest priority at one juncture should be placed upon the improvement of morale within the organization. On the other hand when morale is high he may accentuate problems that are more task-oriented. The ordering of problems is not fixed but usually varies with the demands of the situation.

Furthermore, the problems that an administrator perceives in an organization's task can be defined at different levels of specificity and according to different time perspectives. Some administrators identify as their problem issues crucial to the task; others putter with peripheral details. Some leaders deal in terms of long-range time perspectives; others stumble from day to day, buffeted by the exigencies of each new crisis.

Note that the decision to invoke "group-decision" methods is itself a decision. The leader must also decide within what spheres group decisions will be permitted, and to what extent he will be bound by such decisions. Will the group's role be advisory, or will its decision on every issue be a mandate to the administrator?

Whyte's remarks about group decision in industry apply with equal force to public education:

> This suggests that a hierarchical organization depends upon the allocation of authority and responsibility. The problem is not one of eliminating authority; it is a problem of weaving authority and participation effectively together.
>
> In abandoning the leaderless discussion group in industry, we need not go back to the situation where the boss is the man who has all the ideas and simply states his decisions to his subordinates. Discussions can be utilized with great effectiveness by the executive if he understands their limitations as well as their possibilities. He can utilize discussion to draw from group members knowledge and ideas that he himself does not have. In some cases, he may find that the decision seems naturally to evolve out of the group discussion, but it will still be his role to state that decision for the members. Even if he must state his own decision where no consensus of the group seems to arise in discussion, the discussion may be helpful to him in showing how various men feel about a problem, how strongly they feel about it, and what sorts of decisions will be acceptable to them and what will not be, even though they give their formal assent.
>
> Still, let us not kid ourselves about group process in industry. When all is said and done in group discussion, it is up to the boss to make the decision and accept responsibility for it. A skillful leader will seek to avoid decisions that will needlessly antagonize subordinates. He will weigh their ideas and advice most carefully. And, when necessary, after he has made the

decision, he will seek for it the sort of support that comes from voluntary cooperation.

The skillful executive will utilize the group process to arrive at sounder decisions and to build stronger support for those decisions. He will not saddle on the group the responsibility for making decisions that it is his responsibility to make.

Let us not apologize for the exercise of authority. The large and complicated organizations of our society could not function without putting *upon individuals* the authority and responsibility that goes with their positions. Authority cannot be sloughed off. It need not be exercised in an autocratic and oppressive manner. It can be exercised with great effectiveness if the executive goes beyond the mere giving of orders and learns the skills of leadership in group discussion.[28]

Similarly, the leader must decide what kinds of information about the organization (and its personnel) should be transmitted to the membership, and when and how this information should be transmitted. The leader should also indicate what information about the organization should be transmitted outside the organization, and he should also be concerned with his "timing" in releasing this information.

The Leader as a Group Leader.   As a group leader vis-à-vis his own immediate work group, the leader is committed to two fundamental group goals:

1. Group achievement: measured in respect to how well the group accomplishes the group task.

2. Group maintenance: measured by the extent to which the group remains intact as a group. This may be gauged in terms of morale, cooperation among group members in working with one another, and other indices of job satisfaction.[29]

The investigators responsible for the personnel assessment program of the Office of Strategic Services during World War II recognized this dual aspect of leadership in their definition: Leadership is "a man's ability to take the initiative in social situations, to plan and organize action, and in so doing to evoke cooperation."[30]

Cartwright and Zander have described these two objectives as follows:

It appears that most, or perhaps all, group objectives can be subsumed under one of two headings: (a) the achievement of some specific group goal, or (b) the maintenance or strengthening of the group itself. Examples of member behaviors that serve functions of *goal achievement* are "initiates action," "keeps member's attention on the goal," "clarifies the issue," "develops a procedural plan," "evaluates the quality of work done," and "makes expert information available." Examples of behaviors that serve functions of *group maintenance* are "keeps interpersonal relations pleasant," "arbitrates disputes," "provides encouragement," "gives the minority a chance to be heard," "stimulates self-direction," and "increases the inter-dependence among members."[31]

Similarly, Barnard in his excellent analysis of the functions of the executive has distinguished between the "effectiveness" and the "efficiency" of cooperative action:

The persistence of cooperation depends upon two conditions: (a) its effectiveness; and (b) its efficiency. Effectiveness relates to the accomplishment of the cooperative purpose, which is social and nonpersonal in character. Efficiency relates to the satisfaction of individual motives, and is personal in character. The test of effectiveness is the accomplishment of a common purpose or purposes; effectiveness can be measured. The test of efficiency is the eliciting of sufficient individual wills to cooperate.

The survival of cooperation, therefore, depends upon two interrelated and interdependent classes of processes: (a) those which relate to the system of cooperation as a whole in relation to the environment; and (b) those which relate to the creation or distribution of satisfactions among individuals.

The instability and failures of cooperation arise from defects in each of these classes and processes separately, and from defects in their combination. The functions of the executive are those of securing the effective adaptation of these processes.[32]

The Office of Strategic Services group, Cartwright and Zander, Barnard, and others have described these two major group objectives. But it is not enough to identify these group objectives; the leader *behaviors* associated with the accomplishment of these objectives must also be delineated. This, fortunately, has been done by the Ohio State group, which has identified two major dimensions of leader behavior: Initiating Structure in Interaction[33] and Consideration.

Initiating Structure refers to the leader's behavior in delineating the relationship between himself and members of the work-group, and in endeavoring to establish well-defined patterns of organization, channels of communication, and methods of procedure. Consideration refers to behavior indicative of friendship, mutual trust, respect, and warmth in the relationship between the leader and the members of his staff.[34]

These dimensions of leader behavior were identified on the basis of earlier research with a Leader Behavior Description Questionnaire devised by the Personnel Research Board at The Ohio State University. Hemphill and Coons[35] constructed the original form of this questionnaire. Halpin and Winer in reporting the development of an Air Force adaptation of this instrument have identified Initiating Structure and Consideration as two fundamental dimensions of leader behavior.

The author further describes the technique used in identifying these two dimensions:

These dimensions were delineated on the basis of a factor analysis of the Leader Behavior Description Questionnaire responses of three hundred crew members who described the behavior of their fifty-two B-29 aircraft commanders. This solution of the iterative analysis was guided by a few tentative ideas about the dynamics of leadership. Initially, in the search for a solution to the analysis, a number of "blind" rotations of the axes were made, but to no avail. In each instance only a single large general factor emerged. This factor probably reflected merely a general, vague evaluation of the commander, and contained a sizeable but undefined halo effect. Since the various blind analyses had proven futile, we posited the Initiating Structure and the Consideration dimensions of leader behavior. When the axes were then rotated in respect to these posited dimensions, the empirical data were found to fit the hypothesis.[36]

The two leader behavior dimensions, Initiating Structure and Consideration, parallel the two group goals of Group Achievement and Group Maintenance. As might be expected, "effective" leaders are those who score high on *both* dimensions of leader behavior. Halpin reported this finding in a study of B-29 aircraft commanders flying combat missions over Korea,[37] and Hemphill came to a similar conclusion from his study of the departmental administrators in a liberal arts college.[38] Statements by school board members and teaching staffs in their description of how an ideal school superintendent should behave, and comparable statements about aircraft commanders in respect to their ideal behavior, point to this same conclusion.[39]

The dimensions of Initiating Structure and Consideration are not posited as traits of leadership, for this would violate our preference for the concept of leader behavior as opposed to the more orthodox concept of leadership:

> The distinction between "leader behavior" and "leadership" is more than merely academic, for which term we choose determines the kind of questions we ask, and for this reason also dictates the form our answers will take. For example, to ask "What is leadership?" presupposes the existence of a specified capacity in regard to "leading." This question predicates within the individual an attribute or inherent characteristic of behavior, and implies further that this attribute, like intelligence or clerical aptitude, functions with equal force in a variety of situations. A question so phrased also suggests that individuals differ in their capacity, or potential, for "leadership" and that this potential is probably determined by intrinsic factors in the person. It is an easy step from this position to the inference that this potential is identifiable and hence measurable—that some individuals possess it in high degree and others in lesser degree; and that if we only can discover how to measure it, we shall be able to screen the "leaders" from the "non-leaders." Those who hold this view tend to set little store by the prospect of training individuals in leader-behavior skills, for when leadership is conceived principally as an inherent capacity or potentiality, there is meager justification for devoting time to training for it. The chief personnel task becomes one of discovering the proper formula for identifying and measuring leadership "ability."
>
> In contrast, consider the concept of "leader behavior" and what it implies. First of all, it focuses upon observed behavior

rather than upon a posited capacity inferred from this behavior. No presuppositions are made about a one-to-one relationship between leader behavior and an underlying capacity or potentiality presumably determinative of this behavior. By the same token, no *a priori* assumptions are made that the leader behavior which a leader exhibits in one group situation will be manifested in other group situations. It may be; but the answer to this question is left open for empirical verification rather than incorporated as an implicit assumption into the very terminology we use to define our problem. Nor does the term "leader behavior" suggest that this behavior is determined either innately or situationally. Either determinant is possible, as is any combination of the two, but the concept of leader behavior does not itself predispose us to accept one in opposition to the other. With attention focused upon behavior rather than capacity, there is greater promise of the possibility of training individuals in specified forms of leader behavior. Changes in behavior presumably can be induced through appropriate training, but the concept of capacity, by definition, implies a fixed level of ability and hence thrusts the burden of personnel determination upon selection, not training.[40]

The concept of leader behavior does not preclude the possibility that certain behaviors are more closely associated with effective group achievement and maintenance than others, nor does it shut out the possibility that leaders can transfer some of their skills from one group situation to another. This is neither denied nor affirmed, but the way is left open to determine inductively to what extent and under what conditions these hypotheses are supported by empirical evidence. There is a clear difference in approach: these possibilities are treated as hypotheses to be tested; in the orthodox trait approach to "leadership," these same possibilities are stated gratuitously as premises.

There is a further advantage to the concept of leader behavior over that of leadership. In ordinary parlance the term "leadership" is used in an evaluative sense. To say that a man displays leadership implies that this is "good" or "effective" leadership. But the evaluating of what the leader does is only one aspect of our research objective. The primary task is to describe the behavior of the leader in psychologically meaningful dimensions. If a description of the leader in specific dimensions of behavior and an evaluation of the effectiveness and efficiency of that behavior can be obtained independently, then we can ascertain to what extent each dimension contributes to favorable evaluation. Furthermore, it can be determined whether this contribution changes when the source of criterion of evaluation is changed. This separation of the *description* of what the leader does from the *evaluation* of the effectiveness and efficiency of what he does is of signal importance. Because it focuses upon the description of behavior, the leader behavior concept makes it easier to distinguish between (1) what the leader does, and (2) how what he does is evaluated. What is more, this distinction also reveals the pertinence of two related questions about the leader's behavior: "As described *by whom?*" and "As evaluated *by whom?*"

We do not intend to invite an awkward use of language by abjuring the word "leadership." The term is used adjectivally to refer to leadership acts, leadership ideology, leadership skills, or even leadership behavior. Our intent is to avoid the mistake of treating "leadership" as if it were an entity and of disregarding the coerciveness of situational factors upon leadership behavior.

Hemphill's pioneering study[41] and Stogdill's[42] and Gibb's[43] comprehensive surveys of the research literature on leadership all support the position taken here.

Having briefly defined the four major components of administration—the task, the formal organization, the work group, and the leader—we now will present the paradigm itself.

THE PARADIGM

Identified within the paradigm are the major variables that we must take into account in planning research on administrator behavior. Only those variables most pertinent to our purpose will be selected.[44] We will suggest how these variables can be defined operationally[45] and will indicate the lines of relationship among them. The paradigm is composed of four panels:

Panel I.   The Organization Task: defined in terms of "desirable" *behavior* or behavioral *products.*

Panel II.   Administrator Behavior: the *behavior* of the officially designated leader in his administrative role.

Panel III. Variables Associated with Administrator Behavior: These include behavior on the part of group members other than the leader, products of the behavior of group members, specified conditions under which the administrator and other group members are required to operate, patterns of administrative organization, and community factors that bear upon the formal organization. It is stipulated that these variables be reported objectively and measured reliably.

Panel IV.   Criteria of Administrator "Effectiveness": Two levels of criteria are postulated: (1) intermediate criteria such as evaluations or ratings of the leader's behavior and (2) outcomes of behavior measured in terms of organization products and *changes* in these products.

The panels are a device for differentiating these four broadly defined sets of variables. Although the four components of administration described in the preceding section are not coterminous with the panels, these components are all incorporated into the panel arrangement. The paradigm will be developed step by step according to the following plan. In turn, Panels I, II, and, IV (Figures 2.1, 2.2, and 2.3) will be described, and then they will be combined into a single diagram (Figure 2.4). Next, Panel III will be described separately (Figure 2.5), and finally the total paradigm will be diagrammed with Panel III included (Figure 2.6). This will be supplemented with a streamlined version of the paradigm (Figure 2.7) in which we will omit many of the details of Figure 2.6 in order to stress the salient outline. Finally, in Figure 2.8 we will show how the paradigm can be used in research designed to compare the leaders' behavior in two or more school organizations.

This model is predicated upon three basic assumptions about administrator behavior in education and upon two additional, methodological assumptions. The first three assumptions are:

1. The public school organization is constituted for a purpose, and this purpose can be stated in terms of desired outcomes. Furthermore, these outcomes may be defined either in terms of

"desirable" behaviors or of "desirable" products of behavior. These desired outcomes constitute the organization's task.

2. The individuals who compose the organization are engaged in continuous problem-solving behavior in their effort to accomplish this task.

3. The administrator, as the formally designated leader of the organization, has a key role in this problem-solving behavior; three areas of his behavior are of especial importance:
   (a) His perception of the organization's task.
   (b) His behavior as a decision maker.
   (c) His behavior as a group leader, vis-à-vis his own immediate work group.

The two methodological assumptions are:

1. It is desirable to confine our inquiry to concepts that have definable referents in *behavior* or in the *products of behavior*.

2. It is important to discriminate between *descriptions* of behavior and *evaluations* of behavior.

Panel I—The Organization's Task

In diagramming the paradigm, we will assign variables to different boxes, each designated by a number in parentheses. Because behavior and the events associated with behavior take place through time, a time line is extended horizontally across the paradigm. For convenience, we will consider only $Time_A$ and $Time_B$, but time should be conceived as extending indefinitely into $Time_N$. The task at $Time_A$ is designated as $Task_A$ and is assigned Box 1 in the diagram. Similarly, $Task_B$ denotes the task at $Time_B$ and is placed in Box 2. This schema is given in Figure 2.1.

As noted earlier, the task is the purpose or mission of the

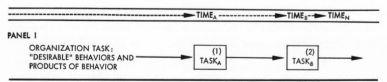

FIGURE 2.1   Panel I of the paradigm.

organization as defined by external observers, and not as perceived by members of the organization. The task should be spelled out in respect to changes that the organization seeks to induce either in behavior or in the products of behavior. It is expressed as a set of "ideal" objectives that specify what the organization *ought* to do rather than what it does do. Thus, to keep the organization on the move, the sights for the task are deliberately set higher than the current standards of the organization's accomplishments.

Here, in dealing with "oughts, *normative* language—in the ethical sense[46]—is used as distinguished from the *descriptive* language of science which is restricted to statements of what "is," or what happens. In planning research, one must be alert to the difference between *descriptive* and *normative* statements. Administrator behavior cannot be discussed without resorting to both kinds of statements; hence a place for both must be found in the paradigm. But it is not enough to provide for these two kinds of statements; they must also be kept straight, so that the researcher is fully aware of when he is dealing with an "is" statement and when he has invoked an "ought" statement. The paradigm takes this distinction into account. Normative statements enter into the definition of the task and have a place in Panel I; but, as we shall explain later, we will scrupulously exclude "ought" statements from Panels II and III. In Panel IV, too, they will have only a limited place.

In stating the task in terms of "oughts," there is the danger of establishing objectives that are equally desirable at the ideal level but mutually exclusive in the world of "real" events—the world that the scientist describes by direct observation. The incompatibility of elements within the task seldom becomes evident until the task requirements have been spelled out in respect to the desired behaviors and products of behavior which the organization is attempting to effect.

Because the organization itself is more stable than the composition of its membership, there is no marked fluctuation in the task over the course of time.[47] Thus Task$_A$, Task$_B$, and Task$_N$ tend to remain stable. Nonetheless, in Figure 2.1 we have differentiated Task$_A$ and Task$_B$ (Boxes 1 and 2) to show that under some circumstances the task may be modified.

Panel II—Administrator Behavior

In this panel we are concerned with three types of behavior on the part of the administrator:
1. His perception of the organization's task.
2. His behavior as a decision maker.
3. His behavior as a group leader vis-à-vis his own immediate work group.

In Figure 2.2 the administrator is designated by an X. He is confronted by the task, and through his perception of the task he defines the organization's problems. This schema takes into account the distinction that Pepinsky makes between the task and the problem.[48] The administrator's perception of the task at Time$_A$ is indicated in Box 3; his perception of the task at Time$_B$, in Box 4. His *perception* of the task at Time$_A$ and at Time$_B$ is more subject to change than is the task itself.

It is through his perception of the task that the leader defines the organization's problems. How do we measure this perception? The most straightforward method is to ask him, to interview him, although this information may also be obtained through questionnaires or by similar techniques. Note, however, that what a man verbalizes as his perception of the task is not necessarily concordant with the evidence of his overt behavior. For example, a man may assert that Issue A is more crucial than Issue B. Because Issue A is at the core of current discussions on public education, he may feel that he *should* reply this way. Yet his actual behavior may show that Issue B is of greater moment to him than A. Consequently, one must be on guard against the administrator's glib use of clichés and slogans. These clichés are common in our professional and trade literature; hence, in seeking to define an administrator's perception of the task, scientists must be adroit in penetrating this "cliché barrier." The best way to break this barrier is to insist that the problem (that is, the administrator's perception of the task) be stated exclusively in behavioral terms. The social scientist can supplement these statements by observing the administrator's behavior—especially at choice points—and by inferring his perception of the task from the observational data. Obviously, these inferences have to be systematized and cross-checked, and precautions against bias have to be built into the procedure. The distinction made here parallels the distinction Woodruff has made between verbalized and functional motives.[49] The same general approach that he has devised for his *A Study of Choices*[50] can be adapted readily to the requirement for distinguishing between an administrator's functional and verbalized perceptions of the organization's task. Stogdill and Shartle,[51] using quite a different approach, have devised other techniques for describing an administrator's perception of the task.

The "administrator's perception of the organization's task" (that is, the problem) is placed in Boxes 3 and 4. Panel II does not deal directly with the task, but with the administrator's perception of the Task. His perception defines the problem, and his behavior both as a decision maker and as a group leader is inexorably mediated through this perception. This relationship is shown in Figure 2.2.

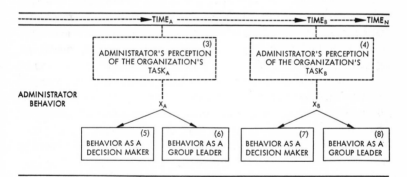

FIGURE 2.2 Panel II of the paradigm.

We should note a few additional points about Figure 2.2. Boxes 3 and 4 have been framed in dotted lines because the administrator's perception of the task is a slightly different order of behavior from that designated in Boxes 5, 6, 7, and 8, in that it is less accessible to direct observation. Note, too, that the administrator's behavior in Panel II is measurable only within the context of a specified formal organization. Characteristics of the administrator as an individual, such as his intelligence, his formal training, or his range of administrative experience, are not treated in Panel II. (Variables of this kind are referred to in Panel III.) Here consideration is given only to the behavior of the individual as Administrator X in Organization Y.

The dichotomy between "behavior as a decision maker" (Box 5) and "behavior as a group leader" (Box 6) is useful despite the fact that one may encounter specific behaviors which are difficult to categorize in this way. In the preceding section, we have already discussed the distinction between these two roles of the administrator. Decision-making often takes place while the administrator is functioning vis-à-vis his group. But his decision-making may also take place in the privacy of his own office and theoretically, at least, without direct contact between himself and the other members of the organization. It is difficult to determine the techniques that an administrator uses in reaching a decision or to ascertain what weight is given to various factors in a given decision-equation. Usually our only access to this aspect of his behavior is through perspicacious interviewing. On the other hand, his behavior as a group leader is more open to direct observation and can be measured in terms of the consensual perception of his behavior by the other members of his work group.

No attempt is made here to expatiate upon different types of decision making. Parsons, for example, has distinguished between *policy* decisions, *allocative* decisions, and decisions that pertain to the *integration* of the organization.[52] This is a useful distinction that can be accommodated by the paradigm, but it will not be discussed here.

To simplify the diagram, we have not shown the lines of interaction, for example, between Boxes 5 and 7, or Boxes 6 and 8. Naturally, X's behavior as a decision maker at $Time_B$ is influenced by the products and "success" of his decisions at $Time_A$. This feedback principle applies to his behavior both as a decision maker and as a group leader.

Panel IV—Criteria of Administrator "Effectiveness"

In keeping with the plan of presentation, we will skip Panel III at this point and describe Panel IV as diagrammed in Figure 2.3.

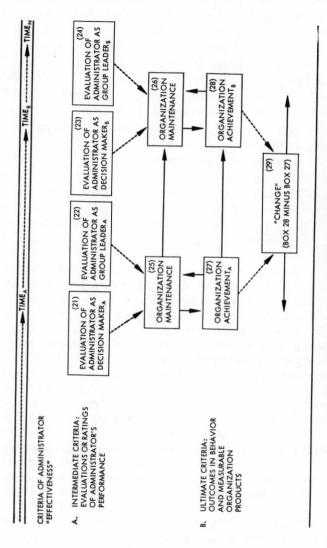

FIGURE 2.3   Panel IV of the paradigm.

The ultimate criteria of administrator effectiveness should be expressed in terms of group or organization achievement, in respect to the *changes* in the organization's accomplishments that can be attributed to the behavior of the administrator. Since changes are being considered, this criterion reflects *differences* between the organization's achievement at Time$_A$ (Box 27) and its achievement at Time$_B$ (Box 28). The variables in these boxes represent measurable products of the organization's accomplishments.[53] The criterion of administrator effectiveness is defined as the *difference* (Box 29) between the organization's achievement at Times *A* and *B*, in respect to whatever products are specified.

This is essentially the same approach to the criterion problem as has been proposed by Cattell, who has coined the term "syntality" to refer to the abstract entity defined by measures of the accomplishment of the organization (or group) as an organization.[54] In short, "syntality" means for the group what personality means for the individual.

> The present proposal for a syntality evaluation calls for shifting the estimate of the goodness of a leader entirely to measurements of the performance of the group acting under his guidance. . . . If the ultimate criterion of leadership is to be the effect of leadership structure upon the actual group performance, i.e., a measurement of behavior, then it is better to measure this directly as such, at the group performance level. . . . "A leader is a person who has a demonstrable influence upon group syntality." And we measure leadership by *the magnitude of the syntality change (from the mean) produced by that person,* i.e., by the difference between syntality under his leadership and the syntality under the leadership of the average or modal leader. It will be evident from these definitions that we can no longer speak of good and bad leaders, but only of leaders that are good and bad with respect to the production of increase in a particular dimension of group syntality. . . . The whole problem of leadership investigation is swung around from "good" and "bad" to the problem of analyzing the leader in terms of increase or decrease of particular syntality dimensions.[55]

Organization achievement (Boxes 27 and 28) should be measured in respect to the same behaviors and behavioral products that have been used to define the task (Boxes 1 and 2). However, whereas the task is defined in terms of "ideal" outcomes, organization achievement should be described not in the normative language of "oughts," but in the scientific language of "what is." For example, one stipulation of the task of the school (that is, one subtask) may be the objective of improving the citizenship of young people. Stated thus, this desired ideal is nebulous. If organization achievement in respect to this ideal is to be measured, one must specify the dimensions of *behavior* by which it is sought to induce change in order to achieve better citizenship. Furthermore, it must be determined that this behavior can be reliably observed and reported. If this requirement is not satisfied, it is impossible to know whether the administrator has or has not accomplished the organization's task. Obviously, an administrator can seduce himself into believing that he has achieved his purpose, simply because he says that he has. This is not uncommon. Although this type of blind faith in his own accomplishments may comfort the administrator, the social scientist engaged in research on administrator behavior requires more tangible evidence than this for evaluating the organization's achievement.

Consequently, it is important to define both the task and the organization's achievement in respect to identical behavioral (and behavior-product) dimensions. Much research on educational administration fails to recognize this point, for there has been an unfortunate tendency to define the task of educational administration in one language and to measure its "effectiveness" in another. Research progress in this field will not be achieved until a tighter articulation between the task (Panel I) and the criteria of administrator effectiveness (Panel IV) has been established. Objectives (the task) and organizational outcomes must be stated in the same language, a language of precision which uses operational definitions and pins down all concepts with unequivocal referents in behavior.

Although differences in the organization's products are the best criteria of the administrator's effectiveness, the social scientist may be temporarily forced to settle for criteria that fall short of this mark. These intermediate criteria usually take the form of ratings of the administrator's effectiveness. Thus members of the Board

of Education or an "outside" jury of professors of educational administration may evaluate the effectiveness of an administrator. Or,
similarly, an investigator may appraise two or more superintendents in respect to their tenure in office. These are intermediate
criteria and are no better than the assumptions on which they are
founded. The rating method assumes that the judges' evaluations
of the administrator are significantly correlated with changes in
the organization's achievement attributable to the administrator.
But it is known that ratings can be contaminated by a "halo effect"
and that a sycophantic, glad-handing superintendent may be rated
very favorably by his Board despite the fact that his contribution
to improving the school program is negligible. Nor is tenure in
office an infallible criterion of administrative effectiveness. Some
superintendents hang onto their jobs because they have neither the
imagination nor the courage to "rock the boat."

Two additional issues complicate the rating approach. First,
from what source are ratings to be drawn? And second, what is
the inter-rater reliability either in describing or evaluating specific
attributes of the administrator's behavior? The author's study of
fifty school superintendents described on the Leader Behavior
Description Questionnaire shows that the board and the staff
groups do not agree in their description of the superintendent's
leadership behavior.[56] If these groups do not agree on straightforward *descriptions* of how the superintendent behaves, we
scarcely can expect them to agree in their *evaluations* of his leadership behavior. Which intermediate criterion, then, should be used?
Ratings by staff, or ratings by board members? If one of these
criteria should prove to be significantly associated with our ultimate criteria, the other, perforce, will fail to show a significant
relationship. Furthermore, ratings from both these sources suffer
from some lack of reliability. The agreement among board members in describing the Initiating Structure behavior of the superintendents is expressed by an unbiased correlation ratio of .52; their
agreement in describing Consideration behavior, by an unbiased
correlation ratio of .63. The corresponding ratios for descriptions
by staff members are .44 and .44. Since these correlations for the
description of the superintendent's behavior reflect an appreciable
lack of interdescriber reliability, we cannot be sanguine in expect-
ing high inter-rater reliability in *evaluations* of his behavior.

Because of these shortcomings of the intermediate criteria in most common use today, in Figure 2.3 we deliberately differentiate between the intermediate and the ultimate criteria. Whenever an intermediate criterion is posited, it must be examined critically and it must be recognized only as a stopgap. Its worth is tenuous until we can demonstrate that it is correlated significantly with objective criteria of changes in the organization's maintenance and achievement.

Included among the ultimate criteria are changes in both organization maintenance and organization achievement. These two kinds of changes have been differentiated because they do not necessarily parallel each other. It is doubtful, for example, whether a desirable change can take place in the organization's achievement without a corresponding change in its maintenance. On the other hand, a favorable change in its maintenance—for example, increased morale—does not guarantee a corresponding change in the organization's achievement.

These "ultimate" criteria are placed at Level *B* in Figure 2.3; whereas the intermediate criteria have been assigned to Level *A*. As noted above, these two sets of criteria must be kept straight, and we must be sure that we do not impute to the intermediate criteria greater "validity" than they possess. In short, if research stops at the intermediate criterion level, the most important part of the job is unfinished. The most crucial research task that lies ahead in educational administration is to prove that the various intermediate criteria of administrator effectiveness now used so glibly are, in fact, significantly correlated with changes in the organization's achievement.

Decisions about the changes measured in Panel IV entail certain value judgments, and at this point the researcher may appear to step out of the social scientist's role. Yet this need not be the case. The educational philosopher and practicing administrator provide the best sources for suggestions about the dimensions of the organization's change that should be measured. The social scientist, *as a scientist*, does not have to evaluate these dimensions; his job is to identify and describe them. It is not for him to say that changes along Dimension *Q* are to be valued as more important than changes along Dimension *K*, but he must define the dimensions in operational terms and must devise reliable techniques for measuring whatever changes do occur. Perhaps his salient contribution is to show the precise ways in which various criteria of the organization's effectiveness fail of unidimensionality. This is no mean accomplishment: it is important to know, for example, that Administrator Behavior X is significantly and positively associated with changes in the organization's achievement along Dimension Q but that there are only chance, or even negative, relationships between Administrator Behavior X and changes along Dimension K. Seeman[57] has reported a finding of this kind in his study of Ohio school superintendents. He found that those superintendents who were most successful in securing salary raises for teachers were described by these teachers as men who did not spend much time in personal contact with them. The teachers perceived these superintendents as a little "stand-offish" from the faculty group. As Seeman points out, the superintendent has only a finite amount of time at his command. To secure salary raises for his teachers, he must do a lot of "politicking" in the community, leaving less time available for interpersonal contacts with individual staff members. It is not the responsibility of the social scientist to declare which objective is more important: higher salaries for the teachers, or a greater feeling of camaraderie between the superintendent and the staff. But the scientist can show, as Seeman has done, that it is unrealistic to expect the superintendent to accomplish both these objectives simultaneously. To accomplish the one objective, the superintendent must divert appreciable effort from the other. This does not mean that the two objectives can never be achieved simultaneously. In order to accomplish this, then, an assistant may have to be added to the administrator's staff to take care of one of the two roles.

Studies such as this one by Seeman permit us to identify the incompatibilities that reside in the statement of the task. When one states a proposition in "ideal" terms, he deals with a level of irreality where "all things are possible at all times." At this ideal level choices are seldom coerced. In real life, where time is finite, each person must make choices and must effect compromises. In dealing with the task of educational administration, it is important to keep clearly in mind this distinction between the unreal and noncoercive character of ideal statements about objectives, and the reality of the world in which administrators operate, where events enforce upon the leader and the group members a continuous series of choices.

This is one of the primary reasons why it is necessary to spell out criteria objectively. Rigorous research in developing dependable criteria will expose the inadequacies of statements of the task; it will help distinguish betweeen wistful hopes for "pie in the sky" and task objectives that are in accord with the reality of the superintendent's job.

The Combination of Panels I, II, and IV

We will now consider the relationship between Panels I, II, and IV, as these have been aligned in Figure 2.4.

Figure 2.4 illustrates the essence of the paradigm: that the fundamental purpose is to delineate the relationship between the *behavior* of the administrator (Panel II) and *changes* in the organization's achievement (Box 29). These changes in organization achievement should be measured in respect to the same task(s) that have been defined for the organization in Panel I. The task is defined in ideal terms, whereas the changes in organization achievement are measured in respect to what actually happens, but always with reference to the objective set forth in the task statement. Accordingly, in a research design that purports to describe the relationship between the behavior of the administrator and the organization's achievement, the behavior of the administrator must be treated as the independent (or experimental) variable and changes in the organization's achievement as the dependent variables. *Let it be emphasized again that, if one fails to establish the relationship between the behavior of the administrator and syntalic measures of the organization's effectiveness, he evades the most fundamental research issue at stake.*

Figure 2.4 also points up the fact that the ultimate criterion of the administrator's effectiveness (Panel IV, Box 29) must be measured in respect to the same dimensions of behavior (or products of behavior) as are used to define the task (Panel I).

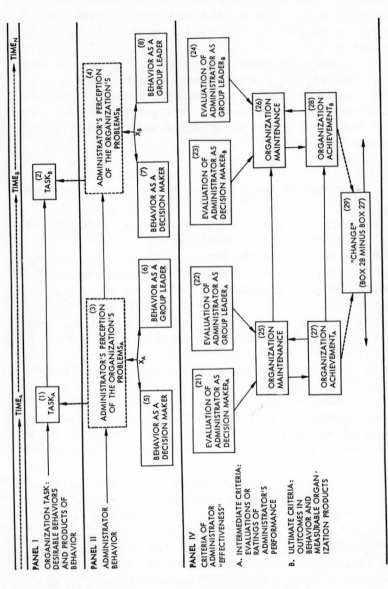

FIGURE 2.4   Panels I, II, and IV of the paradigm.

Panel III—Variables Associated with Administrator Behavior

We now will examine Panel III (Figure 2.5) apart from the rest of the paradigm. After we have done this, we then will consolidate the total paradigm and will discuss its implications.

The variables in Panel III are those which affect the relationship between the administrator behavior variables in Panel II and the effectiveness criteria in Panel IV. They are, in effect, "conditional" variables; variables that define the conditions under which significant relationships may be expected to obtain between the variables in Panel II and Panel IV. These variables are assumed to affect the behavior of the administrator. However, the researcher is not interested in their *general effect* upon the administrator's behavior, but in their focal effect upon those facets of his behavior that are related to pertinent criteria of effectiveness. Schematically, the reasoning may be summarized as follows:

1. Let the correlation between Administrator Behavior Variable X and Criterion Variable Y be designated as r_{xy}.

2. Variable X is measured under the conditions specified by variables $K, L, M \ldots N$ in Panel III; by the presence or absence of specified conditions; or by the degree to which these conditions are present.

3. The correlations between X and $K, L, M \ldots N$ and between Y and $K, L, M \ldots N$ can be computed.

4. From these two arrays of zero-order correlations, the corresponding partial correlations and multiple correlations can then be computed. The multiple regression equations derived from these correlations will then permit the determination of which variables or combinations of variables in the $K \ldots N$ series (all in Panel III) are associated with either increases or decreases in r_{xy}.

The variables in Panel III have been classified into three broad groups: A, B, and C. Each of the three groups has been subdivided horizontally to parallel the broad division in Panel II between "administrator behavior as a decision maker" and "administrator behavior as a group leader." Some variables in Panel III obviously do not fall neatly into this subdivision; for this reason dotted lines have been used to frame the respective pairs of

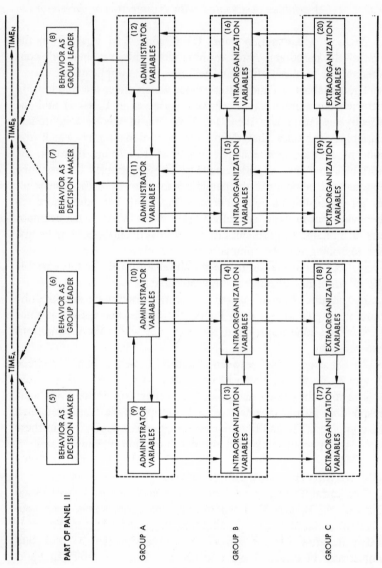

FIGURE 2.5   Panel III of the paradigm: variables.

boxes—for example, 9 and 10, 13 and 14. This division, however, serves to emphasize the two major aspects of administrator behavior.

Group A: Administrator Variables (Boxes 9, 10, 11, and 12). These refer to those attributes and characteristics of the administrator as an individual that can be measured apart from his membership in a specified formal organization. His age, intelligence, academic training, and experience as a teacher or as a school administrator are variables in this category. This list could be expanded considerably. Some of these variables are more closely associated with the administrator's behavior as a group leader than with his behavior as a decision maker. For example, personality characteristics associated with the administrator's "consideration" toward group members are relevant in Box 10, but are probably of little consequence in Box 9. Similarly, some administrator attributes highly associated with his behavior as a decision maker may or may not be associated with his behavior as a group leader. These two vertical channels have been separated deliberately on the chart in order to point up a provocative area for future research on the extent to which skills that contribute to good decision-making also contribute to effective group leadership.

Note the major difference between the variables in Panel II and those in Group A of Panel III. If a variable in Individual X can be measured completely apart from his membership in Organization Y and his assignment as *Administrator Z*, then this variable belongs in Panel III. For example, in prediction studies in educational administration where graduate students are measured on various attributes before they are assigned to jobs in school systems, the variables defined by these measures are examples of those in Group A, Panel III. On the other hand, if the behavior measured depends upon Individual X's assignment as Superintendent S in School T, and if this behavior is measured in respect to the superintendent's decisions for School T and in terms of his interaction with the group members of this school, then the variables that define this behavior should be classified in Panel II rather than in Panel III.[58]

Group B: Intraorganization Variables (Boxes 13, 14, 15, and 16). These refer to measurable characteristics of (1) the organi-

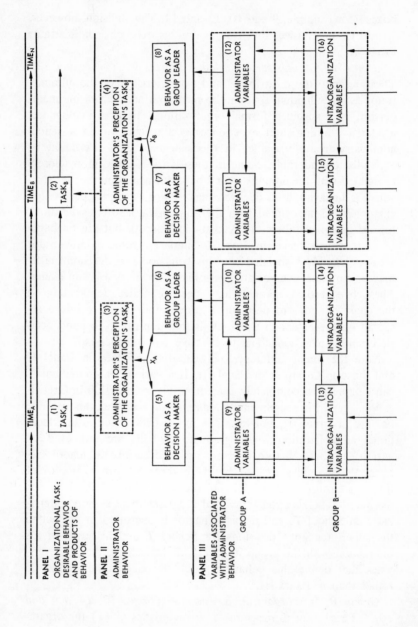

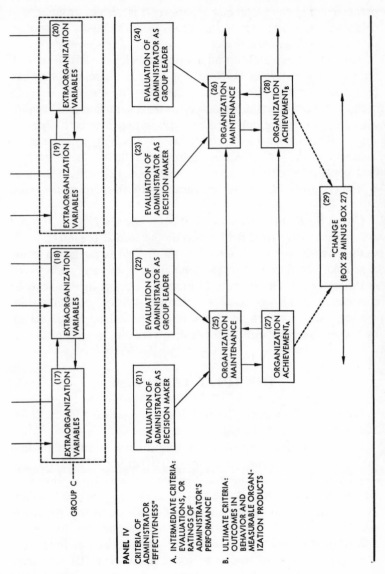

FIGURE 2.6 Paradigm for research on administrator behavior.

zation's administrative structure—for example, whether flat or pyramidal; (2) the group *qua* group—that is, size of group, group cohesiveness, group morale; and (3) group members other than the officially designated leader.

The bulk of research on administrator behavior has dealt with the variables in Group B. Note that some of these variables can be measured before the individual members are constituted into a group, whereas others are based upon the interaction and reciprocal perceptions of group members *qua* group members. For example, the intelligence or the years of teaching experience of Teachers *A, B, C . . . K* can be recorded before these teachers ever come into contact with each other, but their cohesiveness as a faculty group cannot be measured until this group has been constituted.

Group C: Extraorganization Variables (Boxes 17, 18, 19, and 20). These refer to variables outside the formal organization. In studies where the public school is the formal organization being examined, variables that define community "pressures" are placed in this category. The strength of financial support for the schools, community mores on teacher-personnel policies, population increases, racial conflicts, and constraints placed upon the school by "power interests" are all illustrative variables in Group C.

THE TOTAL PARADIGM

We can now examine the paradigm as a whole (Figure 2.6). There are four fundamental points to be noted:

1. The primary purpose is to identify the relationships that exist between the *behavior* of the administrator (Panel II) and *changes* in the organization's achievement (Panel IV-B, Box 29). No matter how successful one may be in defining the relationships in other parts of the paradigm, until he pins down this particular relationship he will have missed the fundamental research issue.

2. Research efforts to date may be characterized as follows:

    (a) They have tended to focus upon Panel III and have restricted their analyses to the relationship among variables *within* this panel.

(b) They have been directed to the study of administrator variables (Boxes 9, 10, 11 and 12) as related to intermediate criteria of administrator effectiveness (Panel IV-A), without either going through Panel II (the behavior of the administrator) or following through from Panel IV-A to IV-B to demonstrate the relationship between evaluations of the administrator and objective criteria of the organization's accomplishments.

3. It is possible to design studies in which administrator behavior variables (Panel II) will be predicted from the variables in Panel III. When this is done, the measures in Panel III must be treated as independent variables and those in Panel II as dependent. Studies of this kind provide useful information, *but this information is of limited value unless one proceeds to the next step of determining the relationship between the behavior predicted in Panel II (from the variables in Panel III) and the criteria in Panel IV.* Research confined to the variables in Panel III, or even to those in Panels II and III, tends to become frustratingly circular because it fails to tackle the criterion issue.

4. Research needs to be done in the areas defined by all four panels, but it would be good strategy to maintain a balance in the energy directed along these four fronts. A great amount of research has been conducted on the variables in Panel III. It is time that we devote as much or more effort to Panels IV and II as has already been poured into Panel III. It is so easy to be tempted down the endless by-paths within Panel III that one is liable to forget that the main highway to research progress runs between Panels II and IV.

To illustrate these points we can refer to the simplified version of the paradigm presented in Figure 2.7. In this figure the time line has been eliminated, and the separate boxes at each horizontal level have been consolidated.

Note the direction of the arrows. Since the task defines the purpose of the organization, the *change* criteria of the organization's achievement are measured in respect to this task. Hence an arrow points from Panel IV to Panel I. The focus of the research is upon the administrator, and since the purpose is to predict changes in organization achievement from his behavior, the arrow

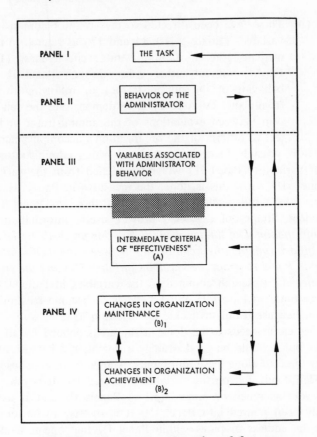

FIGURE 2.7 Condensed version of the paradigm. Note that there is no direct connection between Panels III and IV.

from Panel II points to Panel IV. In Panel IV these flow lines have been split to show that it is preferable to go from II to IV-B. If one goes through IV-A instead, it is still incumbent upon him to demonstrate that there is a significant relationship between IV-A and IV-B.[59] The crux of the problem is to predict events in Panel IV-B on the basis of the variables identified in Panel II. All other relationships are adjuvant.

Panel III variables are studied so as to increase the accuracy of the predictions made from the variables in Panel II. Hence the arrow points from III to II. *Note especially that there is no direct connection between Panels III and IV, that the flow between these two panels must always be mediated through Panel II.* In short, we are interested not in just any variable associated with the administrator's behavior, but only in those variables in Panel III associated with aspects of the administrator's behavior that are, in turn, significantly related to the criteria in Panel IV. This means that the selection of Panel III variables by "shotgun" methods is out of order. Instead, one must start first by identifying those leader behavior variables (Panel II) that are related to changes in the organization's achievement. Then he must select for study only those variables in Panel III that are pertinent to the leader behavior variables which have been identified. The choice of variables to be studied in Panel III must be guided by theoretical formulations that are relatively explicit. This is a sharpshooting rather than a shotgun approach, and one that requires that we name our targets before we start shooting. Failure to appreciate this strategy has resulted in a considerable waste of research time and effort in tinkering with irrelevant variables within Panel III.

The condensed form of the paradigm can be extended to compare two organizations—for example, two school systems (A and B) in which the administrator behavior of Superintendents X and Y is to be studied. This comparison is given in Figure 2.8. Let it be assumed that the task of the two organizations is identical. Let it be further assumed that the intraorganization and extraorganization variables in Panel III are also identical, in both kind and degree, for School Systems A and B. If then, Administrator Y possesses leader behavior skills superior to those of Administrator X, one would predict that the amount of "desirable" change in the achievement of Organization B would be greater than the amount of change in the achievement of Organization A. The desirability of change is defined in respect to the task statement. The measurement of changes in behavior and in behavior products requires that the organization's achievements in these respects be measured at two points in time, herein designated as Time K and Time L. In this research design, it is predicted that where Administrator X's leader behavior skills are less than ($<$) those of Administrator

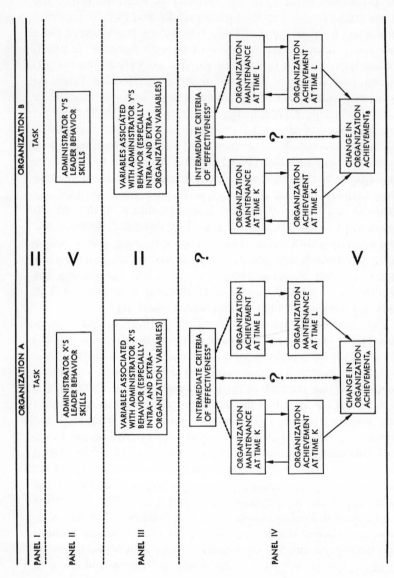

FIGURE 2.8 Comparison of Organizations A and B.

Y and where the task is the same and the associated variables (Panel III) are equivalent, then the desirable changes in Organization *A* will be less than ($<$) those in Organization *B*. But changes in the organization's achievement do not occur along a single dimension. Nor are leader behavior skills unidimensional. Consequently, the primary research objective is to determine what leader behavior variables (that is, skills, attributes) are associated with varying degrees of change along specified dimensions of achievement.

Note that a question mark (?) has been placed between the "intermediate criteria of effectiveness" boxes for Organizations *A* and *B* (Figure 2.8). If the correlations between the intermediate criteria and the ultimate criteria of change are sufficiently high, then with the intermediate criteria we also will find that $A < B$. But if the intermediate criteria are not highly correlated with the change criteria, the relationship at this intermediate level could be expressed either by $A > B$, or $A = B$. Conversely, if we should demonstrate empirically that $A < B$ at the intermediate criteria level, this in itself does not guarantee that $A < B$ in respect to changes in the organization's achievement.

One may object that it is difficult to establish an equivalence of the associated variables in Panel III for Organizations *A* and *B*. It is. Yet this need not force us to reject the fundamental research design, for where it is infeasible for us to control these variables experimentally, we can still have recourse to statistical control through several methods of multivariate analysis.[60]

Figure 2.8 reveals how very important it is to identify and measure pertinent dimensions of *change* in the organization's achievement. In short, one inevitably comes back to the "criterion issue," and he is forced to conclude that in our research on administrative behavior we will be stalemated until we launch a formidable attack upon the whole criterion problem.[61]

At this juncture it is important that we digress a little from the main argument to discuss the concept of "the administrative process," a concept which in current discussions of administration has become almost a slogan. Because "process" is such a tricky term, it is important that we emphasize a warning about it. Unless one is extremely careful, he can be easily tempted into talking about

process as if it were a free-floating affair, detached from the behavior of individuals. We must, therefore, remember that if the
concept of process is to have any usefulness, its referents must be
rooted in behavior and behavior products. An outside observer
can never observe process as process; he can observe only a
sequence of behavior or behavior products from which he can
infer process. This inference is based upon whatever relationship
he discerns in a sequential ordering of behavior and events. But
process always implies purpose, and the observer's perception of
sequence or of the ordering of behavior is cued by his own perception of the ultimate purpose of the actors in the organization.
Process for the sheer sake of process is nonsense; it must always be
directed toward a specified, or at least a dimly perceived, objective.
Accordingly, whenever a sequence of events is observed, the inferences made about the character of the process are structured in
large measure by personal judgments about the greater desirability
of Organization Achievement A as balanced against Organization
Achievement B. These judgments influence one's perception of the
behavior and events that he observes and predispose him toward
making one set of inferences about behavior (that is, one identification of the process involved) rather than another. Yet another
observer, operating from a different set of judgments in respect
to the purpose of the actor's behavior, may identify a totally dif-
erent process that is no less valid or real than the first. Gregg, in
writing about the administrative process, for example, uses
decision-making as the pivot on which he hinges other aspects of
this problem.[62] He could just as readily use a different pivot and
could develop a classificatory schema no less valid than the one
he proposes. Because his choice of rubrics is made on heuristic
grounds, it constitutes a strategic decision to which the orthodox
criteria of "validity" do not apply.

In observing process, it is difficult, if not impossible, to keep
evaluations and descriptions separate. In this regard, the distinction made in the paradigm between the task and the problem(s)
is of particular importance. The task, it will be recalled, is defined
by outside observers, but the problem is defined solely by the
administrator as actor. Similarly, when discussing the administrative process it is important to be aware of the vantage point from

which observations are made: is process described by an outside observer in normative terms (that is, how things "ideally" should operate), or is it described through the perception of an actor within a formal organization (that is, how things do operate)? Hence, it is important that we distinguish between the "oughts" and the "is's" in discussing the administrative process, and that we approach the concept of process with considerable wariness and tentativeness.

IMPLICATIONS

The paradigm presented in this chapter was devised to facilitate research on administrator behavior and to contribute to the formulation of a useful theory of administration. The model proposed is tentative and heuristic; its components are selective rather than exhaustive. It is crude, but if it provides a useful way of thinking about administrator behavior it will have served its purpose.

To keep the presentation simple, we have not discussed many sources of interaction variance among the variables assigned to Panels II, III, and IV. Nor have specific studies to illustrate research on the variables within each panel been cited. We have concentrated upon the major outline of the paradigm (Figure 2.6). In Figures 2.7 and 2.8, the paradigm was reduced to skeletal form in order to emphasize the major argument concerning the *direction* of relationships among the central variables.

Substantially, we have concluded that progress in research on administrator behavior is seriously blocked by our failure to develop objective and dependable criteria of administrative effectiveness. We have argued that it is desirable to define these criteria in respect to *changes* in the organization's achievement.

In presenting the paradigm, several issues in research methodology have been considered. In commenting upon conspicuous limitations in present knowledge about administrative behavior, we have suggested that much research on this topic has gone awry. In conclusion, therefore, we can summarize our criticism of typical research approaches in educational administration:

1. We have failed to recognize the importance of theory and

have relied too heavily upon naked empiricism. This has led to an uneconomical use of shotgun approaches in which we collect data first, and then, at the analysis stage, ask ourselves if anything can be done with the pile of data. In short, we have imputed too much significance to facts per se.

We certainly have used the term "theory" enough—often with deceptive glibness. Yet we have used it naïvely and have betrayed a limited knowledge of the techniques of theory construction in science.[63] We have been inclined to dignify almost any set of speculations with the name of "theory." But a theory is more than a conglomerate of common-sense speculations; it must possess specified logical properties and must be internally consistent.[64] It can be judged best in respect to two major criteria. Can we generate fruitful, testable hypotheses from it? Does this particular theory, as opposed to others, permit us to predict events in the "real world" with greater accuracy? No matter how elegant a theory may appear, it is of dubious worth if it fails to satisfy these criteria.

2. We have directed a disproportionate amount of research energy to isolated problems and peripheral studies rather than to central investigations which yield conclusions of broad generalizability. Our flight from theory and our preoccupation with immediate practical problems have made our research episodic rather than programmatic and have stunted our capacity for research growth. Importuned to be practical and influenced against our better judgment by the thinly veiled contempt of our colleagues toward theorists and other eggheads, we succumb and rationalize our position by saying, "It takes a long time to solve theoretical problems, and meantime there are many practical, everyday problems that we must attend to. Let's take care of them first! We'll get to the more basic problems later." But we seldom do.

Education and the applied social sciences are not alone in this shortcoming; the same difficulty permeates all spheres of science today. But an awakening is taking place, particularly in the physical sciences; more and more energy is being redirected to basic research. A similar shift in emphasis is needed in educational administration. This is not to disparage practical, operational research, but to emphasize that these activities should be balanced by—and perhaps even preceded by—a long-range program of basic research.

3. We have tended to be too parochial in our research outlook. Infatuated with the uniqueness of educational administration, we have often been blinded to the problems that educational administration shares with all other forms of administration. Perhaps it is time for us to move toward a science of administration as *administration*. We have been parochial, too, in not drawing upon the resources of such other disciplines as the social sciences, personnel administration, and political science. The CPEA program[65] has, of course, done a great deal to show us how these other disciplines can contribute to our field, but as yet we have not progressed far in incorporating the insights and techniques of the social sciences into our own research methodologies.

4. We have failed to define our concepts clearly; they lack precision. Because we have not learned the lessons that the general semanticists have tried to teach us, we have persisted in using concepts which have no clear referents in behavior. To be charitable, we can condone this laxity by describing it as a confusion in terminology. But the question arises as to whether it may not be a deeper failure—a lack of rigorous thinking about the objectives of educational administration.

Our problems of language are exacerbated because administration may be approached from the point of view of a normative discipline as well as from that of a descriptive science. Both approaches are important, but the researcher must keep the two realms straight and must know at all times which approach is being used. Administration as a normative discipline deals with how an administrator ought to behave and is predicated upon an ideal situation in which time is theoretically infinite and choices are not coercive. In studying administration as social scientists, our concern is with how administrators actually behave in a real world where time is limited and choices must be made. In choosing one point of view, the other is not necessarily excluded, but the error of confusing the terms and standards of one realm with those of the other must be guarded against. Research on educational administration has been severely impeded because the language of these two realms has been confused.

By heeding these four criticisms we can raise our research standards and can increase our fund of dependable knowledge. This knowledge, in turn, will equip us to do a better job in selecting and training future administrators.

The research objectives which have been proposed in this chapter will not be achieved easily or quickly; nor can we expect that research standards will be raised overnight. Yet the difficulty of the task certainly makes it no less important. The central issue is whether the profession of educational administration is willing to accept responsibility for long-range programmatic research on administrative behavior. To those who may complain that the sights for research have been set too high, here is a reply in the words of T. S. Eliot:

> The fact that a problem will certainly take a long time to solve, and that it will demand the attention of many minds for several generations, is no justification for postponing the study. And, in times of emergency, it may prove in the long run that the problems we have postponed or ignored, rather than those we have failed to attack successfully, will return to plague us. Our difficulties of the moment must always be dealt with somehow: but our permanent difficulties are difficulties of every moment.[66]

NOTES FOR CHAPTER 2

1. From Roald F. Campbell and Russell T. Gregg (eds.), *Administrative Behavior in Education* (New York: Harper & Brothers, 1957), pp. 155-199. Reprinted by permission of the publishers.

2. The term "model" is used in the sense of a theoretical model or mathematical model, and with no connotation of exemplariness.

3. Chester I. Barnard, *The Functions of the Executive* (Cambridge, Mass.: Harvard University Press, 1938).

4. Alexander Leighton, *The Governing of Men* (Princeton, N.J.: Princeton University Press, 1955).

5. Herbert A. Simon, *Administrative Behavior* (New York: The Macmillan Company, 1947).

6. Arthur P. Coladarci and Jacob W. Getzels, *The Use of Theory in Educational Administration* (Stanford, Calif.: Stanford University Press, 1955).

7. Francis G. Cornell, "Socially Perceptive Administration," *The Phi Delta Kappan*, **36**, No. 6 (March 1955), pp. 219-223.

8. Daniel E. Griffiths, "Toward a Theory of Administrative Behavior," in Campbell and Gregg (eds.), *Administrative Behavior in Education*, pp. 354-390.

9. John Walton, "The Theoretical Study of Educational Administration," *Harvard Educational Review*, **25**, No. 3 (Summer 1955), pp. 169-178.

10. Published by the Graduate School of Business and Public Administration (Ithaca, N.Y.: Cornell University).

11. Edward H. Litchfield, "Notes on a General Theory of Administration," *Administrative Science Quarterly*, **1**, No. 1 (June 1956), pp. 3-29.

12. James D. Thompson, "On Building an Administrative Science," *Administrative Science Quarterly*, **1**, No. 1 (June 1956), pp. 102-111.

13. For example, the term "theory" is used in the philosophical sense by Orin B. Graff and Calvin M. Street, "Developing a Value Framework for Educational Administration," in Campbell and Gregg (eds.), *Administrative Behavior in Education*, pp. 120-152.

14. See Herbert Feigl, "Principles and Problems of Theory Construction in Psychology," in Wayne Dennis (ed.), *Current Trends in Psychological Theory* (Pittsburgh: University of Pittsburgh Press, 1951). Feigl's position is discussed in Ch. 1 of the present book.

15. The term "operational definition" is defined by Percy W. Bridgman, *The Logic of Modern Physics* (New York: The Macmillan Company, 1927), Ch. 1. For a more recent discussion of this concept, see Robert H. Ennis, "Operational Definitions," *American Educational Research Journal*, **1**, No. 3 (May 1964), pp. 183-201.

16. Ernst Cassirer, *An Essay on Man* (New Haven, Conn.: Yale University Press, 1944), pp. 208-209. Italics mine.

17. Harrison Brown, "The Case for Pure Research," *Saturday Review*, **39**, No. 12 (March 24, 1956), p. 56.

18. For a discussion of programmatic research in the social sciences, see John G. Darley, "Five Years of Social Science Research: Retrospect and Prospect," in Harold Guetzkow (ed.), *Groups, Leadership and Men* (Pittsburgh: Carnegie Press, 1951). See also Ronald Lippitt, "The Strategy of Socio-Psychological Research," in James G. Miller (ed.), *Experiments in Social Process* (New York: McGraw-Hill Book Co., Inc., 1950).

19. Samuel M. Brownell, in a talk to Phi Delta Kappa Society in 1955, as quoted in *Higher Education,* **13**, No. 1 (September 1956), p. 2.

20. Litchfield, "Notes on a General Theory of Administration," pp. 7-9.

21. Carroll L. Shartle, "Studies in Naval Leadership: Part I," in Guetzkow (ed.), *Groups, Leadership and Men,* pp. 121-122. Italics mine.

For a report on the plan of The Ohio State Leadership Studies, see Ralph M. Stogdill and Carroll L. Shartle, *Methods in the Study of Administrative Leadership* (Columbus, Ohio: Bureau of Business Research, The Ohio State University, 1955).

22. For this distinction I am indebted to the insight of Dr. Harold B. Pepinsky. For an example in which this distinction is discussed and applied, see Harold B. Pepinsky, Pauline N. Pepinsky, and William B. Pavlik, *Motivational Factors in Individual and Group Productivity: I. Successful Task Accomplishment as Related to Task-Relevant Personal Beliefs* (Columbus, Ohio: The Ohio State University Research Foundation, 1956).

23. Ralph M. Stogdill, "Leadership, Membership and Organization," *Psychological Bulletin,* **47**, No. 1 (January 1950), p. 3.

24. Fritz J. Roethlisberger and William J. Dickson, *Management and the Worker* (Cambridge, Mass.: Harvard University Press, 1942).

25. Stogdill, "Leadership, Membership and Organization," pp. 6-7.

26. Mason Haire, "Industrial Social Psychology," in Gardner Lindzey (ed.), *Handbook of Social Psychology,* Vol. II (Cambridge, Mass.: Addison-Wesley Publishing Company, Inc., 1954), p. 1118.

27. Ralph M. Stogdill *et al., A Predictive Study of Administrative Work Patterns,* Research Monograph No. 85 (Columbus, Ohio: Bureau of Business Research, 1956), p. 35.

28. William Foote Whyte, *Leadership and Group Participation,* Bulletin No. 24 (Ithaca, N.Y.: New York State School of Industrial and Labor Relations, Cornell University, May 1953), pp. 41-42.

29. It should be noted that there are certain circumstances under which the accomplishment of the group's objective may call for the dissolution of the group itself. This would be the case, for example, with an *ad hoc* committee. Unfortunately, many *ad hoc* committees persist as inexorably as do some "temporary" government agencies in Washington, D.C.

30. Office of Strategic Services Assessment Staff, *The Assessment of Men* (New York: Rinehart & Company, Inc., 1948), p. 301.

31. Dorwin Cartwright and Alvin Zander (eds.), *Group Dynamics:*

Research and Theory, 2nd ed. (Evanston, Ill.: Row, Peterson & Company, 1960), p. 496.

32. Barnard, *The Functions of the Executive,* pp. 60-61.

33. This is a key concept in the theory of leadership developed by Hemphill. See John K. Hemphill, "Administration as Problem-solving," in Andrew W. Halpin (ed.), *Administrative Theory in Education* (Chicago: Midwest Administration Center, 1958), pp. 89-118.

34. Andrew W. Halpin, *The Leadership Behavior of School Superintendents,* 2nd ed. (Chicago: Midwest Administration Center, University of Chicago, 1959), p. 4. These findings are summarized in Ch. 3 of the present book.

35. John K. Hemphill and Alvin E. Coons, "Development of the Leader Behavior Description Questionnaire," in Ralph M. Stogdill and Alvin E. Coons, (eds.), *Leader Behavior: Its Description and Measurement* (Columbus, Ohio: The Bureau of Business Research, The Ohio State University, 1957), pp. 6-38.

36. Halpin, *The Leadership Behavior of School Superintendents,* p. 4.

37. Andrew W. Halpin, *Studies in Aircrew Composition III: The Combat Leader Behavior of B-29 Aircraft Commanders* (Washington, D.C.: Bolling Air Force Base, Human Factors Operations Research Laboratories; Air Research and Development Command, HFORL Memo No. TN-54-E, 1953).

38. John K. Hemphill, "Patterns of Leadership Behavior Associated with Administrative Reputation of the Department of a College," *Journal of Educational Psychology,* **46**, No. 7 (November 1955) pp. 385-401.

39. Andrew W. Halpin, "The Leader Behavior and Leadership Ideology of Educational Administrators and Aircraft Commanders," *Harvard Educational Review,* **25**, No. 1 (Winter 1955), pp. 18-32.

40. Halpin, *The Leadership Behavior of School Superintendents,* pp. 11-12.

41. John K. Hemphill, *Situational Factors in Leadership* (Columbus, Ohio: Bureau of Educational Research, The Ohio State University, 1949).

42. Ralph M. Stogdill, "Personal Factors Associated with Leadership," *Journal of Psychology,* **25**, No. 1 (1948), pp. 35-71.

43. Cecil A. Gibb, "Leadership," in Gardner Lindzey (ed.), *Handbook of Social Psychology,* Ch. **24**, pp. 877-920.

44. This, of course, is consistent with a fundamental principle of theory construction that the elements of a theory—that is, the major constructs—be chosen parsimoniously.

45. This refers to "operational definitions" as defined by Bridgman. See note 15.

46. Norms, in the ethical sense, refer to something quite different from norms in the field of tests and measurements. In testing, norms constitute a measure of what *is,* in contrast to standards which afford a measure of what *ought to be.* But in philosophy and ethics a norm indicates not what *is,* but what *ought to be.* Note the utter contradiction in the two ways in which the term has been used. In the present context we shall abide by the ethical meaning of the term because this is the customary connotation employed in discussions of scientific method. For a superb analysis of the difference between the descriptive and the normative approach, see F.S.C. Northrop, *The Logic of the Sciences and the Humanities* (New York: The Macmillan Company, 1949).

47. See Eugene L. Belisle and Cyril G. Sargent, "The Concept of Administration," in Campbell and Gregg (eds.), *Administrative Behavior in Education,* Ch. 3, pp. 82-119, for a further discussion of this issue of task stability.

48. Pepinsky *et al., Motivational Factors in Individual and Group Productivity: I.*

49. Asahel D. Woodruff, "The Relationship Between Functional and Verbalized Motives," *Journal of Educational Psychology,* **35**, No. 2 (February 1944), pp. 101-107.

50. Asahel D. Woodruff, *A Study of Choices* (Provo, Utah: Brigham Young University Press, 1948). Copies may be obtained from the author at the College of Education, University of Utah, Salt Lake City.

51. Stogdill and Shartle, *Methods in the Study of Administrative Leadership.*

52. Talcott Parsons, "Suggestions for a Sociological Approach to the Theory of Organizations: I," *Administrative Science Quarterly,* **1**, No. 1 (June 1956), pp. 63-85.

53. These products may include changes in the internal structure of the organization or changes along such dimensions as "morale."

54. Raymond B. Cattell, "New Concepts for Measuring Leadership, in Terms of Group Syntality," *Human Relations,* **4**, No. 2 (1951), pp. 161-184.

55. *Ibid.,* pp. 174-175.

56. Halpin, *The Leadership Behavior of School Superintendents.*

57. Melvin Seeman, "Role Conflict and Ambivalence in Leadership," *American Sociological Review,* **18**, No. 4 (August 1953), pp. 373-380.

58. In Cattell's terminology (see note 54) Group A, Panel III, is made up of "population" parameters, whereas Panel II is composed of "structure" parameters.

59. This, of course, is the point of Cattell's plea that we go directly to syntalic measures.

60. A simple form of such analysis has been outlined earlier in this chapter. The partial correlation technique and other forms of multivariate analysis are explicated in most standard texts in statistics.

61. For a further discussion of this criterion problem in the study of school superintendents, see Halpin, *The Leadership Behavior of School Superintendents,* p. 82. This discussion is summarized in Ch. 3 of the present book.

62. Russell T. Gregg, "The Administrative Process," in Campbell and Gregg (eds.), *Administrative Behavior in Education,* pp. 269-317.

63. Among other things, we have tended to rely upon materialistic rather than upon mathematical models of behavior. For an excellent analysis of the difference between these models, see John Z. Young, *Doubt and Certainty in Science* (Oxford: Clarendon Press, 1951), especially his Sixth Lecture, "The Changing Symbols of Science," pp. 100-112.

64. See Cassirer, *An Essay on Man.*

65. Cooperative Program on Educational Administration, sponsored by the Kellogg Foundation.

66. Thomas S. Eliot, *The Idea of a Christian Society* (New York: Harcourt, Brace, & World, Inc., 1940), p. 3.

PART TWO

Research on Administration

3

How Leaders Behave[1]

We will greatly increase our understanding of leadership phenomena if we abandon the notion of leadership as a trait, and concentrate instead upon an analysis of "the behavior of leaders."

The idea of leadership has been used in a variety of ways, most commonly in referring to the "leader" as an outstanding member of a class. Thus radio and TV commercials proclaim that a certain brand of cigarettes is the leading one, and that a new movie star is the leader of the current covey of actresses. Because of our American predilection for bigness, in no matter what sphere, the leader in this sense refers to the most popular product—or more specifically, to that item with the greatest sales-market potential. Similarly in education, we often confuse leadership with sheer bigness. But this use of the term applies equally to either things or people, and fails to take into account the central psychological characteristic of leader behavior: that this is the behavior of a leader functioning vis-à-vis members of a group in an endeavor to facilitate the solution of group problems. The behavior of the leader and the behavior of group members are inextricably interwoven, and the behavior of both is determined to a great degree by formal requirements imposed by the institution of which the group is a part. For example, Mary Noel, fourth-grade teacher, is the formally designated leader of the children in her class. How she behaves as a leader is influenced by the behavior of the children (which includes their expectations of how a teacher *should* behave as a leader). Moreover, her behavior is conditioned by the policies and regulations, both written and unwritten, of the particular school system in which she is employed. As a result of the year which they spend with her, the children in Mary's class are expected to show certain minimum changes in behavior, especially in respect to scholastic achievement and skill in interpersonal relations. The accomplishment of these objectives is the salient group problem to which Mary must contribute her solution, and it is presumed that her contribution will be greater than that of any other group member in her fourth-grade class. This, of course, is why she was employed.

In accepting her assignment as teacher of the fourth grade, Mary assumes a role as leader of this group. This, however, tells us absolutely nothing about the effectiveness of her performance in this role—that is, how effectively she contributes to the solution of group problems. What, then, are we to mean by leadership? The assumption of a leader's role? The effectiveness with which this role is performed? Or the capacity of the individual to perform this role effectively? These cause a further question to arise: By what criteria are we to judge effectiveness? For research on leader behavior shows that effectiveness in respect to Criterion X is not necessarily correlated with effectiveness in regard to Criterion Y. For example, the behavior of a leader who is effective in maintaining high morale and good human relations within the group is not necessarily effective in accomplishing high production and goal-achievement.

This dilemma of definition emerges from the fact that we have incorporated into the term "leadership" both descriptive and evaluative components, and have thus burdened this single word (and the concept it represents) with two connotations: one refers to a role and the behavior of a person in this role, and the other is an evaluation of the individual's performance in the role. We have compounded this confusion even more by conceptualizing leadership as an essentially innate capacity of the individual manifested with equal facility, regardless of the situation in which the leader finds himself. Yet Stogdill[2] has shown that the trait approach to leadership, as it has been used in most studies reported in the literature, has yielded negligible, and often contradictory, results. Sanford has aptly summarized the situation:

> From all these studies of the leader we can conclude, with reasonable certainty, that:
>
> (a) there are either no general leadership traits or, if they do

exist, they are not to be described in any of our famil[
psychological or common-sense terms,

(b) in a specific situation, leaders do have traits which set
them apart from followers, but *what* traits set *what* leaders
apart from *what* followers will vary from situation to
situation.[3]

In short, the behavior of leaders varies widely from one leadership situation to another. In this connection, Hemphill,[4] in an
elaborate and careful study of approximately 500 assorted groups,
has demonstrated empirically that variance in leader behavior is
significantly associated with situational variance. For example, let
us consider the size of the group as a situational determinative.
Hemphill has analyzed in detail the relation between the leader's
behavior and the size of the group and has concluded that, as
compared with small groups, large groups make more and different
demands upon the leader. In general, the leader in a large group
tends to be impersonal and is inclined to enforce rules and regulations firmly and impartially. In smaller groups, the leader plays a
more personal role. He is more willing (and perhaps also more
able) to make exceptions to rules and to treat each group member
as an individual. Stated baldly, the evidence from these studies
means that it is possible for Mary to function effectively as a leader
in the fourth-grade class of *East* Clambake Elementary School,
and yet operate quite ineffectively as a leader in the fourth-grade
class of *West* Clambake Elementary School. In brief, much depends on the situation.

However, we do not want to overemphasize the determinative
effects of a given situation on a given leader. The question never
is one of whether the results of a leader's efforts are determined
either by the situation *or* by specific behaviors of the leader. Rather
must we phrase our question in a different form: how much of the
variance in group productivity is associated with variance in
Situational Variable *A*? With variance in Situational Variable *B*?
How much of the variance in productivity is associated with
variance in, for example, the Consideration of the leaders? With
variance in the leader's skill in Initiating Structure in his interaction among group members?

We can understand the current status of leadership research

better if we will first stop to analyze briefly the way in which knowledge is accumulated in any scientific area.

Historically, in most disciplines one discovers a tendency for new movements or emphases to arise in revolt against the orthodoxies of a given period. These new movements later tend to crystalize into the orthodoxies of the next period, and fresh countermovements arise in turn. The final position we reach is usually one on middle ground between the original orthodoxy and the first reaction against it. Zig-zag movements of this kind are not uncommon in the progress of science. Leadership research is currently in the process of following this same developmental course. Early research was marked by a search for traits of leadership that would discriminate between leaders and nonleaders. The situational emphasis which has characterized research during the past decade arose as a protest against the earlier trait approach, but in some respects this present emphasis may have been carried to excess. To say that leader behavior is determined exclusively by situational factors is to deny to the leader freedom of choice and determination. This violates common sense and experience. Even now, within research circles, a gradual but growing counter-reaction is taking shape—a drawing away from the extreme situational position, with increasing recognition that the truth probably lies in an area of middle ground.

But now in appraising the trait approach anew, we will have the advantage of a fresh perspective. In the next decade, research workers may be less avid in seizing upon convenient phenotypic data as pertinent variables and may be more willing to explore the relevance of genotypic variables that are not as readily discernible as "givens."[5] In short, in the past we have tended to examine essentially peripheral traits and attributes. Although we have been guided by intuition about possible relationships between these attributes of leaders and other leadership phenomena, we have operated, for the most part, without the benefit of sufficient empirical information about leadership phenomena that would enable us to sharpen our definitions of the variables involved. Herein lies a major benefit of the period of situationally-oriented leadership research: this research has suggested new ways of constituting the more crucial variables that pertain to the individual as a leader.

Eventually, it may be possible to define a few variables of typic order that will prove predictive of leader behavior ___ __ variety of situations. For example, McClelland's[6] series of studies on the achievement motive may throw new light on leadership behavior. Thus Hemphill and his co-workers[7] have conducted a series of experiments on small groups in order to determine the relationship between (1) "need achievement and need affiliation," and (2) the frequency with which group members attempt leadership acts. With the accumulation of a fund of experimental evidence in this area, the new theories of leadership that are generated probably will incorporate ideas which, at least superficially, will resemble those that characterized the original trait approach. The difference in conceptual sophistication is likely, however, to be no less profound than that between pre-Einsteinian and post-Einsteinian physics. All this, of course, rests with the future. The point is made at this juncture simply to underscore one salient feature of good research strategy—that it is sometimes wise to move backwards (or at least in a direction that appears to be backwards) in order to insure greater and more sure-footed strides into the future.

These, then, are the reasons why we prefer at this time to think in terms of leader behavior rather than leadership. Our concept of leader behavior sidesteps a few important issues. It limits us, for instance, to dealing with formal organizations, and focuses attention exclusively upon the "head men" within these organizations. Furthermore, the whole question of the distribution of leadership acts among members of the group is avoided. Nor are our formulations readily adaptable to certain aspects of leadership phenomena that can be observed within informal community groups. Our only defense of such limitations is that we have had to start somewhere. We chose to start with the officially designated leaders of formal organizations. This was an heuristic decision. As more information is gathered and as we gradually begin to build a systematic conceptual framework within which additional hypotheses about leader behavior can be tested, we shall undoubtedly test these hypotheses in informal as well as formal organizations, and with group members other than those officially designated as leaders. The fact that we have not explored these other leadership phenomena implies no skepticism of their importance but is simply an admission that we have not yet found the time and the opportunity (and the funds) to investigate these equally challenging areas.

What, then, do we gain by shifting our emphasis from leadership to the analysis of the behavior of leaders? There are two major methodological advantages. In the first place, we can deal directly with observable phenomena and need make no a priori assumptions about the identity or structure of whatever capacities may or may not undergird these phenomena. Secondly, this formulation keeps at the forefront of our thinking the importance of differentiating between the *description* of how leaders behave and the *evaluation* of the effectiveness of their behavior in respect to specified performance criteria.

DIMENSIONS OF LEADER BEHAVIOR

Evaluations of leadership, on the one hand, can be obtained readily enough by means of various rating schedules. On the other, the measurement of a group's description of its leader's behavior is a less commonly used procedure. Because we can never measure *all* the behavior of an individual, any measurement procedure we adopt must entail some form of selection. We have chosen to measure two specific dimensions of leader behavior: "Initiating Structure" and "Consideration." You will recall that Initiating Structure refers to the leader's behavior in delineating the relationship between himself and members of the work-group, and in endeavoring to establish well-defined patterns of organization, channels of communication, and methods of procedure. Consideration refers to behavior indicative of friendship, mutual trust, respect, and warmth in the relationship between the leader and the members of his staff.

It is important to note that this concept of Consideration does not include what can be best described as merely "spray-gun consideration." The latter behavior is typified by the PTA smile, and by the oily affability dispensed by administrators at faculty picnics and office parties. Promiscuous Consideration defeats its purpose by its very promiscuity. Genuine Consideration must be focused upon the individual recipient and must be tuned to his requirements at a particular time and place.

There is nothing especially novel about these two dimensions of leader behavior. The principles embodied in the concepts of Initiating Structure and Consideration probably have always been used by effective leaders in guiding their behavior with group members, while the concepts themselves, with different labels perhaps, have been invoked frequently by philosophers and social scientists to explain leadership phenomena. Practical men know that the leader must lead—must initiate action and get things done. But because he must accomplish his purposes through other people, and without jeopardizing the intactness or integrity of the group, the skilled executive knows that he also must maintain good "human relations" if he is to succeed in furthering the purposes of the group. In short, if a leader—whether he be a school superintendent, an aircraft commander, or a business executive—is to be successful, he must contribute to both major group objectives of *goal achievement* and *group maintenance*. In Barnard's terms,[8] he must facilitate cooperative group action that is both *effective* and *efficient*. According to the constructs that we have formulated, this means that the leader should be strong in Initiating Structure and should also show high Consideration for the members of his work-group.

These two kinds of behavior are relatively independent but not necessarily incompatible. Cartwright and Zander, for example, have observed:

> Any given behavior in a group may have significance both for goal achievement and for maintenance. Both may be served simultaneously by the actions of a member, or one may be served at the expense of the other. Thus, a member who helps a group to work cooperatively on a difficult problem may quite inadvertently also help to develop solidarity. In another group, however, an eager member may spur the group on in such a way that frictions develop among the members, and even though the goal is achieved efficiently,[9] the continued existence of the group is seriously endangered.[10]

To measure leader behavior and leadership ideology, we have used a Leader Behavior Description Questionnaire[11] devised by the Personnel Research Board at The Ohio State University.

Hemphill and Coons[12] constructed the original form of this questionnaire, and Halpin and Winer,[13] in reporting the development of an Air Force adaptation of this instrument, identified Initiating Structure and Consideration as two fundamental dimensions of leader behavior. These dimensions were identified on the basis of a factor analysis of the responses of 300 crew members who described the leader behavior of their 52 aircraft commanders. Initiating Structure and Consideration accounted for approximately 34 and 50 per cent, respectively, of the common variance.

On the basis of the factor analysis, keys were constructed for these two dimensions of leadership behavior. The original Consideration key of 28 items has an estimated reliability (corrected by the Spearman-Brown formula) of .94. The corresponding estimate for the 29-item Initiating Structure key is .76. In the later, published form of the LBDQ there are only 15 items on each of the keys. The estimated reliabilities are .93 and .86, respectively.

By measuring the behavior of leaders on the Initiating Structure and the Consideration dimensions, we can determine by objective and reliable means how specific leaders differ in leadership style, and whether these differences are related significantly to independent criteria of the leader's effectiveness and efficiency. In sum, the Leader Behavior Description Questionnaire offers a means of defining these leader behavior dimensions *operationally*,[14] making it possible for us to submit to empirical test additional specific hypotheses about leader and group behavior.

The LBDQ is composed of a series of short, descriptive statements of ways in which leaders may behave. The members of a leader's group indicate the frequency with which he engages in each form of behavior by checking one of five adverbs: always, often, occasionally, seldom, or never. Each of the keys to the dimensions contains 15 items, and each item is scored on a scale from 4 to 0. Consequently, the theoretical range of scores on each dimension is from 0 to 60. The 15 items which define each dimension follow:

Initiating Structure

1. He makes his attitudes clear to the staff.
2. He tries out his new ideas with the staff.

3. He rules with an iron hand.*
4. He criticizes poor work.
5. He speaks in a manner not to be questioned.
6. He assigns staff members to particular tasks.
7. He works without a plan.*
8. He maintains definite standards of performance.
9. He emphasizes the meeting of deadlines.
10. He encourages the use of uniform procedures.
11. He makes sure that his part in the organization is understood by all members.
12. He asks that staff members follow standard rules and regulations.
13. He lets staff members know what is expected of them.
14. He sees to it that staff members are working up to capacity.
15. He sees to it that the work of staff members is coordinated.

Consideration

1. He does personal favors for staff members.
2. He does little things to make it pleasant to be a member of the staff.
3. He is easy to understand.
4. He finds time to listen to staff members.
5. He keeps to himself.*
6. He looks out for the personal welfare of individual staff members.
7. He refuses to explain his actions.*
8. He acts without consulting the staff.*
9. He is slow to accept new ideas.*
10. He treats all staff members as his equals.
11. He is willing to make changes.
12. He is friendly and approachable.
13. He makes staff members feel at ease when talking with them.
14. He puts suggestions made by the staff into operation.
15. He gets staff approval on important matters before going ahead.

The form on which the group members describe their leader's behavior is referred to as the "LBDQ-Real, Staff." With modified

* Scored negatively.

instructions, this same instrument may be used to measure the leader's own leadership ideology. On this form each item is worded to indicate how a leader *should* behave, and the leaders answer the questionnaire accordingly. This form is designated as the "LBDQ-Ideal, Self."[15] Similarly, we may ask the staff members to describe how they believe the leader *should* behave. Such scores are termed "LBDQ-Ideal, Staff."

Although group members differ in their perception of the leader's behavior, analyses of variance in which the "between group" variance and the "within group" variance on these dimension scores were compared for several independent samples of leaders have yielded F ratios all significant at the .01 level of confidence. The leader's behavior therefore can be described most succinctly by assigning to him, for each dimension, the mean of the LBDQ-Real scores by which his group members have described him. The correlations between these Consideration and Initiating Structure scores range between 0.38 and 0.45.

The LBDQ can be adapted readily to different group requirements without altering the meaning of the items. For example, with Air Force personnel the term "crew" is used; with educational administrators, "staff" is substituted for "crew." Similarly, for industrial and other situations, minor changes in wording can be made in each item according to the nature of the groups with which the questionnaire is used.

Again, the leader behavior dimensions of Initiating Structure and Consideration are not to be conceived as traits of leadership. They simply describe the behavior of a leader as he operates in a given situation. Nothing in the research completed to date with the LBDQ contradicts this position. The questionnaire measures the leader's behavior in a specified situation—for example, as the commander of an aircrew, or as an administrator in a public school—but does not purport to measure an intrinsic capacity for leadership. But whether individuals tend to employ the same style of leader behavior in different situations is an empirical question that remains to be answered.[16] However, certain organizational climates can coerce the man to change his leadership style simply to save his job, at no matter what cost in his loss of human dignity.

RESEARCH ON LEADER BEHAVIOR

With this background on the theoretical predilections that provided the impetus for The Ohio State Leadership Studies,[17] we now are ready to examine the substantive findings of a group of these studies in which the LBDQ was used.

Most of the developmental work on the Leader Behavior Description Questionnaire was done in a series of studies of aircraft commanders. Related studies have also been conducted in industry and education. Since the industrial studies were concerned primarily with training, they are not directly pertinent to our present purposes. In this section, therefore, we shall first summarize five of the Air Force studies and one educational study; we then will describe in detail the findings of two other educational studies.

Air Crew Studies

1. LBDQ scores were obtained on 52 B-29 commanders during training in the fall of 1950, and 33 of these commanders were subsequently rated on their combat performance in flying over Korea during the summer of 1951.[18] Twenty-nine of these 33 commanders were described again on the LBDQ by their combat crews. For 27 of the crews, a Crew Satisfaction Index was computed on the basis of the member's answer to the question: "If you could make up a crew from among the crew members in your squadron, whom would you choose for each position?" The ratio between the number of nominations an incumbent commander received and the number of nominations made for the aircraft commander position was used as an index of the crew's satisfaction with the incumbent's leadership. The LBDQ scores in training were correlated with this index and with superiors' ratings of the commanders' combat performance. Similarly, the LBDQ scores in the Far East Air Force were correlated with both the index and the ratings. Finally, in each situation—training and combat—partial correlations were computed for the relationship between each dimension and the ratings (or index) with the effect of the other dimension partialled out.

In both the training and combat situations, a trend was found toward negative correlations between the superiors' ratings and the Consideration scores, and positive correlations between these ratings and the Initiating Structure scores. Conversely, the correlations between the Crew Satisfaction Index and the Consideration scores were positive and high. The partial correlations served to accentuate this trend, which was more pronounced in combat than in training. Thus superiors and subordinates are inclined to evaluate oppositely the contribution of the leader behavior dimensions to the effectiveness of leadership. This difference in evaluation would appear to confront the leader with conflicting role expectations.

2. Eighty-Seven B-29 aircraft commanders, flying combat missions over Korea, were the subjects of a study with a design similar to the one reported above.[19] The commanders were rated by their superiors on seven characteristics (for example, "effectiveness in working with others," "attitude and motivation," "over-all effectiveness") and by their crews on three characteristics: "confidence and proficiency," "friendship and cooperation," and "morale." Furthermore, as in the earlier study, a Crew Satisfaction Index was computed. The Consideration and the Initiating Structure scores were correlated with the ratings by superiors and by crew members, and with the Crew Satisfaction Index.

The ratings by superiors yielded significant correlations with the Initiating Structure scores, whereas none of the corresponding Consideration correlations was significant. The crew ratings, including the Index, correlated significantly with both leader behavior dimensions but tended to be higher for the Consideration scores. Two of the Consideration correlations in particular should be noted: .75 with the Crew Satisfaction Index and .84 with the crew ratings of the commanders on "friendship and cooperation." Both correlations differ significantly from the corresponding correlations of .47 and .51 (in themselves significant at the .01 level) with the Initiating Structure scores.

One further hypothesis was tested in this study: that the commanders rated highest by their superiors would score above the mean on both leader behavior dimensions whereas those commanders rated lowest by their superiors would score below the mean on both dimensions. The commanders had been rated on "over-all effectiveness in combat." Two groups of commanders were identified: 13 men in the upper 15 per cent of this rating distribution and 12 in the lower 15 per cent. For each group taken separately, the Consideration and the Initiating Structure scores were plotted into the four quadrants defined by co-ordinates corresponding to the means of the two leader behavior dimensions. These two scatter-plots were then collapsed to construct the 2×2 classification presented in Figure 3.1.

	Below Mean on Both Consideration and Initiating Structure	Above Mean on Both Consideration and Initiating Structure
Upper 15 Percent on Over-all Effectiveness	1	8
Lower 15 Percent on Over-all Effectiveness	6	4

FIGURE 3.1   Number of commanders in high and low groups on ratings of over-all effectiveness scoring above and below the mean on both leader behavior dimensions. [FROM Andrew W. Halpin, "Studies in Aircrew Composition: III," *The Combat Leader Behavior of B-29 Aircraft Commanders,* HFORL Memo. No. TN-54-7. Washington, D.C.: Human Factors Operations Research Laboratory, Bolling Air Force Base, September 1953, p. 15.]

The probability of occurrence of frequencies (Figure 3.1) as deviant from the null hypothesis frequencies—or of greater deviance—is less than 3 in 100. This means that commanders who score above the average on both leader behavior dimensions are evaluated by their superiors as high in over-all effectiveness, whereas those who score below the average on both dimensions are likely to be rated low in effectiveness. In short, the successful leader is the man who furthers both group maintenance and group achievement.

3. The members of 52 newly assembled B-29 crews at Combat

Crew Training School described their commanders on the Leader Behavior Description Questionnaire and rated each other and the crews as units on such items as "crew morale," "friendship," "proficiency," and "willingness to go into combat with each other." These measures of crew attitudes were obtained twice— at the beginning of the training period and toward the end of training. An average period of 10 days intervened between two administrations of the questionnaire. Correlations were computed between *changes in attitude* and the Initiating Structure and Consideration scores on the Leader Behavior Description Questionnaire.[20] It was found that the members of crews whose commanders were described as high on Consideration tended to increase their ratings of each other on such attitude items as "mutual confidence," and "willingness to go into combat together," and that the members of crews whose commanders were described as high on Initiating Structure tended to increase their ratings of each other on "friendship" and "confidence." It was concluded that during this initial period of crew assembly the members of crews whose commanders scored high on both Consideration and Initiating Structure tended to develop more favorable crew attitudes than the members of those crews led by commanders who scored low on both leader behavior dimensions. These findings indicate the influence of leadership style upon early group-learning experience.

4. Rush[21] has reported the relationship between the Leader Behavior Description Questionnaire scores of B-29 and B-50 aircraft commanders and "group dimension" measures of air crews drawn from three independent samples: Combat Crew Training School, Combat Crew Standardization School, and Far East Air Force:

For each sample, crew means on the five dimensions of the Crew Dimension Questionnaire (CDQ)[22] were correlated with mean scores for the two LBDQ dimensions. Results were highly consistent across samples and appeared meaningful in terms of the definitions of the various dimensions. Perhaps the best way to summarize the results of this analysis is to discuss the correlations for each of the CDQ dimensions as follows:

Control—Scores on this dimension were negatively related to Consideration in all three samples, while the correlations with

Initiating Structure were not significant. *One possible interpretation of these results is that when crew members perceive the AC* [that is, the aircraft commander] *as a controlling agent, they construe his behavior as not considerate.*

Intimacy—Initiating Structure was not significantly related to this dimension but Consideration showed significant positive correlations. Crews which describe themselves as more intimate tend to judge their AC's as being more considerate.

Harmony—Scores on this dimension correlated positively with Consideration while the correlations with Initiating Structure were not significant. This would seem to point to the influence of leader behavior in establishing certain interpersonal relationships among crew members. The amount of effort he spends in organizing crew relations and defining the roles of crew members doesn't seem to make much difference in the harmony of the crew. However, the *way* in which he goes about his duties does appear to be a factor in the development of compatible relationships.

Procedural Clarity—This characteristic of crews, which refers to the way procedures and duties are defined for each crew member, was related to Initiating Structure in a positive direction. Correlations with Consideration were not significant. Thus the *manner* in which the leader acts toward crew members does not appear significant in establishing a well-defined set of relationships among crew members. But the frequency with which he engages in acts construed as Initiating Structure is related to the clarity of duties and functions in the crew.

Stratification—Scores on this dimension were highly related to Consideration in a negative direction, while correlations with Initiating Structure were not significant. In other words, crews which describe their leader as relatively less considerate tend to be characterized by greater awareness of status hierarchies within their crew.

In general, these results point to the interaction between group dimensions and leader behavior. It seems clear that if we are to understand the psychological characteristics of crews, we must deal not only with *what* the AC does, but also *how* he does it. In air crews, the actions of the AC may set the style, so to speak, for the interpersonal relations of crew members.[23]

5. In a study of 132 B-29 and B-50 commanders, a comparison was made between commanders' ideologies of leadership behavior and their crews' descriptions of their actual behavior in relation to

the two leader behavior dimensions.[24] The ideology scores were computed from the commanders' own responses to the LBDQ-Ideal. In expressing their leadership ideology, the commanders clearly recognized the desirability of scoring high on both dimensions of leader behavior, but the correspondence between their statements of how they should behave and their behavior as described by their crews was negligible. In the case of the Initiating Structure dimension, the correlation did not differ significantly from zero. Although the corresponding correlation of .14 for the Consideration dimension was significant at the .05 level of confidence, this represented only a low degree of association. The moderate reliability of the Initiating Structure and Consideration scales, and the fact that the distributions are not entirely normal, probably contribute to the low magnitude of the correlations obtained. *Nevertheless, the evidence suggests that the aircraft commander's knowledge of how he should behave as a leader has little bearing upon how he is perceived as behaving by the members of his crew.*

Educational Study

So much for the Air Force studies; now let us examine an important early study by Hemphill, using the LBDQ in education.[25]

The members of 18 departments in a liberal arts college described their department heads and indicated on the LBDQ-Ideal how they believed a department head should behave.[26] They also ranked the five departments in the college that had the general reputation on the campus of being best led or best administered and the five departments that were least well led or least well administered. In making these rankings, each respondent excluded his own department. The correlations between the reputation scores and the LBDQ-Real scores were .36 for Consideration and .48 for Initiating Structure, with .47 required for significance at the .05 level. When discrepancy scores—measuring the absolute difference between the Real and the Ideal scores on each of the leader behavior dimensions—were correlated with the reputation scores, the obtained coefficients, —.52 and —.55, respectively, were both statistically significant. The greater the departure of the actual behavior of the department head (on either leader behavior dimension) from the norm of how ideal behavior on this dimension was conceived by the members of his department, the poorer was the administrative reputation of the department.

A cutting score of 41 on Consideration and 36 on Initiating Structure for the split on one co-ordinate, and the median reputation score for the split on the other, were used to distribute the 18 cases into quadrants as illustrated in Table 3.1.

TABLE 3.1

THE RELATIONSHIP BETWEEN THE REPUTATION ACHIEVED BY COLLEGE
DEPARTMENTS AND THE CONSIDERATION AND INITIATING
STRUCTURE SCORES OF DEPARTMENT CHAIRMEN
TAKEN CONJUNCTIVELY (N = 18)

	Number of Chairmen	
Chairman's Leadership	*Below Median Reputation*	*Above Median Reputation*
Score of 41 or larger on Consideration and a score of 36 or more on Initiating Structure	1	8
Score of less than 41 on Consideration or less than 36 on Initiating Structure	8	1

SOURCE: After John K. Hemphill, "Leadership Behavior Associated with the Administrative Reputation of College Departments," *The Journal of Educational Psychology*, 46, No. 7, November 1955, p. 396. Reprinted by permission of the publisher.

The import of these data is clear: the departments with high reputation are those whose chairmen score high on *both* leader behavior dimensions.

It is appropriate at this point to summarize five principal findings of this series of leader behavior studies.

1. The evidence indicates that Initiating Structure and Consideration are fundamental dimensions of leader behavior, and that

the Leader Behavior Description Questionnaire provides a practical and useful technique for measuring the behavior of leaders on these two dimensions.

2. Effective leader behavior is associated with high performance on both dimensions. The aircraft commanders rated highest by their superiors on "over-all effectiveness in combat" are alike in being men who (a) define the role which they expect each member of the work-group to assume, and delineate patterns of organization and ways of getting the job done, and (b) establish a relationship of mutual trust and respect between the group members and themselves.

3. There is, however, some tendency for superiors and subordinates to evaluate oppositely the contribution of the leader behavior dimensions to the effectiveness of leadership. Superiors are more concerned with the Initiating Structure aspects of the leader's behavior, whereas subordinates are more concerned with (or "interested in") the Consideration the leader extends to them as group members. This difference in group attitude appears to impose upon the leader some measure of conflicting role-expectations.

4. Changes in the attitudes of group members toward each other, and group characteristics such as harmony, intimacy, and procedural clarity, are significantly associated with the leadership style of the leader. High Initiating Structure combined with high Consideration is associated with favorable group attitudes and with favorable changes in group attitude.

5. There is only a slight positive relationship between the way leaders *believe* they should behave and the way in which their group members *describe* them as behaving. *For this reason, those engaged in leadership training programs should be especially wary of accepting trainees' statements of how they should behave as evidence of parallel changes in their actual behavior.*

We have seen that the most effective leaders are those who score high on *both* dimensions of leader behavior. These dimensions may be diagrammed according to the scheme in Figure 3.2; the ordinates are defined by the averages of the respective dimensions, and the four quadrants are designated by Roman numerals.

The leaders described in Quadrant I are evaluated as highly

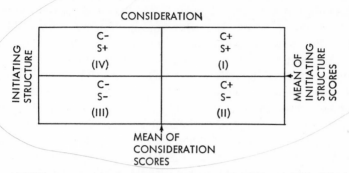

FIGURE 3.2 A quadrant scheme for describing leaders' behavior on the Initiating Structure and Consideration dimensions. [FROM Andrew W. Halpin, "The Superintendent's Effectiveness as a Leader," *Administrator's Notebook,* **7,** No. 2, October 1958.]

effective, whereas those in Quadrant III, whose behavior is ordinarily accompanied by group chaos, are characterized as most ineffective. The leaders in Quadrant IV are the martinets and the "cold fish" so intent upon getting a job done that they forget they are dealing with human beings, not with cogs in a machine. The individuals described in Quadrant II are also ineffective leaders. They may ooze with the milk of human kindness, but this contributes little to effective performance unless their Consideration behavior is accompanied by a necessary minimum of Initiating Structure behavior.

Educational Administrators and Aircraft Commanders

Having presented this background material on the LBDQ, we will now discuss two studies that deal directly with school superintendents. The first of these two compares superintendents and aircraft commanders.[27]

It is presumed that every leader, irrespective of the institutional setting within which he operates, engages to some extent in both forms of leader behavior—Initiating Structure and Consideration. Consequently, in comparing groups of leaders from different institutional settings we should expect to find some degree of overlap in leadership behavior. But where the institutional settings differ markedly—as in the case of public education and the Air Force— we also should expect to discover significant differences between groups of leaders drawn from two such settings. The leaders whom we have studied—educational administrators and aircraft commanders—function within institutional settings that traditionally would appear to emphasize different aspects of leader behavior. On the basis of predicated differences between these two settings, the following hypothesis was formulated: that educational administrators will demonstrate, in both leader behavior and leadership ideology, more Consideration and less Initiation of Structure than aircraft commanders. Accordingly, the purpose of this study is to determine whether these two groups of leaders differ significantly in their leadership ideology and their leadership style.

The sample was composed of two groups of subjects: 64 educational administrators and 132 aircraft commanders.

The 64 educational administrators were drawn from two sources. Thirteen of the group were participants in an interdisciplinary graduate seminar on "Leadership for Educational Administrators"[28] conducted during the Winter Quarter, 1954, and sponsored by the School-Community Development Study at The Ohio State University. Eight of the 13 members were principals; the others, local superintendents and supervisors. The remaining 51 members of this sample were all superintendents of Ohio schools studied during the spring of 1954. Sixty-two of the sample were men, and two were women. These 64 administrators answered the LBDQ-Ideal, and also were described on the LBDQ-Real by 428 members of their respective staffs. The LBDQ-Real and the LBDQ-Ideal were administered by members of a research team with the guarantee that the anonymity of each respondent would be protected. On the average, 6.7 descriptions ($\sigma = .8$) were secured for each administrator.

The 132 aircraft commanders were in charge of B-29 and B-50 crews. The two aircraft are essentially similar, with an eleven-man crew on the B-29 and a ten-man crew on the B-50. Seventy-six of the commanders were studied in the Far East Air Force at the time they were flying combat missions over Korea.[29] The other

56 were members of select Strategic Air Command crews undergoing evaluation in this country.[30] These two groups of commanders did not differ significantly either in leadership ideology or in leader behavior as measured here, and hence have been combined into a single sample. The 132 commanders answered the LBDQ-Ideal and were described on the LBDQ-Real by 1099 members of their respective crews. On the average, 8.3 descriptions ($\sigma = 1.6$) were secured for each commander.

For the combined sample, the primary data consist of the responses of 196 group leaders to the LBDQ-Ideal and descriptions of these leaders on the LBDQ-Real by the 1527 members of their respective groups.

The 1723 LBDQ's were scored on the Consideration and Initiating Structure dimensions. The leader's own scores on the Ideal form were used to represent his ideology in respect to the two dimensions. With the LBDQ-Real, it was appropriate to determine first how well group members agreed in describing their respective leaders. Accordingly, for each sample and separately by dimension, between-group versus within-group analyses of variance were made. The F ratio was significant at the .01 level of confidence in each instance. The extent of agreement among group members in describing their leaders may be expressed by the unbiased correlation ratio (epsilon). These ratios for the Consideration dimension are .49 and .61 for the administrators and commanders, respectively. The corresponding ratios for Initiating Structure are .49 and .44. For the LBDQ-Real, group-mean Initiating Structure scores were therefore used as indices of the leader's behavior on these dimensions.

For each leader, and on each dimension, one score (the LBDQ-Ideal) expresses his own ideology, and another (the LBDQ-Real) describes his behavior as perceived by the members of his own group. The comparisons of the leadership ideology and leader behavior of the administrators and the commanders have been made exclusively in terms of group differences, and have been analyzed in two ways: first, by *t* ratios of the mean difference between the number of leaders from each group who scored either above or below the mean of the pooled samples on each (and both) of the dimensions; secondly, the differences in leadership

TABLE 3.2

LEADER BEHAVIOR DESCRIPTION QUESTIONNAIRE (REAL AND IDEAL) MEANS, STANDARD DEVIATIONS, AND *t* RATIOS OF MEAN DIFFERENCES, FOR EDUCATIONAL ADMINISTRATORS AND AIRCRAFT COMMANDERS

| | Real | | | | Ideal | | | | t*(Ideal-Real) | |
| | Considera-tion | | Initiating Structure | | Considera-tion | | Initiating Structure | | Considera-tion | Initiating Structure |
	Mean	σ	*Mean*	σ	*Mean*	σ	*Mean*	σ		
Educational Administrators (N = 64)	44.7	6.0	37.9	4.4	52.4	3.9	43.8	6.4	8.95	7.28
Aircraft Commanders (N = 132)	39.7	8.0	40.9	4.9	48.7	5.3	51.0	4.6	11.69	18.50
t* (EA—AC)	4.38		−4.11		4.93		−8.97			

* All reported *t*'s are significant at the .001 level of confidence.
SOURCE: From Andrew W. Halpin, "The Leader Behavior and Leadership Ideology of Educational Administrators and Aircraft Commanders," *Harvard Educational Review*, **25**, Winter 1955, p. 24.

styles have also been analyzed according to number and per cent of cases in each sample that fall into the quadrants listed in Table 3.4.

Table 3.2 presents a comparison of the mean LBDQ-Real and the mean LBDQ-Ideal scores of the educational administrators and the aircraft commanders.

In Table 3.3 are listed, by sample, the correlations between the leader behavior dimension scores on the LBDQ-Real and the LBDQ-Ideal, and the correlations between the Real and the Ideal scores on each dimension.

The findings in Table 3.2 support the hypothesis that leaders who function within these two different institutional settings exhibit differences in their leadership ideology and differences in their style of leadership behavior. Specifically, the administrators,

TABLE 3.3

PRODUCT-MOMENT CORRELATIONS BETWEEN LEADER BEHAVIOR DESCRIPTION QUESTIONNAIRE REAL AND IDEAL SCORES FOR EDUCATIONAL ADMINISTRATORS AND AIRCRAFT COMMANDERS, AND BETWEEN CONSIDERATION AND INITIATING STRUCTURE SCORES ON THE REAL AND ON THE IDEAL

	Educational Administrators $(N = 64)$	*Aircraft Commanders* $(N = 132)$	t
Consideration—Real, Consideration—Ideal	.09	.17*	.53
Initiating Structure—Real, Initiating Structure—Ideal	.34**	.14	1.37
Consideration—Real, Initiating Structure—Real	.13	.45**	2.28*
Consideration—Ideal, Initiating Structure—Ideal	.22	.29**	.48

* Significant at the .05 level of confidence.
** Significant at the .01 level of confidence.

SOURCE: From Andrew W. Halpin, "The Leader Behavior and Leadership Ideology of Educational Administrators and Aircraft Commanders," *Harvard Educational Review*, 25, Winter 1955, p. 24.

in both leadership ideology and leader behavior as measured by the LBDQ, show more Consideration and less Initiation of Structure than the commanders. These differences are all significant at the .001 level of confidence.

The leaders in both samples indicate that they should show more Consideration and greater Initiation of Structure than their group members perceive them as doing. These differences, too, are significant at the .001 level of confidence. The differences between the two samples on the Ideal are in the same direction as those on the Real, so that the pattern of Ideal means corresponds to the pattern of Real means.

But this similarity in pattern of group means does not imply a necessary relationship between how individual leaders behave and how they believe they should behave. It has been noted previously that a leader's beliefs about his leadership behavior are not highly associated with his leadership behavior as described by his own group members. In general, this is confirmed by the present findings (two top rows of Table 3.3).

The commanders, both on the LBDQ-Real and on the LBDQ-Ideal, show significant correlations between the Consideration and the Initiating Structure scores, whereas the administrators do not. Although the interdimension correlations do not differ significantly in the case of the Ideal, the difference between the interdimension correlations on the LBDQ-Real is statistically significant. This indicates that the administrators, to a greater extent than the commanders, treat the two dimensions as if they were independent.

The differences between the leadership styles of the administrators and the commanders may be analyzed also according to the number and per cent of cases in each sample that fall into each of four quadrants: (1) "above the mean on Consideration" and "above the mean on Initiating Structure," (2) "below the mean on Consideration" and "below the mean on Initiating Structure," (3) "above the mean on Consideration" but "below the mean on Initiating Structure," and (4) "above the mean on Initiating Structure" but "below the mean on Consideration." The two means are based upon the pooled samples of administrators and commanders and may be constructed as coordinates which define these four quadrants. For the LBDQ-Real, the number and per cent of cases in each sample that fall into each quadrant are presented in Figure 3.3.

CONSIDERATION

		Below Mean			Above Mean		
INITIATING STRUCTURE	Above Mean	EA AC	5 37	(7.8%) (28.0%)	EA AC	21 57	(32.8%) (43.2%)
	Below Mean	EA AC	8 29	(12.5%) (22.0%)	EA AC	30 9	(46.9%) (6.8%)

Mean = 39.9

Mean = 4.14

FIGURE 3.3 Number and per cent of educational administrators (N = 64) and aircraft commanders (N = 132) with LBDQ-Real Scores above and below the mean on Initiating Structure and Consideration. [FROM Andrew W. Halpin, "The Leader Behavior and Leadership Ideology of Educational Administrators and Aircraft Commanders," *Harvard Educational Review*, **25**, Winter 1955, p. 25.]

Earlier findings with aircraft commanders have suggested that the most effective leaders are those represented in the upper right quadrant, and the least effective those in the lower left quadrant. The leaders represented in the other two quadrants may be conceived as falling within a middle range of effectiveness. In the one instance, represented by those leaders in the lower right quadrant, there is a tendency to show sufficient Consideration but not enough Initiation of Structure; in the other, the converse holds—the leaders are strong in Initiating Structure but fail to show enough Consideration for the members of the group.

The statistical significance of the difference between the number of administrators and the number of commanders who scored in each quadrant was determined by the chi-squared test. The χ^2 values and corresponding *p* values are presented in Table 3.4.

At the .05 level of confidence, the two groups of leaders do not differ significantly in respect to either the number of highly effec-

TABLE 3.4

χ^2 AND p VALUES FOR DIFFERENCE BETWEEN THE NUMBER
OF EDUCATIONAL ADMINISTRATORS AND THE NUMBER
OF AIRCRAFT COMMANDERS WHOSE LBDQ-REAL
SCORES FALL IN EACH QUADRANT

Quadrant	χ^2	p^*
Above Mean on Both Initiating Structure *and* Consideration	3.80	$> .05$
Below Mean on Both Initiating Structure *and* Consideration	2.54	$> .05$
Above Mean on Consideration *but* Below Mean on Initiating Structure	43.61	$< .001$
Above Mean on Initiating Structure *but* Below Mean on Consideration	10.43	$< .01$

* With 1 *df*, require 3.84 at $p=.05$, 6.64 at $p=.01$, and 10.83 at $p=.001$.

SOURCE: From Andrew W. Halpin, "The Leader Behavior and Leadership Ideology of Educational Administrators and Aircraft Commanders," *Harvard Educational Review*, **25**, Winter 1955, p. 26.

tive or highly ineffective leaders. It should be noted, however, that the χ^2 value in the upper right quadrant (3.80) does approach the value required (3.84) for significance at the .05 level of confidence. This suggests that according to the posited criterion of effectiveness the commanders show a greater tendency toward effective leadership than is demonstrated by the administrators.

The principal differences between the two groups of leaders are found in the off-quadrants. Those leaders among the administrators who score in neither the highly effective nor the highly ineffective quadrant tend to cluster in the lower right quadrant, and are characterized by high Consideration but low Initiation of Structure. Conversely, those leaders among the commanders who score in neither the highly effective nor the highly ineffective quadrant tend to cluster in the upper left quadrant, and are characterized by high Initiation of Structure and low Consideration. In both instances, the differences are highly significant. In short, these findings suggest that the leaders in these two groups who are not effective differ systematically in the nature of their shortcomings. *The aircraft commanders are inclined to show less Consideration than is desirable, whereas the educational administrators tend to be remiss in not initiating sufficient structure.*

A similar analysis was made for the LBDQ-Ideal scores. The number and per cent of administrators and commanders who score in each quadrant are given in Figure 3.4; and the χ^2 and the corresponding p values for tests of the significance of the difference between the incidence of cases in each group are listed by quadrant in Table 3.5.

CONSIDERATION

		Below Mean		Above Mean		
Above Mean	EA	5	(7.8%)	EA	10	(15.6%)
	AC	49	(37.1%)	AC	47	(35.6%)
Below Mean	EA	10	(15.6%)	EA	39	(61.0%)
	AC	26	(19.7%)	AC	10	(7.6%)

INITIATING STRUCTURE   Mean = 48.6

Mean = 49.9

FIGURE 3.4   Number and per cent of educational administrators (N = 64) and aircraft commanders (N = 132) with LBDQ-Ideal Scores above and below the mean on Initiating Structure and Consideration. [FROM Andrew W. Halpin, "The Leader Behavior and Leadership Ideology of Educational Administrators and Aircraft Commanders," *Harvard Educational Review*, **25**, Winter 1955, p. 27.]

The administrators and the commanders differ significantly in their leadership ideology. The most pronounced difference occurs in the lower right quadrant of Figure 3.4 in which are found the scores of 61.0 per cent of the administrators but of only 7.6 per cent of the commanders. Conversely, in the other off quadrant (Low Consideration and high Initiation of Structure) are found the scores of 37.1 per cent of the commanders but of only 7.8 per cent of the administrators. The probability of obtaining differences of this magnitude by chance alone is less than .001.

TABLE 3.5

χ^2 AND p VALUES FOR DIFFERENCE BETWEEN THE NUMBER
OF EDUCATIONAL ADMINISTRATORS AND THE NUMBER
OF AIRCRAFT COMMANDERS WHOSE LBDQ-IDEAL
SCORES FALL IN EACH QUADRANT

Quadrant	χ^2	p^*
Above Mean on Both Initiating Structure *and* Consideration	8.32	< .01
Below Mean on Both Initiating Structure *and* Consideration	.50	> .05
Above Mean on Consideration *but* Below Mean on Initiating Structure	65.46	< .001
Above Mean on Initiating Structure *but* Below Mean on Consideration	18.46	< .001

* With 1 *df*, require 3.84 at $p=.05$, 6.64 at $p=.01$, and 10.83 at $p=.001$.

SOURCE: From Andrew W. Halpin, "The Leader Behavior and Leadership Ideology of Educational Administrators and Aircraft Commanders," *Harvard Educational Review,* **25,** Winter 1955, p. 27.

Finally, instead of comparing the two groups of leaders by this quadrant method we may simply note the per cent of each group that scores above the mean of both samples on each leader behavior dimension, both Real and Ideal. The juxtaposition of the data for this purpose, as given in Table 3.6, highlights the fact that an essentially similar pattern of differences between the administrators and the commanders obtains in respect to both the LBDQ-Real and the LBDQ-Ideal.

The findings support the basic hypothesis that educational administrators differ from aircraft commanders in both leadership ideology and leadership style. The administrators tend to show greater Consideration and less Initiating of Structure than the commanders. These differences are presumably associated with differences between the institutional settings within which the two groups of leaders operate.

Since the concept of institutional setting possesses a certain heuristic value, further comparative studies of leaders drawn from

TABLE 3.6

PER CENT OF EDUCATIONAL ADMINISTRATORS AND OF AIRCRAFT
COMMANDERS WHO SCORE ABOVE THE COMBINED MEANS
OF BOTH GROUPS ON INITIATING STRUCTURE AND
CONSIDERATION, REAL AND IDEAL

| | | Per Cent of Cases | | | |
		Educational Administrators	*Aircraft Commanders*	χ^2	p^*
Initiating	Real	40.6	71.2	17.03	< .001
Structure	Ideal	23.4	72.7	42.45	< .001
Consideration	Real	79.7	50.0	15.80	< .001
	Ideal	76.6	43.2	19.37	< .001

* With 1 *df*, require 10.83 at $p=.001$.

SOURCE: From Andrew W. Halpin, "The Leader Behavior and Leadership Ideology of Educational Administrators and Aircraft Commanders," *Harvard Educational Review*, **25**, Winter 1955, p. 27.

different institutional settings should increase our understanding of leadership behavior. These studies need not be confined to the American culture, for cross-cultural studies of leadership afford an equally important area for investigation. For example, are the present findings about the leader behavior of educational administrators peculiar to American educators; or is the same leadership style characteristic of school administrators in Germany or in England? But in spite of its heuristic value, the concept of institutional setting is limited by its lack of specificity. To know that different institutional settings foster different leadership styles is important, but we also need to know what specific factors in each setting are associated with these differences. Therefore, it would be preferable to study various specific conditions of group operation that are imposed upon both the leader and his group. Some conditions are clearly a function of the institutional setting; others are defined by the mission of the group; and others are determined by local mores and regulations, and by temporal exigencies. It should be possible, however, to isolate particular conditions of group operation and determine their relationship to different leadership styles. For example, what is the relationship between the specificity with which a group goal has been defined and the way the leader behaves? What effect does the visibility of group products have on the leader's behavior? The speed with which the leader and the group receive feedback information on these products? In education—where goals ordinarily are broadly defined, where the responsibility for their accomplishment is diffused, where the products of group effort are not readily visible, and where considerable time often elapses before the leader and the group receive feedback on the success of the group's efforts—do these conditions prompt the administrator to stress Consideration more than the Initiation of Structure? The limitations in the design of this study permit only speculation about these questions. They deserve, however, further careful investigation.

It has been noted that the leader's belief in how he should behave is not strongly associated with how his group members describe his behavior. In examining the pattern of the four correlations in the two top rows of Table 3.3, we note, however, that the Real *versus* Ideal correlations are significant for the commanders on Consideration, and for the administrators on Initiating Structure. Although these correlations are low, they suggest an interesting speculation. In public education where a high value is placed upon Consideration, and Initiating Structure is not a dominant theme of the institutional mores, we find a significant relationship between the Real and the Ideal scores on Initiating Structure. Conversely, in the Air Force where a high value is placed upon Initiating Structure behavior, and Consideration is not a major theme of the institution, we find a significant relationship between the Real and Ideal scores on Consideration. *In both institutional settings the relationship between the Real and the Ideal scores tends to be greater for that aspect of leadership behavior which is least supported by the institutional mores.* This suggests that the leader's belief in how he should behave is reflected in his behavior—as perceived by his own group members—most clearly in respect to that aspect of leadership behavior which is *least* endorsed by the institutional norms. Whether this is due to a closer parallel between the leader's ideology and his actual behavior on this score, or whether it is due instead to a closer relationship between his ideology and the discrimination with which the group members perceive his leader behavior, is a question for further research. In either event, the implications for leadership training programs are provocative, for if this finding is corroborated by other cross-institutional studies of leader behavior, then we should expect to find that changes in an individual's leadership ideology will be reflected in his leader behavior principally in those aspects of behavior that are least endorsed by the norms of the specific institution within which he functions.

The Leader Behavior of the School Superintendent

The preceding series of studies provided the chief impetus for the next investigation of 50 Ohio school superintendents.[31] Although the findings of earlier investigations had indicated that effective leaders are those whose performance is high both in Initiating Structure and Consideration, we are not directly concerned in this effort with *evaluating* the superintendents. Our objective is simpler and, in one sense, more fundamental: to determine the relationship between the superintendent's own perception of how he behaves on the Initiating Structure and Consideration dimensions, as contrasted with the board and staff perception; and, furthermore, to discover the corresponding relationship between his, the board's, and the staff's beliefs concerning how he *should* behave as a leader. This, of course, implies several additional questions. To what extent do board members agree in their descriptions of the superintendent's leader behavior? Is there greater agreement about how he *should* behave than about how he *does* behave? These are the major questions that we shall examine in this study.

The superintendent, as the officially designated leader in charge of the school organization, is confronted by two major sets of responsibilities. He is responsible to the board of education, but he also must be responsive to the members of his own professional staff. Both reference groups, the board and the staff, impose upon him expectations of how he should behave as a leader. When these expectations are essentially similar, he probably encounters no difficulty in orienting his behavior to them. But to the extent that they are incompatible, he is placed in a position of potential role-conflict. How should he behave as the leader? Should he respond principally to the expectations of his board or to those of his staff? Or should he "be his own man" and persist in his own style of leadership irrespective of what either board or staff may wish? These practical questions plague most school administrators and are of equal concern to those responsible for their pre-service and in-service training.

This investigation is closely related to the whole question of evaluating the performance of school superintendents. Objective measures of the superintendent's job performance or of the effectiveness of his leadership are extremely rare, for the development of such measures is a sorely neglected area of research. Evaluations of the superintendent's job performance customarily take the form of subjective ratings of his effectiveness. These ratings are seldom made with the help of a well-constructed rating schedule that elicits evaluations of his performance in specified areas of his job; instead, they usually entail little more than global judgments of whether the superintendent's performance is "good" or "bad." This is not the place to explore the ramifications of the criterion problem in educational administration. But one troublesome question must be raised: If we discover an appreciable lack of relationship between the descriptions of the superintendent's behavior given by his board members and by his staff, and also find that the agreement among board members about how the superintendent behaves is far less than perfect, with what degree of confidence can we then accept, as a dependable criterion of the superintendent's performance, an evaluation of his behavior given by a single board member?

Accurate and judicious evaluation of an individual's performance admittedly involves a more complex process than a straightforward description of what he does—of how he behaves. A valid criterion of ideal behavior should provide the foundation for whatever evaluation is made of the effectiveness of the behavior of a particular individual. Hence, to such extent that a given rater's information about how a person does behave is unreliable, his evaluation of the effectiveness of that behavior is suspect. In short, if board members do not possess sufficient information about how the superintendent actually behaves to permit them to describe his behavior consistently among themselves and in reasonable agreement with the consensus of staff members, then a serious question can be raised about using board members' evaluations of the superintendent as the *sole* criterion of how effectively he performs his job. There is need for empirical research designed to explore this aspect of the criterion problem. Obviously, the present investigation provides no final answer on this score. Nevertheless, we shall examine the findings in terms of the question: What are the implications of these results for improving our present methods of evaluating the job performance of superintendents?

This study of the leadership behavior of 50 Ohio school superintendents deals again with the same dimensions of leader behavior: Initiating Structure and Consideration. The superintendents' behavior in respect to these two dimensions of behavior has been measured with the LBDQ-Real on which the staff and board respondents and the superintendents themselves indicate the frequency with which the superintendent engages in specific forms of leader behavior. The leadership ideology of the members of these same three respondent groups was measured by having each respondent indicate on the LBDQ-Ideal how he believed an Ideal superintendent *should* behave. The items on the LBDQ-Real and the LBDQ-Ideal are identical.

The LBDQ's were administered in each community by a member of the research team. The meetings with the staff and the board were held separately but not necessarily on the same day. Each team member assured the participants that the anonymity of their answers would be protected. Although the general purpose of the study was explained to all participants, *no reference whatsoever was made to the concepts of Initiating Structure and Consideration as dimensions of leader behavior.*

The raw data consisted of the responses on 1274 questionnaires divided equally between LBDQ-Real and LBDQ-Ideal. Each questionnaire was scored on the Initiating Structure and Consideration dimensions. The LBDQ-Self scores, both Real and Ideal, were secured directly from the superintendents themselves. Each of the fifty superintendents received an Initiating Structure score and a Consideration score that expressed his description of his own behavior in respect to these two dimensions. Similarly, his two LBDQ-Ideal scores indicated what he believed his behavior should be on these dimensions. The staff scores were obtained by having seven members of each superintendent's staff (that is, members of the work-group that reported directly to him) describe his leader behavior. The average of the seven scores by which his staff members described his Initiating Structure behavior was designated as his LBDQ-Real staff score on Initiating Structure. Likewise, an LBDQ-Real staff Consideration score was computed for each superintendent. The corresponding LBDQ-Ideal staff scores were determined in the same way. Scores for the boards' descriptions of the superintendents' behavior (LBDQ-Real, board) and scores that expressed their leadership ideology (LBDQ-Ideal, board) were computed by an analogous procedure. On the average, five board-member descriptions were obtained for each superintendent.

By this procedure the responses from the 1274 questionnaires were reduced to 600 scores, with 12 scores for each of the 50 superintendents:

1. LBDQ-Real, Self   Initiating Structure
2. LBDQ-Real, Self   Consideration
3. LBDQ-Real, Staff   Initiating Structure
4. LBDQ-Real, Staff   Consideration
5. LBDQ-Real, Board   Initiating Structure
6. LBDQ-Real, Board   Consideration
7. LBDQ-Ideal, Self   Initiating Structure
8. LBDQ-Ideal, Self   Consideration
9. LBDQ-Ideal, Staff   Initiating Structure
10. LBDQ-Ideal, Staff   Consideration
11. LBDQ-Ideal, Board   Initiating Structure
12. LBDQ-Ideal, Board   Consideration

The data were then analyzed in respect to these 12 scores. The findings can be summarized as follows:

1. On each leader behavior dimension, the staff respondents tend to agree in the description of their respective superintendents.

Likewise, the board respondents tend to agree in the description of their respective superintendents. *Although the staff and the board members each agree among themselves as a group in their description of the superintendent's leadership behavior, the two groups do not agree with each other.* Thus knowledge of the superintendent's leadership behavior as perceived by his board does not permit us to predict with greater than chance accuracy how these same aspects of the superintendent's behavior will be perceived by the members of his immediate staff. Hence, if we intend to use descriptions of the superintendent's leadership behavior as a criterion of performance, we need to take into full account the source of the description. It is evident that such descriptions should be secured from both board and staff. Neither source by itself provides a complete description of the superintendent's behavior. We conclude from these findings that the superintendents tend to adopt different behavioral roles in dealing with the members of staff and board groups.

2. Although the boards, on the whole, show statistically significant agreement among their members in their descriptions of their superintendents' leadership behavior, this agreement is far from perfect. The unbiased correlation ratio is .52 for Initiating Structure and .63 for Consideration. This finding raises a provocative question: if board member agreement in describing the leadership behavior of superintendents is no greater than these correlations indicate, then how much confidence can we place in an evaluation of the superintendents' effectiveness based upon board members' ratings? The same argument applies to staff member descriptions of the superintendent's behavior. Here again, the unbiased correlation ratio (.44 for each dimension), though statistically significant, reflects far less than perfect agreement.

3. In respect to Consideration, consistency in the superintendent's role behavior in dealing with the several members of his board shows only a chance association with the consistency the superintendent displays in dealing with the several members of his staff. In short, the superintendent may reveal a consistent "front" of Consideration to all members of his board, but it does not follow from this that he displays a similarly consistent "front" of Consideration to all members of his staff.

4. *In respect to Consideration, the superintendents do not see themselves as either their staffs or boards see them.* The staffs see the superintendents as showing less Consideration than they are described as showing either by the boards or by the superintendents themselves.

5. There is significant but low correlation (.44) between the superintendents' self-descriptions and the staff members' descriptions of their Initiating Structure behavior.

6. The boards describe the superintendents as Initiating Structure to a greater extent than they are perceived as doing by either the staffs or the superintendents themselves.

7. *On both dimensions, the board descriptions show only chance relationship with both the staff and the self descriptions.* The boards tend to describe the superintendents as higher on both Consideration and Initiating Structure than they are described by the staffs and in this sense show greater inclination than the staffs to view their superintendents as effective leaders. This suggests that the superintendents "play up to the boards"—behave, in fact, more effectively as leaders in dealing with their boards than in working with their own staffs. Even though the superintendent may possess good leadership skills as evidenced in his relationship with his board, he seems inclined to "let down a little" in his dealings with his staff.

8. The boards do not differ significantly from school to school in their expectation of how the superintendent should behave on either dimension.

9. There are significant differences between boards and staffs in the extent of their agreement about how the superintendent should behave on Consideration. But in respect to Initiating Structure, the within-group agreement for boards and for staffs is approximately the same for all staffs and all boards.

10. The staffs do not differ significantly from school to school in their expectation of how much Consideration the superintendent should show, but there is a slight difference in their expectation of how much Structure he should Initiate.

11. For the most part, staff and board conceptions of how an Ideal superintendent should behave do not differ from school to school. These conceptions constitute general norms of how staffs,

boards, and superintendents believe a superintendent should behave. All three groups of respondents characterize an Ideal superintendent as one who scores high on both Consideration and Initiating Structure.

12. The superintendents set for themselves higher standards of Consideration than either the staffs or the boards set for them. *The boards, in fact, expect the superintendents to show greater Consideration to their staffs than the staffs themselves posit as Ideal.*

13. The boards believe that a superintendent should be very strong in Initiating Structure. The superintendents themselves and the staffs both believe that the superintendents should Initiate far less Structure than the boards expect. The staffs, in turn, prefer less Structure than the superintendents believe they should Initiate.

14. The perceived leadership behavior of the fifty superintendents differs significantly from the ideal behavior of a superintendent as conceived by all three respondent groups. Whereas only 19 superintendents are described by their staffs in the "high-high" quadrant (Figure 3.1), 48 out of 50 of these staffs believe that this quadrant characterizes the leadership behavior of an Ideal superintendent. Conversely, though eight of the superintendents are described in the "low-low" quadrant, the staffs unanimously agree that an Ideal superintendent would *not* behave in this fashion. Similar differences between the Real and the Ideal distributions by quadrant occur for both other respondent groups.

15. An analysis was made of the number of superintendents classified in the two quadrants on the main diagonal according to the descriptions of their behavior given by both their boards and their staffs. Eleven of the 50 superintendents (22 percent of the sample) were described as effective leaders by both their staffs and their boards—that is, were described as scoring high on both Consideration and Initiating Structure. On the other hand, only two of the 50 superintendents were described by both their staffs and their boards as ineffective leaders—that is, low on both dimensions. This quadrant analysis technique provides a useful way of evaluating the leadership effectiveness of superintendents and appears especially applicable in those instances where the

description of the superintendent's leadership behavior by *both* his staff and his board indicates that he can be classified in either the "high-high" or the "low-low" quadrants.

The leadership ideology of board and staff members, and of the superintendents themselves, is essentially the same. Effective or desirable leadership behavior is characterized by high scores on both Initiating Structure and Consideration. Conversely, ineffective or undesirable leadership behavior is marked by low scores on both dimensions. These findings on the leadership ideology of superintendents, staff members, and board members agree with the results of the earlier Air Force study in which it was found that aircraft commanders rated effective both by superiors and crew score high on both leader behavior dimensions. These results are also consistent with Hemphill's finding that college departments with a campus reputation for being well administered are directed by chairmen who score high on both leader behavior dimensions. In short, the effective leader is one who delineates clearly the relationship between himself and the members of the group, and establishes well-defined patterns of organization, channels of communication, and way of getting the job done. At the same time, his behavior reflects friendship, mutual trust, respect, and warmth in the relationships between himself and the members of the group.

The findings indicate that the superintendents differentiate their role behavior. In dealing with their boards they tend to be effective as leaders, but they are inclined to be less effective in working with their staffs. Even when superintendents possess sufficient skill to be highly effective as leaders, they often "let down" a little in dealing with their staffs. Here it is important to note that the superintendent has less frequent direct contacts with his board than with his staff. This affords him more time for planning the strategy of his behavior in working with the board. Because the board is in a stronger power position than the staff, the superintendent evidently puts this time to good use. In his relationship with his staff, on the other hand, the superintendent is frequently forced to meet exigencies, with the result that he may not have sufficient time to apply to each new problem his full potentiality for leadership.

It is difficult, but not impossible, to overcome the pressure of events. To avoid being crowded by time, many executives delegate to associates a large share of authority and responsibility. This transfer of authority is in itself, of course, an essential aspect of Initiating Structure in the interaction of group members. Hence the present findings confirm our subjective impression that far too many superintendents allow their principal responsibilities to become obscured by trivia, with the result that they abdicate their leadership role and allow themselves to degenerate into mere functionaries. Routine and perfunctory activities have a specious attractiveness because they often allay anxieties that are inherent in the superintendent's leadership role. But we must avoid the mistake of confusing sheer routine activity with the productivity and creativity required for effective leadership.

The superintendent's tendency to play different roles with board and staff is revealed by the lack of relationship between the board and staff descriptions of the superintendent's leader behavior. Although the members of each of these two reference groups show statistically significant agreement in their perceptions of the superintendent's behavior, the agreement is far from perfect. This finding has important implications for research on the effectiveness of the superintendent's job performance. The salient implication concerns the use of board member ratings as the criterion of leadership effectiveness. Our findings have provided two cogent arguments against this practice. First, we have noted that the board members show considerably less than perfect agreement in simply *describing* how the superintendent behaves, a finding which casts serious doubt upon how much board member agreement we can expect to find among independent *evaluations* of the superintendent's leadership effectiveness. This criticism applies especially to global judgments made without the benefit of a carefully constructed rating schedule of known reliability. Second, in evaluating the superintendent, we must take into account information from all relevant reference groups. When the descriptions of the superintendent's behavior emanating from two relevant reference groups such as the board and staff are not significantly correlated, it is all the more imperative that data from *both* sources be examined as potential criteria. In the present study, we have not exhausted the reference groups that can furnish independent and pertinent criterion information on the superintendent's performance. We have confined our inquiry to reference groups focal to the superintendent's efforts in the internal administration of the schools. Similar studies could be developed to examine the superintendent's behavior in external administration—that is, in community and public relations activities.

Our findings point up the need for a multiple-criteria approach to the study of the leadership effectiveness of school superintendents. This means that we must first establish several independent, objective criteria of the superintendent's effectiveness and then determine the relationship between (1) these criteria and selected predictor variables and (2) the criteria themselves. Predictor variables can be posited readily enough. What we lack are dependable, *objective* criteria of effective school administration. Criteria, by definition, entail value-judgments. For this reason, whenever we are confronted by several criteria that do not have a high correlation with each other, a further value-judgment may be required to rank the relevance of the separate criteria. The responsibility for a judgment of this kind should rest with the board of education as the official body representing the community in matters of public education. The social scientist, as a scientist, is not required to make these value-decisions, but he can make an equally important, and perhaps even more fundamental, contribution. He can demonstrate to what extent the various criteria proposed are dependable and whether they are in any way incompatible with each other. He can show, for example, that Leadership Style *A* is effective in terms of Criterion *A*, and Leadership Style *B* is effective in respect to Criterion *B*. He may also note, however, that Leadership Styles *A* and *B* are incompatible, perhaps even antithetical. For instance, the superintendent who must spend a lot of time "politicking" in the community in order to put through a salary raise for his teachers may be forced to spend so little time with his teachers that they characterize his behavior as low in consideration. If the board or the staff should insist that the superintendent be active in securing better salaries for teachers (Criterion *A*), and also that he be perceived by his staff as Considerate (Criterion *B*), then the superintendent may be faced by a real dilemma. For if he is to be perceived as considerate by the staff he must devote time to personal interaction with individual staff members. If this same time is demanded for community contacts to gain support for a salary increase for teachers, the superintendent has to make a choice. There are only 24 hours in a day, and the superintendent, like every executive, must choose how he can best allocate the time at his disposal. Under such circumstances as these, if the board demands that the superintendent satisfy both Criterion *A* and Criterion *B*, they may impose upon him an intolerable burden of role-conflict. On this point Seeman[32] has provided an illuminating discussion of role-conflict and ambivalence in the leadership behavior of school superintendents. As we have said, the choice of the criteria of effective administration is a prerogative of the local community, but it should be an informed choice in which conflicting or incompatible demands upon the administrator are clearly recognized as such. It is here that research can make a trenchant contribution by furnishing dependable, objective data that will permit communities to make wiser and better-informed decisions in establishing criteria for evaluating the performance of their school superintendents.

The fact that the superintendents play a different role with their boards from that which they assume with their staffs does not necessarily imply that they are confronted by role-conflict. Some administrators undoubtedly compartmentalize their behavior, and in so doing minimize the likelihood of role-conflict. Others, however, may find themselves torn by what they perceive as differential expectations imposed upon them by board and staff. In the present study we have not attempted to explore the dynamics of the superintendent's behavior in the matter of role differentiation. To do this would require a clinical, case-study approach similar to that employed by Seeman.[33] As he has clearly demonstrated, this is an important area for further research in educational administration, and one in which the methods of the present study can be used in conjunction with straightforward case-study techniques.

Until such time as we are sure of the ultimate criteria we seek, we may be wise to settle for "intermediate" criteria that have strong presumptive evidence in their favor. The LBDQ-Real scores may be construed as an intermediate criterion of this kind. Inasmuch as we lack suitable objective criteria of the effectiveness of school executives at this time, we may assume tentatively that the relationship between leader behavior dimension scores and effectiveness which has been found in the Air Force and in higher education studies we have cited applies with equal force to school superintendents. Our present findings on leadership ideology support this assumption. *If we are willing to accept it, then we may use LBDQ-Real scores secured from board and staff as an intermediate criterion for evaluating the effectiveness of the superintendent's behavior.* Obviously it is a rough measure, but it does provide a first approach to the objective appraisal of leadership effectiveness. We would suggest that those who are interested in experimenting with this approach use the quadrant analysis technique that we have described.

Although the three respondent groups of the present study all agree on the Ideal, the behavior of this sample of 50 superintendents—as described by the boards, the staffs, and the superintendents themselves—falls significantly short of the ideal. This discrepancy should not necessarily be conceived as an indictment of these superintendents; for ideals, by definition, are objectives difficult to attain. It is heartening to find that approximately one-fifth of the superintendents in the sample approach the ideal in the eyes of their boards *and* staffs. At the opposite end of the scale, only 4 per cent of these superintendents are categorized, both by their boards and staffs, as ineffective leaders.

In what way do the superintendents tend to fall short of the Ideal? On the one hand, these administrators demonstrate good leader behavior in their high Consideration for members of their staffs; on the other, they fail to Initiate Structure to as great an extent as is probably desirable. As a group, they appear somewhat disinclined to Initiate Structure in their interaction with group members. One may speculate about possible reasons for this. In some of our discussions with administrators we have encountered a tendency to view Consideration and Initiating Structure as incompatible forms of leader behavior. Some administrators act as if they were forced to emphasize one form of behavior at the expense of the other. Yet the correlation between the LBDQ-Real dimension scores for this sample is .23 (not significant) for the staff descriptions and .61 (significant at the .01 level) for board descriptions. Hence there is nothing negative or antithetical in this interdimensional relationship.[34] The fact that the interdimension correlation for the board's descriptions is higher than the corresponding correlation for staff descriptions suggests that the superintendents can stress both dimensions of behavior when they believe that this is sufficiently worth their effort—especially in dealing with members of the board.

Why, then, the apparent disinclination to place similar stress upon both aspects of behavior in dealing with the staff? This reluctance may be a reflection of some of the current emphasis in education upon "human relations." The human relations approach and the burgeoning interest in group dynamics have developed in part as a protest against reactionary and even authoritarian leadership styles that have prevailed in far too many school situations. But in our enthusiasm for the new approach, have we perhaps swung the pendulum too far?

In applying the human relations approach it is important that we do not overlook the responsibility imposed upon every official leader by the institutional realities of the formal organization of which he is a part. The official leader has a responsibility and, in fact, a contractual obligation to accomplish a specified mission, and certain aspects of this mission may be beyond the purview of decision by the immediate work group. It therefore is imperative for us to re-examine our ideas about the proper balance between human relations—that is, Consideration—and Initiating Structure behavior within formal organization, and to become more critical about applying generalizations adduced from experience with informal groups to groups embedded within formal hierarchical organizations. Some principles may apply to both kinds of groups, but there is insufficient research evidence to permit us to assume a priori that leadership styles that succeed in informal, autonomous groups will be equally effective in formally organized workgroups.

The swing of the pendulum seems also to be associated with a tendency to judge the Initiation of Structure as being nondemocratic. This point of view is ill-founded, for there is no necessary negative relationship between democratic leadership and the Initiation of Structure. In fact, it is our impression—and here we are speculating—that what ordinarily is referred to as democratic administration or democratic leadership is precisely what we have defined "operationally" as leadership behavior characterized by high Initiation of Structure and high Consideration. This we have evaluated as effective leadership. Where the Initiation of Structure is weak, however, it is doubtful that there exists sufficient leadership—whether democratic or nondemocratic—to be dignified by the name. Democratic leadership is highly desirable, but, for a leader's behavior to earn this description, it is not sufficient for the leader to be democratic—he must also demonstrate definite acts of leadership.

Having diagnosed the superintendent's leadership skills, what can we do to help him improve these skills? It is regrettable that there is no pat answer; we must read the notes as well as we can and let our own psychological insights suggest the tune. Role-playing can help, and professional counseling can accomplish a great deal. Practice in situational analysis and case-study methods are often useful. But the training task is formidable; nor are we always sure that the training methods achieve what was intended in the first place. Yet the situation is not entirely hopeless; on the basis of present knowledge, we can avoid several false starts. For example, a glib prescription for men low on Consideration is to "give them a course on Consideration." I do not believe this will work, for we cannot make men more considerate by teaching them these skills directly; the necessary changes need to be induced through a therapeutic relationship.

Industrial consultant organizations have devised ingenious ways for improving executive skills; these methods often include a professional counseling relationship between the executive and the consultant. It may be time for us to examine similar possibilities in education—and this does not mean that we must install a psychoanalyst's couch in each superintendent's office! Furthermore, we are at a point where we can start some important basic research on better training procedures for school administrators. Increasingly, however, we have learned that how-to-do-it recipes are not enough; that we shall have to pay greater attention to administrative theory.[35]

The LBDQ technique provides one method for evaluating certain aspects of the superintendent's effectiveness as a leader. The project on effectiveness criteria for elementary principals has developed important techniques for evaluating principals.[36] Several additional evaluation procedures are being devised at other universities. The question now is whether school administrators do, in fact, want to have their own effectiveness evaluated.

Our findings have clear implications for the training of educational administrators to the extent that we can describe those forms of leadership behavior which the board, the staff members, and the superintendents themselves consider most desirable, and which also are the most effective. Furthermore, we can specify the character of the role differentiation used by the superintendents vis-à-vis their boards and their staffs. But at this point, about all that we can say to the trainee or to the superintendent in service is, "This is how we believe you should behave." The chief shortcoming to be found with this is that exhortation is a notoriously poor training method. Little is accomplished by merely telling trainees how they should behave; we must also establish conditions in the training situation itself that will be conducive to behavioral change in the desired direction. Training in administrative skill involves many subtleties and is a complex process. We cannot inoculate a trainee with high Consideration and high skill in Initiating Structure in the same way that we inoculate a child with the virus of the Salk vaccine. The required leadership skills must be learned, and, as with all learning, ample opportunity for practice must be provided.

In leadership training we must examine our assumptions very cautiously. It has been theorized, for example, that human relations training will increase the Consideration that trainees show their work-group members. But Fleishman,[37] in a study for the International Harvester Company, has demonstrated that the success of human relations training depends upon a variety of factors, not the least of which is the "social climate" in which the trainee functions in performing his job. An orthodox human relations training program can, under some circumstances, not only fail to achieve its stated purpose, but even boomerang upon its initiators by instilling in trainees apathetic, and often negative, attitudes toward human relations objectives. In short, we cannot assume on faith that the training we conduct will achieve the purposes we have in mind. Nor can we measure the effectiveness of training by the good intentions our trainees profess. The ultimate test of the success or failure of training lies in the changes that take place in the trainees' behavior.

Evidence from this inquiry and findings from an earlier Air Force study show that the leader's description of his own leadership behavior and his concept of what his behavior should be have little relationship to others' perceptions of his behavior that others have. In the case of the superintendents, this is especially true in respect to Consideration. For this reason we must be extremely wary about using statements made by the trainees as an index of the success of training. What a man says about himself is not the most dependable measure of changes that have assertedly taken place in his behavior. On the other hand, changes which his direct associates perceive in his behavior would appear to constitute a suitable index of the results of training. Our present evidence indicates that the LBDQ-Real is well adapted to this purpose and can provide a reliable gauge of the superintendent's leadership behavior in respect to the Initiating Structure and Consideration dimensions. It should be possible to conduct training experiments in which the difference between the LBDQ pre-training scores and the LBDQ post-training scores is used as an indicator of change by which we can evaluate the effectiveness of the training program. This technique, however, cannot be used for pre-service training of school administrators because a dependable pre-training LBDQ measure is unobtainable. But for the in-service training of men currently employed as administrators, such a method of evaluating training should prove quite valuable. It can even provide a means for comparing the relative effectiveness of various training procedures.

SUMMARY

The evidence from these inquiries shows that effective leadership is characterized by high Initiation of Structure and high Consideration. These two dimensions of leader behavior represent fundamental and pertinent aspects of leadership skill. The LBDQ-Real provides an objective and reliable method of describing the leader's behavior on these two dimensions. It should be possible to train leaders in the skills that compose these dimensions, but the methods for accomplishing this training have yet to be developed. We have noted two practical applications of the present approach: (1) the use of LBDQ-Real scores as an intermediate criterion of the leadership effectiveness of superintendents and (2) the use of differences between pre-training and post-training LBDQ-Real scores as an index of changes in behavior attributable to specific training programs.

The dimensions of leadership behavior we have delineated obviously do not exhaust the field. It would be fatuous to imply that these dimensions constitute *the* criterion of leadership effectiveness. They do not. However, they probably do represent *a* criterion that should be taken into account in evaluating the leadership skills of superintendents. Ours is only one approach to the study of the leader's behavior. Other investigators will, in turn, supplement our findings, and will take into account additional variables which we were not ready to include in the present series of studies.

NOTES FOR CHAPTER 3

1. In this chapter I have drawn heavily upon material from four earlier publications: (a) *The Leadership Behavior of School Superintendents* (Columbus, Ohio: College of Education, The Ohio State University, 1956); 2nd ed. (Chicago: Midwest Administration Center, University of Chicago, 1959); (b) "The Leader Behavior and Leadership Ideology of Educational Administrators and Aircraft Commanders," *Harvard Educational Review,* **25** (Winter 1955), pp 18-32; (c) "The Behavior of Leaders," *Educational Leadership,* **14**, No. 3 (December 1956), pp. 172-176; and (d) "The Superintendent's Effectiveness as a Leader," *Administrator's Notebook,* **7**, No. 2 (October 1958). I gratefully acknowledge the publishers' permission to republish the material here.

2. Ralph M. Stogdill, "Personal Factors Associated with Leadership: A Survey of the Literature," *Journal of Psychology,* **25,** No. 25 (1948), pp. 35-71.

3. Fillmore H. Sanford, "Research on Military Leadership," in John C. Flanagan (ed.), *Psychology in the World Emergency* (Pittsburgh: University of Pittsburgh Press, 1952), p. 51.

4. John K. Hemphill, *Situational Factors in Leadership,* Bureau of Educational Research Monograph No. 32 (Columbus, Ohio: Bureau of Educational Research, The Ohio State University, 1949).

5. The distinction between a phenotypic and a genotypic research approach is described in Ch. 1 of Kurt Lewin, *Dynamic Theory of Personality* (New York: McGraw-Hill Book Co., Inc., 1935).

6. David C. McClelland *et al., The Achievement Motive* (New York: Appleton-Century-Crofts, 1953).

7. John K. Hemphill *et al., Leadership Acts I: An Investigation of the Relation Between Possession of Task Relevant Information and Attempts to Lead* (Columbus, Ohio: The Ohio State University Research Foundation, 1954).

For a detailed discussion of Hemphill's theory of leadership, see John K. Hemphill, "Administration as Problem-solving," in Andrew W. Halpin (ed.), *Administrative Theory in Education* (Chicago: Midwest Administration Center, University of Chicago, 1958), pp. 89-118.

8. Chester I. Barnard, *The Functions of the Executive* (Cambridge, Mass.: Harvard University Press, 1938).

9. In Barnard's terminology, this would read "effectively" rather than "efficiently."

10. Dorwin Cartwright and Alvin Zander (eds.), *Group Dynamics: Research and Theory,* 2nd ed. (Evanston, Ill.: Row, Peterson & Company, 1960), p. 496.

11. Published by the Bureau of Business Research, The Ohio State University, Columbus 10, Ohio. This questionnaire may not be used, either as a whole or in part, without permission.

12. John K. Hemphill and Alvin E. Coons, *Leader Behavior Description* (Columbus, Ohio: Personnel Research Board, The Ohio State University, 1950).

13. Andrew W. Halpin and B. James Winer, *The Leadership Behavior of the Airplane Commander,* Technical Report III prepared for Human Resources Research Laboratory, Department of the Air Force under Contracts AF 33 (038)-10105 & AF 18 (600)-27 (Columbus, Ohio: The Ohio State University Research Foundation, 1952), mimeo.

14. This refers to operational definitions in science as described by Percy W. Bridgman, *The Logic of Modern Physics* (New York: The Macmillan Company, 1927), especially Ch. 1.

15. The reliability estimates for the LBDQ-Ideal are lower than for the LBDQ-Real. Thus, for the LBDQ-Ideal-Self, the reliabilities are only .66 for Consideration and .69 for Initiating Structure.

16. Some studies suggest that the leader does take a good share of his own style with him from job to job. See Edwin F. Harris and Edwin A. Fleishman, "Human Relations Training and the Stability of Leadership Patterns," *Journal of Applied Psychology*, **39** (1955), pp. 20-25; and Ralph M. Stogdill *et al.*, *A Predictive Study of Administrative Work Patterns*, Research Monograph No. 85 (Columbus, Ohio: Bureau of Business Research, 1956), p. 35.

17. The Ohio State Leadership Studies were initiated and directed by Dr. Carroll L. Shartle.

18. Andrew W. Halpin, "The Leadership Behavior and Combat Performance of Airplane Commanders," *Journal of Abnormal and Social Psychology*, **49** (January 1954), pp. 19-22.

19. Andrew W. Halpin, "Studies in Aircrew Composition: III," *The Combat Leader Behavior of B-29 Aircraft Commanders*, HFORL Memo. No. TN-54-7 (Washington, D.C.: Human Factors Operations Research Laboratory, Bolling Air Force Base, September 1953).

20. Charlotte A. Christner and John K. Hemphill, "Leader Behavior of B-29 Commanders and Changes in Crew Members' Attitudes Toward the Crew," *Sociometry*, **18** (February 1955), pp. 82-87.

21. Carl H. Rush, Jr., *Group Dimensions of Aircrews* (Columbus, Ohio: Personnel Research Board, The Ohio State University Research Foundation, 1953.

22. Crew Dimension Questionnaire, adapted from the Group Dimension Questionnaire described by John K. Hemphill and Charles M. Westie, "The Measurement of Group Dimensions," *Journal of Psychology*, **29**, No. 29 (1950), pp. 325-342.

23. Rush, *Group Dimensions of Aircrews*, pp. 132-136. Italics mine.

24. Andrew W. Halpin, "The Leadership Ideology of Aircraft Commanders," *Journal of Applied Psychology*, **39** (April 1955), pp. 82-84.

25. John K. Hemphill, "Leadership Behavior Associated with the Administrative Reputation of College Departments," *The Journal of Educational Psychology*, **46**, No. 7 (November 1955), pp. 385-401.

26. Note that this use of the LBDQ-Ideal differs from that employed

in the last study cited where the leader himself stated how he *should* behave. In Hemphill's study the "Ideal" is used with the group members who state how they believe the leader *should* behave.

27. Andrew W. Halpin, "The Leader Behavior and Leadership Ideology of Educational Administrators and Aircraft Commanders," *Harvard Educational Review,* **25** (Winter 1955), pp. 18-32.

28. See Roald F. Campbell, "The Interdepartmental Seminar for School Administrators," *Graduate School Record* (Columbus, Ohio: The Ohio State University, 1954), **7**, No. 9, pp. 4-6.

29. Dr. John K. Hemphill and Lt. Col. Fred E. Holdrege, as members of a Human Resources Research Laboratories team, collected these data as one part of a larger study conducted in the Far East Air Force during the summer of 1951.

30. Data collected at MacDill Air Force Base, Tampa, Florida, during 1951.

31. Andrew W. Halpin, *The Leadership Behavior of School Superintendents* (Columbus, Ohio: College of Education, The Ohio State University, 1956).

32. Melvin Seeman, "Role Conflict and Ambivalence in Leadership," *American Sociological Review,* **18** (August 1953), pp. 373-380.

33. Melvin Seeman, *Social Status and Leadership: The Case of the School Executive* (Columbus, Ohio: Bureau of Educational Research and Service, The Ohio State University, 1960).

34. Similarly, for crew descriptions of the leader behavior of 249 aircraft commanders, an interdimension correlation of 0.38 was found.

35. See, for example, Andrew W. Halpin (ed.), *Administrative Theory in Education.*

36. John K. Hemphill, Daniel E. Griffiths, and Norman Frederiksen, *Administrative Performance and Personality* (New York: Teachers College, Bureau of Publications, Columbia University, 1962).

37. Edwin A. Fleishman, *"Leadership Climate" and Supervisory Behavior* (Columbus, Ohio: Personnel Research Board, The Ohio State University, 1951), lithoprinted.

4

The Organizational Climate
of Schools[1]

Anyone who visits more than a few schools notes quickly how schools differ from each other in their "feel." In one school the teachers and the principal are zestful and exude confidence in what they are doing. They find pleasure in working with each other; this pleasure is transmitted to the students, who thus are given at least a fighting chance to discover that school can be a happy experience. In a second school the brooding discontent of the teachers is palpable; the principal tries to hide his incompetence and his lack of a sense of direction behind a cloak of authority, and yet he wears this cloak poorly because the attitude he displays to others vacillates randomly between the obsequious and the officious. And the psychological sickness of such a faculty spills over on the students who, in their own frustration, feed back to the teachers a mood of despair. A third school is marked by neither joy nor despair, but by hollow ritual. Here one gets the feeling of watching an elaborate charade in which teachers, principal, and students alike are acting out parts. The acting is smooth, even glib, but it appears to have little meaning for the participants; in a strange way the show just doesn't seem to be "for real." And so, too, as one moves to other schools, one finds that each appears to have a "personality" of its own. It is this "personality" that we describe here as the "Organizational Climate" of the school. Analogously, personality is to the individual what Organizational Climate is to the organization.

This observation of how schools differ in their Organizational Climate provided the major impetus for the present research. We knew from direct experience that schools differed markedly in their "feel." This was no new discovery. But we wanted to go beyond this. We sought to map the domain of organizational climate, to identify and describe its dimensions, and to measure them in a dependable way which would minimize those limitations that necessarily inhere in every instrument which must, in the final instance, rely upon some form of subjective judgment.

A second impetus was our dissatisfaction with the concept of morale and with the sloppy way in which this concept had been used in typical studies of schools and school systems. Statements about the morale in a school failed to tell us enough about the school's Organizational Climate.

A third impetus was a direct outgrowth of our experience with the LBDQ studies. Experience had shown us how futile it was to assign a principal with high scores on both Consideration and Initiating Structure to a school whose faculty was not quite ready to accept a leader who, at least from our point of view, was likely to be effective. The group could immobilize him, especially in a situation where the teachers held tenure and the principal did not. Obviously, some kind of matching had to be made between a leader's style and how ready the group members were to accept his style. Accordingly, such information as the LBDQ gave about a leader needed to be supplemented with related information about the organization itself. There was precedent for this view. Hemphill's *Studies in Aircrew Composition*[2] had included both types of measures, and an earlier study by Hemphill and Westie[3] had produced a Group Description Questionnaire which could be used as a prototype for the OCDQ that Croft and I sought to construct.

A fourth impetus was our interest in Organizational Climate as such, whether in a school, in a hospital, a military unit, or a business corporation. Fortuitous circumstances made it convenient for us to begin the study of Organizational Climate with schools. We surmise that, if we had started instead with business corporations, we would have identified a similar set of subtests and a similar array of climates. (A recent study by Muliak shows that the OCDQ is, indeed, applicable to a hospital setting.[4]) Our interest in the general topic of Organizational Climate rather than in the specific topic of the Organizational Climate *of schools* caused us to search for dimensions and concepts which would not be chained to the school situation.

These, then, were the four motivations that prompted Croft and me to study the Organizational Climate of schools. Specifically, what did we do?

THE RESEARCH PLAN

We constructed an Organizational Climate Description Questionnaire (OCDQ) that permits us to portray the Organizational Climate of an elementary school. The OCDQ is composed of 64 Likert-type items which teachers and principals can use to describe the climate of their school. The questionnaire is given in a group situation; it requires no more than 30 minutes for administration. The OCDQ is of intrinsic interest to the faculty, and the findings from it can be used for purposes of faculty self-evaluation. The scores that we have devised for describing the climate make good "factorial" sense. But more than this, they also make practical sense and are consistent too with present theoretical knowledge about the nature of organizations.

We analyzed the climate of 71 elementary schools chosen from six different regions of the United States. This analysis was based upon the description of these schools given by 1151 respondents. The 64 items in the OCDQ were assigned to eight subtests which we had delineated by factor-analytic methods. Four of these subtests pertain to characteristics of the faculty group as a group, the other four to characteristics of the principal as a leader. From the scores on these eight subtests we then constructed, for each school, a profile, or psychograph, which depicts the school's Organizational Climate. By comparing the profiles of different schools we can spot the distinguishing features of their respective Organizational Climates. Furthermore, by analyzing the profile for a given school, we can estimate the quality of its climate.

The eight subtests are:

CHARACTERISTICS OF THE GROUP
1. Disengagement
2. Hindrance

3. Esprit
4. Intimacy

BEHAVIOR OF THE LEADER

5. Aloofness
6. Production Emphasis
7. Thrust
8. Consideration

The mere names of the subtests can only suggest the behavior that each taps. Later we will define each subtest in greater detail.

We next examined the profiles for the 71 schools to see whether the profiles themselves constellated in a fashion that would allow us to differentiate meaningful types of Organizational Climates. They did. We were able to identify six Organizational Climates, and found that these could be arrayed along a continuum defined at one end by an *Open* Climate, and at the other, by a *Closed* Climate. The continuum that we devised does not possess porcelain perfection; it has a few chips and nicks along the edges. Specifically, it is not quite fair to say that the six climates can be *ranked* on this continuum; at best, they can be arrayed in respect to it. Yet, for heuristic purposes, in conducting the research by which the OCDQ was constructed, we treated the data *as if* the climates could be ranked. The ranking schema was a working convenience and thus provided a useful approximation to the way that we roughly conceptualized the data. But the ranking schema is, at best, only an approximation, and the use of a continuum—which, perforce, assumes a linearity of relationship—oversimplifies the facts. This schema has proven to be a highly useful oversimplification, but its usefulness does not wed us to it. In short, during the initial, exploratory study of Organizational Climates, our primary purpose was to "rough out" the map and identify on it whatever major climates we could demarcate. Refinements could come later. Accordingly and quite arbitrarily, Croft and I were willing to treat our data with the assumption of linear relations. If a useful way of identifying and describing Organizational Climates could be devised on the basis of the assumption of linearity, we felt confident that either we, or other investigators, could at a later date sharpen our hypotheses about the climates by taking into fuller account the possibility of various nonlinear relationships among the variables. Progress in this area of inquiry, as in all areas of scientific inquiry, must take place by means of a series of successive approximations. Ours is only a first approximation, and we insist upon treating it as no more than this.

So much for this note of caution.

To repeat, we identified six Organizational Climates. We termed these the "Open," the "Autonomous," the "Controlled," the "Familiar," the "Paternal," and the "Closed." At this point we simply will compare the most Open Climate with the most Closed (Figure 4.1).

All eight points—one for a school's score on each of the eight OCDQ subtests—define a particular climate. Thus, the difference between the Open and the Closed Climate is defined by the difference between the two profiles charted in Figure 4.1. Although all eight points define each profile, it is evident that two of the subtests possess especial significance in this definition: Esprit and Thrust. Esprit corresponds closely to what is referred to in everyday language as "morale." Thrust is almost self-explanatory. An important point to note is that Thrust represents a critical attribute of a leader's behavior, and an attribute which had failed to emerge from the original studies with the LBDQ.

The names that we assigned to the climates purport to be only descriptive. But we would have to be either blind or fatuous to assume that words such as Open and Closed do not also carry with them evaluative connotations. Of course they do. At the outset, Croft and I thought that we might be able to stick to describing climates without evaluating them. That was an innocent thought. The more we worked with the findings, the more did judgments about the climates force themselves upon our attention. The difference in the quality of the different climates became too vivid and too compelling to be ignored. In short, we were forced to admit that the Open Climates were "the good guys," while the Closed Climates were "the bad guys."

But the dialogue of the cowboy drama is not quite accurate. Rather does the Open Climate represent "the fortunate guys," while the Closed Climate represents "the unfortunate guys." "Good" and "bad" imply an element of intent and a distinction

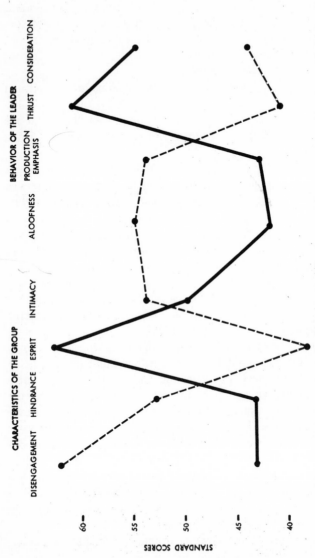

FIGURE 4.1 Comparison of an Open and a Closed organizational climate on the eight subtests of the Organizational Climate Description Questionnaire (Form IV). The Open Climate is represented by the solid line and the Closed Climate by the dotted line. Standard scores are shown with a mean of 50 and a standard deviation of 10.

between "virtue" and "evil." But a Closed Climate can occur without evil or malice on anybody's part. It can result from a combination of fortuitous events over which the members of a particular school have little or no control.

The point we press here is no mere quibble with words. In respect to action designed to improve the openness of a given school, the distinction we stress is both subtle and critical: the members of schools with Closed Climates are not sinners to be castigated, but victims to be helped. Furthermore, their resistance to benefiting from help is not to be construed as motivated by sheer cussedness or stupidity. A psychotherapist who views a neurotic patient's resistance in such fashion is doomed to failure, and the patient is doomed to agony. The wise therapist knows that the patient's resistance is seldom rooted in rational factors. And he knows, too, that the patient's prognosis also depends upon situational factors, and upon his skill in extinguishing habit residuals. Present scientific knowledge about the techniques to be used for changing an organizational climate is frightfully skimpy. Yet we do know that certain approaches will not work. Didactic instruction, pep talks and other methods of exhortation, and efficiency expert procedures do not accomplish the required changes. What little research has been done on organizational change suggests that, to be effective, any technique we use must take into full account the irrational element in man, must recognize psychodynamic factors within individual group members as well as within the organization as such, and must reflect—at the level of the organization itself—a pattern of relationship similar to that which obtains between a patient and a psychotherapist.

The recognition of how exceedingly difficult it is to change an organizational climate permits us to use such terms as "Open" and "Closed" with greater temperance. True, these terms are more than descriptive. But although we use them to evaluate the organizational climate of schools, we do so with no intent to either praise or damn the climate of a particular school. Obviously, we believe that a Closed Climate is undesirable, that it is crippling for both the faculty and the students. Yet we prefer to view a Closed Climate as unhealthy or sick—not as evil. Not too many centuries ago, the inmates of mental institutions were regarded as possessed by the devil, and treatment was focused on literally beating the devil out of them. Many executives today are not much more advanced than this in their attitudes toward their organizations and their employees; when things go wrong, these executives want to "beat the devil" out of the help. We want to be certain that administrators who use the OCDQ do not adopt a similar punitive attitude toward whatever Closed Climate schools they may find in their schools system. Throughout this chapter we will refer to Open and Closed Climates, but we use these terms with temperance and forbearance and, I hope, even with kindness. It is imperative that these terms be read and understood with the same temper.

THE PITFALLS OF LANGUAGE

In a genuine sense we did not discover these Organizational Climates; we *invented* them. This notion of scientific inquiry as a method of invention rather than of discovery runs counter to many commonly accepted ideas about the scientific process. Accordingly, our report of the procedures which we used in the actual research will be understood better if we first digress briefly to discuss a few points about the relationship between the events and phenomena that we observe in nature and the language we use to describe these events.

Why, indeed, did we finally choose as a major dichotomy the Open versus the Closed Climate? Why did we settle for the particular names that we assigned to the other four climates? Why six climates rather than seven, or for that matter, 50? Why eight rather than ten or 20 subtests? And how do these eight subtests happen to have been assigned the particular names that we have given them? Why speak of the Thrust behavior of the principal? This is a new term. Why introduce it at all? Are there not other terms that are more commonly used in everyday discussions of leadership sufficient to explain what we seek to explain? Why complicate matters by introducing new terms, and new concepts? Are the new terms and the new jargon presented here introduced just for the sheer sake of being different? Is their introduction simply a matter of caprice?

Questions of this kind deserve to be answered, and it is wise to try to answer them promptly. The full answers must reside in the complete report given in this chapter, for each of the concepts that we introduce is defined literally by the complete set of operations that we have used to measure it. This is the operational definition of each concept. Yet each concept contains a further meaning which we later infuse into it on the basis of linkages that we make between the stark empirical findings and our theoretical knowledge about the nature of organizations and human personality. Such knowledge is drawn not merely from the context of the research reported here, but also from other sources and disciplines that provide insights which can illuminate our own findings. Consequently, questions of this kind cannot be answered fully at this point; they must be answered at different points during the presentation with the hope that each successive approach to these questions will fill in a greater number of details about the answers and will do this within the context of the specific research procedures and the actual findings. Yet, even before we proceed to describe the research procedures, a few comments on these questions are in order.

These questions all hinge on the same point: why did we, in effect, *invent* a language to describe Organizational Climates? And why did we not content ourselves with a concept such as morale, or with other concepts drawn more directly from the language of common sense? To answer these questions it will be helpful if we first examine a few stages in the history of research on human personality.

During the first two decades of this century, efforts to study human personality were focused mainly on the identification of human instincts. Instincts, or, perhaps more accurately, alleged instincts, were dutifully listed and catalogued. This approach to the explanation of that domain of behavior ordinarily described as personality produced arrays of instincts which differed greatly in respect to their specificity, their susceptibility to observation, and their usefulness as predictors of human behavior. For the most part, this instinct approach provided only *ex post facto* "explanations." Different psychologists promulgated different lists of basic human instincts, and these lists contained anywhere from three to more than 150 postulated basic human instincts. The length of many of these lists appeared to be a direct function of the investigator's dexterity with a dictionary. The instinct movement, as an attempt to explain human personality, fell of its own weight. The most critical failure of this effort to explain personality was that it failed to give a psychotherapist any "purchase"; a therapist could do nothing with it. The instinct approach was only pseudodynamic, it confined itself mainly to phenotypic variables, and it was, in essence, fatalistic—in almost a Calvinist sense.

During the twenties and early thirties, other American psychologists devised temperament scales, and constructed personality tests which mapped the domain of personality according to such attributes as extroversion versus introversion, or dominance versus submissiveness. The language which the investigators invented for these explanations of personality differed from the language that had characterized the instinct approach. The concepts that these psychologists had invented were at least operationally defined. The human attributes which the concepts denoted were still more phenotypic than genotypic in character. Yet, within a certain range of use, the language that this group of investigators had used to map the domain of human personality did permit them to make useful predictions about human behavior. We grant that these predictions probably were more useful in the areas of personnel selection and educational guidance than in a psychiatrist's or clinical psychologist's office. The important point to note here is that the language which this group of psychologists had invented was more *useful* than the language which the "instinct psychologists" had invented. And note, too, that both groups of psychologists sought to deal with the same domain of events: human personality. Each group mapped this domain differently, and each used different language— *and hence different concepts*—to construct its map.

Meantime, in Europe, Freud and his disciples invented another new language for mapping the psyche. Freud conceptualized human personality in a way alien to any that had previously been used by academic psychologists. For the language which he invented, Freud drew heavily upon the language of mythology, especially Greek mythology. The concepts that he postulated, such as the ego, the id, the libido, and anxiety, were of a thoroughly different order than those invented either by the "instinct psychologists" or by the American academic psychologists of the twenties and thirties. Many of these psychoanalytic concepts suffer from the fact that Freud and his colleagues did not give them strict operational definitions. Nor did the Freudian constructs readily permit predictions that could be verified by research methods which academic psychologists customarily use for verification. Yet psychiatrists and other therapists who used these concepts found them viable and useful as a basis for action in treating patients. Furthermore, other workers, not always as orthodoxly Freudian as Freud, were able to use the essential rationale of the Freudian conceptualization of the psyche to construct devices which enabled them to map the domain of human personality in yet another way. The two best known examples of these efforts are the Rorschach Ink-Blot Test and the Thematic Apperception Test. The portraits, or profiles, of human personality that a skilled clinician can secure from these tests are useful for predicting aspects of the patients' subsequent behavior, and also are useful in determining appropriate avenues of treatment. Yet the language of the Thematic Apperception Test, and certainly of the Rorschach, is not the common sense language of everyday life. Indeed, in devising procedures to evaluate patients' responses to the ink blots, Rorschach found it necessary to invent a language for which there was no counterpart in the words of everyday experience.

This brief background about a few of the different levels of sophistication that have been used in the study of human personality is presented only so that we now can draw a rough parallel between the levels of sophistication available in the study of human personality and possible levels of sophistication at which the domain of Organizational Climate can be studied. One obvious approach to the domain of Organizational Climate is the attempt to encapsulate everything important to be said about the climate within the single global concept of morale. With this approach the best that we can hope to do is to estimate how high or how low the morale of a given organization is. This reading on the thermometer of morale can tell us whether the organization is sick, but it scarcely can provide us with a basis for making a differential diagnosis of the sickness. The difficulty, of course, is that this approach rests upon the a priori assumption that a single dimension—that is, morale, can usefully summarize the essence of the variations that occur in organizational climates. By definition, these variations are thereby restricted to a single, narrow continuum, even as the mercury in a thermometer is physically restricted to a narrow, vertical channel. But the assumption of this approach is untenable, for research on morale has yielded, above all, one unequivocal finding: morale, whatever it may or may not be, is not unidimensional in its structure. Whatever is being described by the term "morale" is multifaceted; any attempt to describe this "something" as if it had but a single face does violence to the phenomena that we seek to understand. This direct, frontal attack upon the domain of organizational climate resembles, in its primitiveness and its meager sophistication, some of the earlier attempts to measure human personality.

An equally unsophisticated way of tackling the domain of organizational climate is to use a tactic precisely opposite to that of assuming that morale, and hence climate, can be described unidimensionally. The investigator who uses this tactic proceeds to generate elaborate lists of adjectives which presumably can be used to describe a host of possible aspects of organizational climates. (These adjectives can then, for example, be arranged in the form of a checklist.) Obviously, these adjectives do describe the climate, but since they have been generated *ad hoc*, without an organizing principle, the investigator can group the behaviors to which the adjectives refer on only an arbitrary basis. Indeed, he is not able to declare with assurance that the arbitrariness of any one grouping is either better or worse than the arbitrariness of another. Precisely why does this tactic lead to a dead end? Because the aspects of organizational climate chosen for study, and the adjectives chosen to define these aspects, are determined not empirically and not by means of a strict theoretical formulation of the nature of organizations, but are determined solely by means of armchair speculation. (Sometimes, of course, these speculations are secured from a group-think "armchair.") Since the aspects of the organizational climate thus chosen for study are derived speculatively, their number is limited only by the investigator's verbal facility and his imagination. He has no way of knowing whether

the aspects are mutually exclusive, whether—in a semantic sense—
they fall at a comparable level of ordinality,[5] or whether it is
possible to identify sets of observable *behaviors* which correspond
to the respective aspects that have been chosen.[6] In short, to use
this tactic is to make the very mistake that the instinct psychologists
had made.

The assumption of a unidimensional model of organizational
climate violates the facts, and the assumption of a multidimen-
sional model derived deductively and speculatively repeats the
methodological errors of the instinct psychologists. What, then, is
the fundamental flaw in both of these naïve approaches to the task
of conceptualizing the domain of organizational climate? The
identification of this flaw will help us to understand what we should
not do. Thus, specifically, wherein lies the flaw? Very simply, the
flaw lies in a mistaken view of how the relationship between language and events should be handled in the process of scientific
inquiry. In particular, the language of common sense, in itself, will
not suffice as a way of telling us what variables should be used
when we seek to map the domain of organizational climate. Common sense alone cannot tell us how many or how few categories
we should—for any given purpose—draw directly from the language of everyday life. The blunder of the common sense approach
lies in the faulty and rather silly assumption that the *word* for
whatever we may seek to study is somewhere in the catalogue; all
we need do is find the event or the phenomenon which corresponds
to the word. This view is coupled with a devout conviction that
for every word there *must* exist in nature an event or set of events
that are meaningfully and monotonically related to the word. But
this is not the way of scientific progress. In scientific inquiry, we
first must observe the event or events as carefully as possible and
then, and only then, should we venture to name these events. If
the words at hand, with their present connotations, do not fit the
events, then so much the worse for the words. Their connotations
will need to be qualified or extended, or perhaps new words or
new word combinations will need to be invented and will have to
be invested with fresh meanings that are strictly consonant with
the phenomena which the words purport to describe. Everyday
common sense language is rich enough for everyday life, but the

attempt to apply common sense terms to scientific concepts often exposes the poverty areas of everyday language. Newton had to invent the concept of "gravity" before he could name it. Freud had to identify the role of anxiety in symptom formation before he could name it. Not that the word *Angst* had not existed before Freud. But since Freud, the connotation of *Angst* has changed; it has become different and richer.

What is the relevance of this discussion to the actual research that Croft and I conducted on the Organizational Climate of Schools? Fortunately, we think, we started out with an especially acute awareness of the relationship between words and events. We tackled the problem of Organizational Climate with the determination that we would be neither premature nor precipitate in identifying and naming the variables which seemed to constitute our domain of inquiry—that is, Organizational Climate. When we first spoke to colleagues, teachers, and superintendents about measuring the Organizational Climate of schools, the typical response we received was, "Oh, you mean the morale of the school? Is this what you are working with?" To which we could only say that the answer was both "Yes" and "No," that we were dealing paradoxically enough with both more *and* less than what is commonly referred to as morale. We were seeking to map the same domain of inquiry that other investigators have described as morale, but we were seeking to conceptualize—or, if you will, to map—this domain in a different way.

We wanted first to observe the *behavior* that defined different Organizational Climates and were willing to name these climates only *after* we had analyzed the specific behaviors. In short, we were committed to an inductive, empirical approach. In terms of the parallel noted earlier in the development of methods for conceptualizing human personality, we hoped, in our effort to conceptualize Organizational Climates, that we could be lucky enough to hit upon a method that would be less like the mere listing of instincts and more like the order of formulation that had gone into the Rorschach and the Thematic Apperception Test. This aspiration should not be viewed as indecent presumptuousness. We knew that present knowledge about Organizational Climates and our own limited abilities would not permit us to reach the sophistica-

tion that characterizes the Rorschach and the Thematic Apperception Test. Nor were we seeking to develop a projective device for
measuring Organizational Climates. But we did hope to capture
at least the spirit of those later attempts to map the domain of
human personality—efforts which had drawn richly from the
psychoanalytic movement, and efforts which also had refused to
accept as the most pertinent variables those which appeared most
readily and glaringly on the surface. We knew from the experience
of others, and from earlier experiences of our own, that the
obvious "givens" of everyday language and experience can prove
to be snares. In short, we sought a conceptualization of Organizational Climates that was not superficial, that was not rooted in the
snares of the obvious. However, the final test of the concepts that
we have invented must be heuristic. Do the concepts that we have
chosen to describe our domain of inquiry permit us to describe the
events in this domain more "usefully" than we could describe these
events without the benefit of the particular concepts which we
have created? In short, in respect to both future research and
action, how seminal are the concepts that we have invented?

THE DEVELOPMENT OF THE OCDQ

At the very beginning of the study we decided that in constructing the OCDQ it would be best for us to use a set of Likert-type
items. This approach had proved useful in the development of the
LBDQ, and we believed that it would be equally satisfactory in
the construction of the OCDQ. We did give consideration to the
idea of using some form of a forced-choice technique, but rejected
this notion for two reasons. First, a forced-choice questionnaire
would, of necessity, be a long one; hence it would not engender
hearty cooperation from the teachers to whom we would give it
at the end of a school day. And second, before we could use a
forced-choice questionnaire, we first would have to identify the
dimensions of Organizational Climate that we sought to measure;
for this purpose, a Likert-type questionnaire was the preferable
instrument. Now that we have identified the dimensions of Organizational Climate, and have specified a set of Climates, it obviously

would be possible to move to the more complex task of constructing a forced-choice questionnaire. Such a questionnaire would have greater refinements than a Likert-type test and perhaps might provide measurements of greater stability, but we are not convinced that the effort required to construct a forced-choice instrument would, *at this time*, yield commensurate increments of fresh knowledge about Organizational Climates. There are other studies that should be done first.

We prepared a set of simple statements and asked the respondent to indicate to what extent each statement characterized his school. The following items illustrate the kind of statements we used:

1. The principal insures that the teachers work to their full capacity.
2. The principal is in the building before teachers arrive.
3. The principal helps teachers solve personal problems.
4. Teachers ask nonsensical questions in faculty meetings.
5. Most of the teachers here accept the faults of their colleagues.

The scale against which the respondent indicated the extent to which each statement characterized his school was defined by four categories:

1. Rarely occurs.
2. Sometimes occurs.
3. Often occurs.
4. Very frequently occurs.

These four categories of responses can be scored by simply assigning to the respective categories any four successive integers. Thus the responses can be punched for scoring just as they are listed above: 1, 2, 3, and 4, respectively. Or they could be punched as 6, 7, 8, and 9. Actually, we punched them as 6, 7, 8, and 9. This was an arbitrary choice made for no more recondite reason than that we had reserved the first five digits for use in the identification columns on the IBM cards. Obviously, scores can be converted from one scale to another by merely adding or subtracting a constant, and this can be done without affecting the variance. In the present chapter we will not report the distribution of scores in raw data form, but only in the form of doubly standardized scores (that is, normatively and ipsatively) as given in Figure 4.2. *Current* raw-score distributions and the procedures for scoring the OCDQ by computer can be secured from Don B. Croft, at the Administrator Training Project, School of Education, University of New Mexico.

Although the scale is marked according to frequency of occurrence, the essential question is simply, "How true is this of your school?" And this, indeed, is how the teachers and the principals respond to the items. Obviously, each teacher's perception of the school's climate is mediated through his own set of personal values and needs. Yet, as in the case of the LBDQ, the members of any given faculty show consistency among themselves in their perception of what is "out there." When, for example, a faculty describes the Organizational Climate of its school as Open, the question "Is it *really* Open?" is unanswerable and irrelevant. The climate is Open if the faculty perceives it as Open. Accordingly, the OCDQ items are measures of attitudes, or alternatively, of perceptions. (To speak of perceptual attitudes is to descend to redundant jargon.) We are satisfied to take the position that the faculty's consensus in its perception of the school's climate can be used as a dependable index of what is "out there."

In constructing the OCDQ we started by building a bank of about 1000 items. We screened these items in various ways, but principally by constructing and actually testing three preliminary forms of the OCDQ. The major analysis was done with data on Form III of the OCDQ, secured from 1151 respondents in a total of 71 elementary schools. Form III contained 80 items, but our analysis showed that we could prune it to 64 items. The present, "final" version, Form IV, is composed of these 64 items, to which five buffer items were added solely to fill out the space on the IBM mark-sensing cards on which we had printed the OCDQ items. The cards were prepunched for identification purposes; the respondents marked their answers with electromatic pencils. The 69 items of the OCDQ, Form IV, are presented in Table 4.1.

By factor analysis we identified eight dimensions of Organizational Climate. We assigned the items which loaded on each of

TABLE 4.1

The Organizational Climate Description Questionnaire, Form IV

1. Teachers' closest friends are other faculty members at this school.
2. The mannerisms of teachers at this school are annoying.
3. Teachers spend time after school with students who have individual problems.
4. Instructions for the operation of teaching aids are available.
5. Teachers invite other faculty members to visit them at home.
6. There is a minority group of teachers who always oppose the majority.
7. Extra books are available for classroom use.
8. Sufficient time is given to prepare administrative reports.
9. Teachers know the family background of other faculty members.
10. Teachers exert group pressure on nonconforming faculty members.
11. In faculty meetings, there is the feeling of "let's get things done."
12. Administrative paper work is burdensome at this school.
13. Teachers talk about their personal life to other faculty members.
14. Teachers seek special favors from the principal.
15. School supplies are readily available for use in classwork.
16. Student progress reports require too much work.
17. Teachers have fun socializing together during school time.
18. Teachers interrupt other faculty members who are talking in staff meetings.
19. Most of the teachers here accept the faults of their colleagues.
20. Teachers have too many committee requirements.
21. There is considerable laughter when teachers gather informally.
22. Teachers ask nonsensical questions in faculty meetings.
23. Custodial service is available when needed.
24. Routine duties interfere with the job of teaching.
25. Teachers prepare administrative reports by themselves.
26. Teachers ramble when they talk in faculty meetings.
27. Teachers at this school show much school spirit.
28. The principal goes out of his way to help teachers.

29. The principal helps teachers solve personal problems.
30. Teachers at this school stay by themselves.
31. The teachers accomplish their work with great vim, vigor, and pleasure.
32. The principal sets an example by working hard himself.
33. The principal does personal favors for teachers.
34. Teachers eat lunch by themselves in their own classrooms.
35. The morale of the teachers is high.
36. The principal uses constructive criticism.
37. The principal stays after school to help teachers finish their work.
38. Teachers socialize together in small select groups.
39. The principal makes all class-scheduling decisions.
40. Teachers are contacted by the principal each day.
41. The principal is well prepared when he speaks at school functions.
42. The principal helps staff members settle minor differences.
43. The principal schedules the work for the teachers.
44. Teachers leave the grounds during the school day.
45. The principal criticizes a specific act rather than a staff member.*
46. Teachers help select which courses will be taught.
47. The principal corrects teachers' mistakes.
48. The principal talks a great deal.
49. The principal explains his reasons for criticism to teachers.
50. The principal tries to get better salaries for teachers.
51. Extra duty for teachers is posted conspicuously.
52. The rules set by the principal are never questioned.
53. The principal looks out for the personal welfare of teachers.
54. School secretarial service is available for teachers' use.
55. The principal runs the faculty meeting like a business conference.
56. The principal is in the building before teachers arrive.
57. Teachers work together preparing administrative reports.
58. Faculty meetings are organized according to a tight agenda.
59. Faculty meetings are mainly principal-report meetings.
60. The principal tells teachers of new ideas he has run across.
61. Teachers talk about leaving the school system.
62. The principal checks the subject-matter ability of teachers.
63. The principal is easy to understand.
64. Teachers are informed of the results of a supervisor's visit.

TABLE 4.1

(Continued)

THE ORGANIZATIONAL CLIMATE DESCRIPTION
QUESTIONNAIRE, FORM IV

---

65. Grading practices are standardized at this school.*
66. The principal insures that teachers work to their full capacity.
67. Teachers leave the building as soon as possible at day's end.*
68. The principal clarifies wrong ideas a teacher may have.*
69. Schedule changes are posted conspicuously at this school.*

---

* These five items are merely "buffer" items used to fill out the IBM cards; these five items are not scored. The questionnaire scores are based on 64 items.

the eight dimensions to eight corresponding subtests. The first four subtests refer primarily to the behavior of the teachers; the second four, to the behavior of the principal. The eight dimensions of Organizational Climate are described in Table 4.2. The OCDQ, Form IV, items which compose each of the eight corresponding subtests are listed in Tables 4.3 and 4.4. The items in Table 4.3 refer to the teachers' behavior; those in Table 4.4, to the principal's behavior.

TABLE 4.2

THE EIGHT DIMENSIONS OF ORGANIZATIONAL CLIMATE

Teachers' Behavior

1. *Disengagement* refers to the teachers' tendency to be "not with it." This dimension describes a group which is "going through the motions," a group that is "not in gear" with respect to the task at hand. It corresponds to the more general concept of *anomie* as first described by Durkheim.* In short, this subtest focuses upon the teachers' behavior in a task-oriented situation.

2. *Hindrance* refers to the teachers' feeling that the principal burdens them with routine duties, committee demands, and other requirements which the teachers construe as unnecessary "busywork." The teachers perceive that the principal is hindering rather than facilitating their work.

3. *Esprit* refers to morale. The teachers feel that their social needs are being satisfied, and that they are, at the same time, enjoying a sense of accomplishment in their job.

4. *Intimacy* refers to the teachers' enjoyment of friendly social relations with each other. This dimension describes a social-needs satisfaction which is not necessarily associated with task-accomplishment.

Principal's Behavior

5. *Aloofness* refers to behavior by the principal which is characterized as formal and impersonal. He "goes by the book" and prefers to be guided by rules and policies rather than to deal with the teachers in an informal, face-to-face situation. His behavior, in brief, is universalistic rather than particularistic; nomothetic rather than idiosyncratic. To maintain this style, he keeps himself—at least, "emotionally"—at a distance from his staff.

6. *Production Emphasis* refers to behavior by the principal which is characterized by close supervision of the staff. He is highly directive and plays the role of a "straw boss." His communication tends to go in only one direction, and he is not sensitive to feedback from the staff.

7. *Thrust* refers to behavior by the principal which is characterized by his evident effort in trying to "move the organization." Thrust behavior is marked not by close supervision, but by the principal's attempt to motivate the teachers through the example which he personally sets. Apparently, because he does not ask the teachers to give of themselves any more than he willingly gives of himself, his behavior, though starkly task-oriented, is nonetheless viewed favorably by the teachers.

8. *Consideration* refers to behavior by the principal which is characterized by an inclination to treat the teachers "humanly," to try to do a little something extra for them in human terms.

---

* Emile Durkheim, *Le Suicide* (Paris: Librarie Felix Alcan, 1930), p. 277. *Anomie* describes a planlessness in living, a method of living which defeats itself because achievement has no longer any criterion of value; happiness always lies beyond any present achievement. Defeat takes the form of ultimate disillusion—a disgust with the futility of endless pursuit.

TABLE 4.3

OCDQ, Form IV—Items That Compose Four Subtests:
Teachers' Behavior

I. Disengagement

   1.* The mannerisms of teachers at this school are annoying.

   2. There is a minority group of teachers who always oppose the majority.

   3. Teachers exert group pressure on nonconforming faculty members.

   4. Teachers seek special favors from the principal.

   5. Teachers interrupt other faculty members who are talking in staff meetings.

   6. Teachers ask nonsensical questions in faculty meetings.

   7. Teachers ramble when they talk in faculty meetings.

   8. Teachers at this school stay by themselves.

   9. Teachers talk about leaving the school system.

  10. Teachers socialize together in small select groups.

II. Hindrance

  11. Routine duties inferfere with the job of teaching.

  12. Teachers have too many committee requirements.

  13. Student progress reports require too much work.

  14. Administrative paper work is burdensome at this school.

  15. Sufficient time is given to prepare administrative reports.**

  16. Instructions for the operation of teaching aids are available.**

III. Esprit

  17. The morale of the teachers is high.

  18. The teachers accomplish their work with great vim, vigor, and pleasure.

  19. Teachers at this school show much school spirit.

  20. Custodial service is available when needed.

  21. Most of the teachers here accept the faults of their colleagues.

  22. School supplies are readily available for use in classwork.

  23. There is considerable laughter when teachers gather informally.

  24. In faculty meetings, there is the feeling of "let's get things done."

  25. Extra books are available for classroom use.

26. Teachers spend time after school with students who have individual problems.

IV. Intimacy

27. Teachers' closest friends are other faculty members at this school.
28. Teachers invite other faculty members to visit them at home.
29. Teachers know the family background of other faculty members.
30. Teachers talk about their personal life to other faculty members.
31. Teachers have fun socializing together during school time.
32. Teachers work together preparing administrative reports.
33. Teachers prepare administrative reports by themselves.**

---

* These numbers are used solely to list the items here by subtest. The numbers do not correspond to the sequence in which the items actually appear in Form IV. See Table 4.1, p. 148.
** Scored negatively.

TABLE 4.4

OCDQ, FORM IV—ITEMS THAT COMPOSE FOUR SUBTESTS:
PRINCIPAL'S BEHAVIOR

V. Aloofness

34.* Faculty meetings are organized according to a tight agenda.
35. Faculty meetings are mainly principal-report meetings.
36. The principal runs the faculty meeting like a business conference.
37. Teachers leave the grounds during the school day.
38. Teachers eat lunch by themselves in their own classrooms.
39. The rules set by the principal are never questioned.
40. Teachers are contacted by the principal each day.
41. School secretarial service is available for teachers' use.**
42. Teachers are informed of the results of a supervisor's visit.**

VI. Production Emphasis

43. The principal makes all class scheduling decisions.
44. The principal schedules the work for the teachers.
45. The principal checks the subject-matter ability of teachers.
46. The principal corrects teachers' mistakes.

TABLE 4.4
(Continued)

OCDQ, Form IV—Items That Compose Four Subtests:
Principal's Behavior

---

47. The principal insures that teachers work to their full capacity.
48. Extra duty for teachers is posted conspicuously.
49. The principal talks a great deal.

VII. Thrust

50. The principal goes out of his way to help teachers.
51. The principal sets an example by working hard himself.
52. The principal uses constructive criticism.
53. The principal is well prepared when he speaks at school functions.
54. The principal explains his reasons for criticism to teachers.
55. The principal looks out for the personal welfare of teachers.
56. The principal is in the building before teachers arrive.
57. The principal tells teachers of new ideas he has run across.
58. The principal is easy to understand.

VIII. Consideration

59. The principal helps teachers solve personal problems.
60. The principal does personal favors for teachers.
61. The principal stays after school to help teachers finish their work.
62. The principal helps staff members settle minor differences.
63. Teachers help select which courses will be taught.
64. The principal tries to get better salaries for teachers.

---

* These numbers are used solely to list the items here by subtest. The numbers do not correspond to the sequence in which the items actually appear in Form IV. See Table 4.1, p. 148.

** Scored negatively.

THE ANALYSIS OF THE EIGHT SUBTEST SCORES

Thus far, we had analyzed the data entirely at the *item* level. By means of iterative cluster analyses and factor analyses, we had identified the eight, relatively independent dimensions which we chose to use as indexes of the Organizational Climate of a school.

We had come out with 64 "live" items, and we had assigned those items which composed each of the eight "climate" dimensions to the eight respective subtests of the OCDQ.

The next task was to move from the *item* level to the *subtest* level. To compute each respondent's eight subtest scores, we simply summed his item scores, subtest by subtest, and divided each of the eight sums by the number of items in the corresponding subtest. Next, we rounded off each quotient to a two-digit score for each subtest. This procedure gave us eight subtest scores for each of the 1151 respondents.

We computed the mean and the standard deviation for each subtest (summing across all 1151 respondents) and converted the raw scores into standard scores, with an arbitrary mean of 50 and a standard deviation of ten. We now had eight standard scores for each respondent. The correlations between these eight subtest scores are presented in Table 4.5.

TABLE 4.5

CORRELATIONS BETWEEN EIGHT SUBTEST SCORES
OF THE OCDQ, FORM IV, 64 ITEMS (N = 1151)

OCDQ Subtest	1	2	3	4	5	6	7	8
Teachers' Behavior								
1. Disengagement	1.00	.27	—.36	00	.18	.17	—.22	.04
2. Hindrance		1.00	—.32	—.07	.15	.08	—.25	—.15
3. Esprit			1.00	.31	—.09	.12	.60	.42
4. Intimacy				1.00	—.06	.11	.18	.31
Principal's Behavior								
5. Aloofness					1.00	.13	—.07	—.10
6. Production Emphasis						1.00	.17	.19
7. Thrust							1.00	.49
8. Consideration								1.00

At this point we should note that, whenever one constructs a battery of tests, one must be concerned with three standards: (1) that each test measures a relatively different "thing," or type of behavior; (2) that the battery, as a whole, taps enough common behavior to permit the investigator to describe the pattern in terms of a few, more "general" factors (that is, fewer, certainly, than the number of subtests); and (3) that the general factors which he extracts for a particular domain of inquiry are not discordant with those which previously have been reported in the literature.

But before we report the results of factor-analyzing the OCDQ subtests, let us first state what is meant by a factor loading and outline the procedure which we used to identify the factors measured by the OCDQ battery of eight subtests. The loading (the numerical value, expressed as a correlation) which a given subtest receives on a particular factor shows to what extent that subtest measures the same type of behavior as is represented in a more general form by the factor itself. Whenever a subtest yields a high loading on a given factor, *be it either positive or negative,* that subtest can be viewed as a "good" measure of the factor. Contrariwise, if a subtest secures only a zero loading on a factor, then that subtest obviously is not measuring the same thing as the factor presumably is measuring. In other words, the loadings tell us to what degree each subtest is saturated with each of the factors.

When one examines, across factors, the pattern of loadings on each of several factors, one finds that several of the subtests (that is, dimensions) load high on only one factor, whereas other subtests load high on several factors. Naturally, the most readily identifiable factor patterns are those in which groups (or clusters) of subtests load high on one factor yet yield close to zero loadings on the other factors. In examining the content of those subtests which do load high on a given factor, the investigator's task is to determine in what fundamental way these particular subtests are conceptually alike. He then must name this similarity; thus does he "create" the concept denoted by the factor.

To proceed, then, we factored the intercorrelations among the eight subtest scores. We used a principal-components method of analysis. The unrotated factor loadings and the corresponding *eigenvalues*[7] for each of the eight factors, together with the estimates of variance attributed to each factor, are listed in Table 4.6.

TABLE 4.6

UNROTATED FACTOR MATRIX FOR EIGHT SUBTESTS,
OCDQ, FORM IV, 64 ITEMS (N = 1151)

OCDQ *Subtest*	I	II	III	IV	V	VI	VII	VIII	h^2
1. Disengagement	−.40	.65	−.27	−.07	−.47	−.09	−.32	.10	1.00
2. Hindrance	−.49	.42	.14	−.08	.63	−.40	−.03	.04	1.00
3. Esprit	.84	−.03	.17	.09	.14	−.05	−.22	.44	1.00
4. Intimacy	.46	.30	−.48	.60	.16	.24	−.04	−.13	1.00
5. Aloofness	−.23	.44	.69	.49	−.11	−.14	.10	−.02	1.00
6. Production Emphasis	.19	.67	.22	−.38	.18	.54	.07	00	1.00
7. Thrust	.79	.10	.21	−.19	.01	−.27	−.28	−.37	1.00
8. Consideration	.67	.37	−.22	−.12	−.22	−.32	.43	.06	1.00
Eigenvalue	2.5	1.5	.97	.82	.75	.72	.43	.36	
% of Variance	.31	.19	.12	.10	.09	.09	.05	.05	$\Sigma = 1.00$

(Again, we followed Kaiser's recommendation and entered a value of 1.00 in the diagonal of the matrix before we computed the factor solution.)

The *eigenvalues* for the first three factors shown in Table 4.6 were sufficiently large (approximately 1.00 or higher) to suggest that the "best" factorial solution would be found in either a two- or a three-factor, rotational solution. Our next task, therefore, was to try both the two-factor and the three-factor solutions so that we could then determine which of the two solutions would provide us with a better understanding of the "higher," or the more "general," factors by which all eight of the subtests could be defined. In short, the purpose of this effort was to describe the composition of each of the subtests in terms of the smallest number of higher-order concepts (in other words, factors) which would, at the same time, yield maximum additional information about the "psychological" composition of each of the eight subtests.[8]

Now, let us look at both rotational solutions and see which helps us to interpret more incisively the various possible patterns of subtest scores.

THE TWO-FACTOR ROTATIONAL SOLUTION

The two-factor varimax rotational solution for the eight OCDQ subtests is given in Table 4.7. Note that Intimacy and Consideration load solely upon Factor I, while Disengagement and Aloofness load only on Factor II. We have observed earlier that Intimacy and Consideration both describe social-needs oriented behavior; in the case of Intimacy, satisfaction is derived from group membership, whereas Consideration can be construed as emanating from the leader. Moreover, Disengagement and Aloofness both depict behavior which is primarily task-oriented, and which therefore is related to a form of social control. Accordingly, we have named Factor I "Social Needs" and Factor II "Social Control." In reading Tables 4.7 and 4.8, it is important to note that the critical interpretation of the signs is to be made by vertical comparisons, up and down each column, not by comparisons across the rows for each subtest. (In short, the important relationship is that which obtains among those variables that load high on each of the factors.)

In a crude way, most of the social behavior which occurs in an organization can be classified either as oriented to social needs, or as associated with social control. For this reason the two-factor solution is very appealing. It allows us to describe the association among the subtests in a way which heeds the factorial data and yet also makes good sense in terms of organizational theory.

All eight subtests are saturated, to at least some degree, with either Social Control or Social Needs behavior (or both). Naturally, some of the subtests provide "purer" measures of one of these factors while other subtests reflect different combinations of the behaviors described as Social Control and Social Needs.

The two-factor solution is helpful. Yet this solution accounts for only 50 per cent of the common variance. Furthermore, some of the communalities (the squared sum of the factor loadings in

TABLE 4.7

TWO-FACTOR VARIMAX ROTATIONAL
SOLUTION FOR TOTAL SAMPLE
(N = 1151 Respondents)

OCDQ Subtest	Social Needs I	Social Control II	h^2
1. Disengagement	—.06	—.76	.58
2. Hindrance	—.24	—.60	.42
3. Esprit	.73	.41	.70
4. Intimacy	.55	—.06	.30
5. Aloofness	—.01	—.50	.25
6. Production Emphasis	.47	—.51	.48
7. Thrust	.75	.27	.64
8. Consideration	.77	—.02	.59
Factor Value	2.27	1.69	
% of Variance	.28	.22	$\Sigma = .50$

a row) are rather low. Nonetheless, the factor values (the squared sum of the factor loadings in a column) are clearly above 1.00. This, of course, indicates that both of the factors are "good" factors.

THE THREE-FACTOR ROTATIONAL SOLUTION

Now let us examine Table 4.8, the three-factor rotational solution for the scores on the OCDQ subtests, to see how the subtest loadings change when we seek to "explain" these scores according to three independent factors, instead of two.

We believe that the three-factor "solution" provides the "best" description of the factors tapped by the OCDQ. As compared to the two-factor solution, the three-factor solution is more concordant with orthodox procedures for factor analysis. Furthermore, in the three-factor solution, the high communalities found for each

TABLE 4.8

THREE-FACTOR VARIMAX ROTATIONAL SOLUTION
FOR TOTAL TEACHER SAMPLE
(N = 1151)

OCDQ Subtest	Social Needs I	Esprit II	Social Control III	h^2
1. Disengagement	.20	—.76	.20	.66
2. Hindrance	—.04	—.64	.16	.44
3. Esprit	.47	.70	.11	.73
4. Intimacy	.71	—.06	—.17	.53
5. Aloofness	—.31	—.09	.79	.72
6. Production Emphasis	.35	—.15	.62	.53
7. Thrust	.49	.62	.24	.68
8. Consideration	.78	.17	.06	.64
Factor Value	1.83	1.92	1.18	
% of Variance	.23	.24	.15	$\Sigma = .62$

of the individual subtests provide estimates—and encouragingly high estimates—of the reliability of the eight subtests.[9]

Intimacy and Consideration, the key subtests of social-needs orientation, secure high loadings on Factor I. Because Factor I indicates to what extent each subtest score is associated with "pure" social needs, we again named this factor Social Needs. But the three-factor solution, in contrast to the two-factor one, illuminates the further point that Factor I seems to measure *individual* Social Needs. The respondents describe on those subtest items which compose Intimacy and Consideration, their "individual" attitudes toward the organization. Specifically, each person describes *his own* friendly relations with the group rather than the friendly relations that presumably obtain *among the group members*. An analysis of the content of these subtest items supports the view that these items are answered primarily from an *individual* frame of reference.

Esprit and Thrust yield high positive loadings on Factor II, whereas Disengagement and Hindrance yield high negative loadings on this factor. Because Factor II of this solution describes the degree to which each subtest is associated with Esprit, we have named this factor Esprit. In examining those items that compose the subtests which load high on this factor, we note that the respondents are describing the behavior of the group *qua* group, and not their own "individual" behavior. For this reason we view Esprit as a "group" measure.

Aloofness and Production Emphasis secure the highest loadings on Factor III; these subtests represent the principal's orientation toward directing and controlling the behavior of his teachers. Since the highest loadings on this factor are secured by those subtests which describe the principal's behavior, we infer that this factor measures social control, as exerted by the principal. Consequently, we have named Factor III "Social Control"; we treat it as a measure of the *principal's* behavior.

Scrutiny of the three-factor rotational solution shows that these three measures do, indeed, comprehensively cover the domain: Social Needs is an *individual* factor, Esprit is a *group* factor, and Social Control is a *leader* factor. This, of course, is merely a restatement of the obvious observation that the major components of a school's Organizational Climate are associated with individuals *qua* individuals, with the group *qua* group, and with the principal as the leader.

The three general factors of Organizational Climate which we have identified—Social Needs, Esprit, and Social Control—describe the types of behavior that occur among members of elementary school faculties. Furthermore, each of the eight subtests reflects a different "saturation" of each of these three major types of behavior. Thus the three-factor solution provides an effective way of "explaining" the composition of the eight subtests which define the Organizational Climate profiles. Interestingly enough, Kaiser's[10] conclusion that the best rotational solution can be obtained by rotating only those factors with *eigenvalues* above 1 proved amazingly applicable to the present study.[11]

Now let us seek to relate the three general factors which we have delineated in the OCDQ to other factors already reported in the literature. Schutz[12] has identified in the FIRO tests three factors of interpersonal needs which seem to parallel the three factors which we have identified in the OCDQ. They are Affection, Inclusion, and Control.

Affection is defined as behavior directed toward the satisfaction of the interpersonal need for affection, and refers to behavior characterized by the following terms: "like," "personal," and "friendship" and, contrariwise, by such terms as "dislike," "cool," and "emotionally distant."

Control is defined as behavior directed toward the satisfaction of the interpersonal need for control, and refers to behavior that connotes "dominance," "authority," and "rules" and, contrariwise, that connotes "rebellion," "resistance," and "submission."

Inclusion is defined as behavior directed toward the satisfaction of the interpersonal need for inclusion, and refers to behavior that connotes "belonging," "communication," and "togetherness" and, contrariwise, to behavior that is described as "isolated," "lonely," "ignored," and "excluded."

The factor which we have identified as Social Needs corresponds to Schutz's Affection. Social Control is similar to the Control factor which Schutz has described. However, there is an important difference between the OCDQ factor of Esprit and Schutz's factor of Inclusion. Esprit reflects the interaction between the group and the leader, whereas Inclusion seems to describe primarily a measure of interaction *within* the group. We surmise that if we were to analyze the data for second-order factors, we would find that all the eight subtests probably could be "explained" in terms of one general factor—Esprit. Such an explanation at first blush would appear to represent a return to a unidimensional conceptualization of morale. But this is not quite true. Refined of its common variance with Factors I and III, Esprit connotes something more highly specific than what normally has been construed as morale; Esprit seems to measure the "genuineness" of the relationship between the group and its leader, the principal. The term "genuineness," as used in this context, requires comment; it describes that condition under which the group feels that the principal's behavior is "for real." Such a description refers to the leader's integrity in the most fundamental meaning of the term: Is he all of a piece? Are the verbal messages which he transmits to others concordant with his nonverbal behavior? Or do the group members feel that he transmits a great many "mixed messages" in that what he *says* and what he *does* do not appear to coincide? Does he seem to stand for something? Or is he a willow bent by each passing breeze?

In our judgment, Inclusion can be described equally well in terms of a combination of Control and Affection, or—to use our nomenclature—in terms of Social Control and Social Needs.

Let us examine the roles that Social Control and Social Needs play in an organization. For the most part, the exercise of Social Control is assigned as one of the major responsibilities of the principal; it represents his behavior in directing and controlling the activities of the group in order to accomplish the organization's goals. The group may perceive this control as behavior which "includes" the group ("democratic" control) or as behavior which "excludes" the group ("autocratic" control). Thus each group member may feel either included or not included, according to how he perceives the processes by which the organization makes decisions.

On the whole, Social Needs describes the behavior of individuals directed toward the satisfaction of their own individual needs, or toward the establishment of positive social relations with others (that is, friendship). In a social organization the principal can facilitate the formation of friendly relations among the members of the organization, and he himself can act also in a friendly fashion toward the members. According to how he behaves, the individual members of the organization will perceive that they are either "included" in the social interaction of the organization—that they do, indeed, possess and maintain satisfying friendships with others —or that they are "excluded" from the social life of the organization. Thus, inclusion is a function of both Control and Affection.

Recently, Muliak has analyzed the equivalence between personality factors and semantic factors. He identifies three second-order personality factors: Evaluation, Surgency, and Power. He comments:

> Halpin and Croft similarly found three factors when they factor analyzed the correlations between scores on subtests consisting of factorially homogeneous items in a questionnaire pertaining to the behavior of teachers and principals in public schools. These factors were named *Social Needs, Esprit,* and *Social Control.* The first of these, *Social Needs,* appears to be very similar to the *Evaluation* factor found in this investigation. It pertains to the closeness and consideration for others manifested by teachers and principals, respectively. The second of these factors, *Esprit,* appears to be related to the *Surgency* factor in this investigation. *Esprit* refers to the morale, enthusiasm, and zest with which teachers and principals work to get things done. Finally, the third factor, *Social Control,* appears to be similar to the *Power* factor found in this investigation. It refers to the production emphasis of a principal and is manifested in task-oriented behavior wherein he leads and makes decisions and plans others' activities on his own.[13]

Furthermore, the three semantic factors that emerge from Muliak's study are identical to those delineated by Osgood, Succi, and Tannenbaum, in their major, and by now, classic report on the semantic differential.[14]

We conclude that the three factors of social interaction which occur in an elementary school are, indeed, similar to the factors delineated by Schutz and described as basic factors in all social interaction, and that they also are consonant with the factors which Muliak has identified. It therefore appears that the specific findings which we have noted, *in the school situation,* can probably be generalized to other organizations as well.

The *item* factor analysis of the subtests showed that each subtest was relatively independent of the other seven. This was important for the construction of a *battery* of subtests, for the very concept of a battery is meaningless unless each part of the battery does, in fact, tap a *different* segment of the range of behavior to be explored. Yet we did not want to become so obsessive about establishing independence among the subtests that we would find ourselves confronted with what can be described metaphorically as a randomly scattered set of pebbles on the beach. We also wanted to know where each pebble was in respect to the others, and we wanted to know, too, on what beach they were scattered. Why? Because we intended later to construct a profile of each school's Organizational Climate, and we recognized that it would be foolhardy to draw such a profile unless we could be confident that the points which defined the profile were comparable in that they could be scaled from the same base. In brief, to depict the Organizational Climate, we needed to know the *degree* to which the behavior defined by each of the eight subtests characterized a given school, and to what extent this characterization of any one school compared with the characterization of the total sample of 71 schools.

RECAPITULATION

The analysis of the *item* level had identified the eight most pertinent dimensions of Organizational Climates, while the analysis at the *subtest* level had identified the higher, or the more general components, of *all* eight of the subtests. Stated somewhat differently, in the *item* analysis we had concentrated upon independence and specificity, while in the *subtest* analysis we had sought to identify the most dependable, higher-order abstractions which could be delineated within the total set of subtests—in spite of such independence as did obtain among them.

We knew by now that the eight subtests of the OCDQ could, in fact, be viewed as a battery of tests, and that the information secured from this battery could be articulated into the present corpus of knowledge about organizational theory.

To this point, in constructing and testing the OCDQ, we had been concerned with the analysis of *items* and *subtests* and with the responses of *individual* respondents. But our major purpose in the study was to describe the Organizational Climate of *schools* as perceived by their respective *staffs*. In other words, thus far we had been dealing with eight separate subtests, and with the answers given by 1151 individual respondents. Now, we need to shift our "set."

Accordingly, in the next section, we will deal with the OCDQ as a test battery and will move from the individual level of response to the consensual description of each school by its respective staff.

THE IDENTIFICATION OF THE SIX
ORGANIZATIONAL CLIMATES

Here we will report the analysis of the data, not at the *item* level or subtest level, but at the *school* level. For each school we constructed a profile whose eight points were defined by the scores on the eight subtest scores. This gave us 71 profiles—one, of course, for each school. The next task was to determine whether the profiles themselves constellated into differentiable clusters. By applying the Q technique[15] of factor analysis to the 71 profiles, we found that we could, indeed, classify these profiles into six major clusters, each of which could be used to depict a different type of Organizational Climate.

How, then, did we identify these six major Climates? We will report this process in four steps:

Step 1. We constructed school-profiles based upon the raw scores on the eight subtests of the OCDQ and then converted these raw scores into standardized scores which we standardized in two ways: normatively and ipsatively.

Step 2. We factor-analyzed the 71 school-profiles, extracted three profile factors, found six major *patterns* of factor loadings among the profiles, and then categorized each school-profile in respect to one of these six sets (that is, patterns).

Step 3. For each of the six sets of school-profiles we computed the mean-profile for those profiles within the set which were distinguished by a high loading on only one of the three profile factors. We designated these six profiles as prototypic profiles and defined the six Organizational Climates in terms of these six prototypes.

Step 4. We ranked these six Organizational Climates in respect to Openness versus Closedness and then used the content of the subtest items (and, of course, the prototypic scores for each of the eight subtests) to describe, for each climate, the behavior which characterizes the principal and the teachers.

We now will deal with each of these steps in turn.

Step 1: The Construction and Standardization of the School-Profiles.

To construct the school-profiles, we first computed, school by school, a school-mean subtest score for each of the eight subtests. These scores define the "average" response of the teachers for each respective subtest. Hence, the profile of scores shows how most of the teachers in a school characterize the Organizational Climate of their particular school. Specifically, the scores indicate how often certain types of behavior "occur" among the teachers and with the principal.

The 71 profiles, at this stage, had been expressed in terms of raw scores. The next step was to convert these raw scores into standard scores and to plot each profile in standard scores. Since we planned to intercorrelate the profile scores among the schools (using the Q technique), it behooved us to standardize the scores for each school *twice*: first, normatively, and second, ipsatively.

Normatively, we standardized the subtest scores across the sample of 71 schools so that we could compare each of the eight subtest scores on a common scale. Thus each subtest was standardized according to the mean and standard deviation of the total sample for that subtest.

Then we took these standardized scores and standardized them again—this time, ipsatively. Accordingly, all the subtest scores were standardized with respect to the mean and standard deviation of the profile scores *for each school.*

For both standardization procedures we chose a standard-score system based upon a mean of 50 and a standard deviation of ten. These standardized scores now told us two things. For example, we knew that a score above 50 on a particular subtest indicated, first, that the given school scored above the mean of the sample on that subtest, and second, that the score on that subtest was above the mean of the school's other subtest scores. The converse, of course, applied to scores below 50. The distribution of the school-mean standard scores is presented in Figure 4.2.

By standardizing the raw scores both normatively and ipsatively we had approximated a double-centered matrix.[16] This double standardization technique allows us to examine the relationship between the scores on the subtests, with the differences among the means of the subtest scores for each school in the sample held statistically constant. In short, the interschool variance and the intraschool variance are not confounded.[17]

Step 2: The Factor Analysis and the Delineation of Six Sets of School-Profiles.

With the OCDQ scores appropriately standardized, we next computed the intercorrelations among the school-profiles and factor-analyzed this matrix. Because we had found in the previous R factor analyses at the subtest level that the eight subtests seemed to be measuring three "things," we rotated three factors, using the Q factor analysis.[18]

Now, to see whether the school-profiles constellated into differentiable clusters, our first task was to categorize similar profiles into groups. Because we suspected that the factor loadings would help us achieve this end, we examined the factor matrix and noted that some of the 71 profiles secured either high positive loadings or high negative loadings primarily on only one of the three profile factors. Hence, we separated these school-profiles into six sets: two sets for each factor; one set obtained a high positive loading on the factor; the other, a high negative loading on the

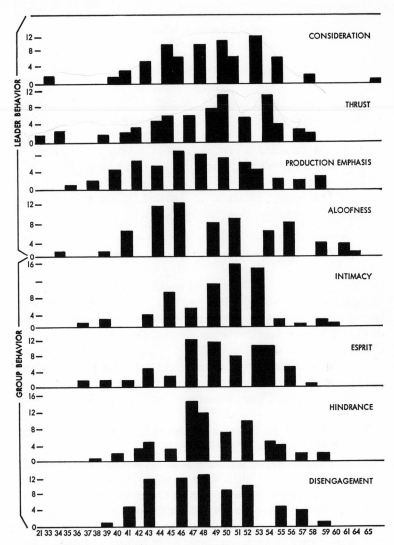

FIGURE 4.2 School-mean standard scores (N = 71) with a mean of 50 and a standard deviation of 10.

same factor.[19] We have presented this matrix in Table 4.9. For the sake of clarity, we have listed the profiles in six sets, defined by the similarity among the factor loadings within each set.

Step 3: The Specification of the Six Prototypic Profiles

The next task was to compute for each of the six sets of school-profiles a single prototypic profile[20]—or a specified set of eight subtest scores—which would best depict those schools whose profiles we had classified within each set. We simply computed the average score, subtest by subtest, for those school-profiles within each set which were distinguished by a high loading on *only one* factor. These scores, presented in Table 4.10, represent the best estimate of the prototypic profile for each set.

Step 4: The Six Organizational Climates of Schools

These prototypes can be viewed as descriptions of six different Organizational Climates, which we have named and ranked in order from Open to Closed. Even as one can regard minds as open or closed, so can we view Organizational Climates. Nor does our conceptualization differ very much, in essence, from Lewin's[21] hypothesis about the structure of "mind." To use Lewin's terms, we can describe the Open Climate as marked by "functional flexibility," and the Closed Climate as distinguished by "functional rigidity."

The ranking of the climates on Openness roughly parallels the scores which the schools receive on Esprit, the best single indicator of morale. As we trace the loadings on Esprit through the six climates, we note that these loadings become increasingly smaller as we move from the more Open to the more Closed Climates. We therefore have chosen to regard Esprit as the key subtest for describing a school's Organizational Climate. We infer that high Esprit reflects an "effective" balance between task-accomplishment and social-needs satisfaction.[22]

If we should choose to deal with cruder rubrics, we could collapse the six categories into three major groups: (1) composed

TABLE 4.9

THREE-FACTOR ROTATION FOR SCHOOL-PROFILE SCORES
(N= 71)

	Factor			
School Number	*I*	*II*	*III*	h^2
OPEN CLIMATE				
69*	91	19	20	91
45*	87	25	—02	82
6*	87	17	11	80
15	78	53	25	95
33*	87	14	—22	83
12	74	35	01	67
31	74	57	01	88
38	62	46	07	60
46	70	32	40	75
26*	68	—12	22	52
50	65	30	—33	63
64	60	03	—39	51
4	65	—35	—18	57
60	63	—44	—47	81
70	73	01	13	55
9	73	—58	13	89
41	49	—09	14	27
AUTONOMOUS CLIMATE				
22*	47	22	81	93
25*	35	25	88	97
20*	43	01	85	91
16*	28	31	87	93
21*	01	28	74	63
23	46	27	62	68
24	—21	—42	78	83
19	01	23	66	49
18	—17	32	55	45
CONTROLLED CLIMATE				
8*	11	—91	—11	87
32*	—12	—87	—29	86

TABLE 4.9
(Continued)

THREE-FACTOR ROTATION FOR SCHOOL-PROFILE SCORES
$(N= 71)$

| School Number | Factor | | | h^2 |
	I	II	III	
5*	18	—92	—25	95
28	58	—71	11	86
7	—34	—78	28	80
66*	17	—67	49	72
1	—29	—66	—03	52
2	—28	—48	—01	31
3	—02	—49	—01	24
65	—37	—49	22	42
34	—11	—40	—22	22
44	—11	—49	20	29
FAMILIAR CLIMATE				
37*	21	87	08	81
13*	02	90	03	81
39*	—10	80	—07	64
55*	31	79	06	72
61	—07	41	—04	17
53	—32	58	—32	55
PATERNAL CLIMATE				
51*	—20	55	—68	81
49*	—50	42	—63	83
27	—44	58	—52	81
62*	—08	—45	—73	74
68*	10	27	—70	58
71	—50	51	—51	76
54	38	27	—68	68
52	43	27	—64	67
57	—05	—51	—83	96
59	10	—16	—57	37
48	—04	08	—36	14
42	31	—44	—60	65

TABLE 4.9
(Continued)

THREE-FACTOR ROTATION FOR SCHOOL-PROFILE SCORES
(N= 71)

School Number	Factor			h^2
	I	II	III	
CLOSED CLIMATE				
58*	—88	21	—39	97
56*	—83	26	06	76
47	—83	03	15	72
63*	—86	09	21	79
30	—84	—43	—12	89
35	—76	—14	—41	76
36*	—75	36	—26	77
14	—70	—19	16	55
67	—67	37	05	58
10*	—70	—26	—04	57
40	—61	35	—06	51
17	—68	—30	45	76
29	—67	—54	—25	80
43	—42	—11	47	41
11	—25	—54	—16	39
Eigenvalue	20.9	14.6	12.2	
% of Variance	29	21	17	$\Sigma = 67\%$

* "Key" profiles which were used in computing the "prototypic" profiles shown in Table 4.10.

of the first two, relatively Open, climates; (2) composed of the third and fourth climates, each of which stresses only one of the two major organizational requirements (group maintenance or task accomplishment); and (3) composed of the fifth and sixth climates, both of which are Closed. To note this distinction, we have, in Table 4.10, drawn horizontal lines at the two points of separation.

TABLE 4.10

<small>Prototypic Profiles* for Six Organizational Climates
Ranked in Respect to Openness vs. Closedness</small>

	Group's Characteristics				Leader's Characteristics			
Climates	Disen-gage-ment	Hin-drance	Esprit	Inti-macy	Aloof-ness	Produc-tion Em-phasis	Thrust	Con-sider-ation
Open	43**	43	63	50	42	43	61	55
Autonomous	40	41	55	62	61	39	53	50
Controlled	38	57	54	40	55	63	51	45
Familiar	60	42	50	58	44	37	52	59
Paternal	65	46	45	46	38	55	51	55
Closed	62	53	38	54	55	54	41	44

* These profiles are based solely on those schools in the sample which secured a high loading on only one profile-factor.
** The numbers represent double-standardized scores (both normatively and ipsatively), with a mean of 50 and a standard deviation of ten.

VIGNETTES OF THE SIX ORGANIZATIONAL CLIMATES

Let us now describe, in turn, each of the six Organizational Climates, based upon the content (that is, the behavior tapped by the items) of each of the eight subtests which constitute the six prototypic profiles.

The Open Climate

The Open Climate depicts a situation in which the members enjoy extremely high Esprit. The teachers work well together without bickering and griping (low Disengagement). They are not burdened by mountains of busywork or by routine reports;

the principal's policies facilitate the teachers' accomplishment of their tasks (low Hindrance). On the whole, the group members enjoy friendly relations with each other, but they apparently feel no need for an extremely high degree of Intimacy. The teachers obtain considerable job satisfaction, and are sufficiently motivated to overcome difficulties and frustrations. They possess the incentive to work things out and to keep the organization "moving." Furthermore, the teachers are proud to be associated with their school.

The behavior of the principal represents an appropriate integration between his own personality and the role he is required to play as principal. In this respect his behavior can be viewed as genuine.[23] Not only does he set an example by working hard himself (high Thrust) but, depending upon the situation, he can either criticize the actions of teachers or go out of his way to help a teacher (high Consideration). He possesses the personal flexibility to be genuine whether he be required to control and direct the activities of others or to show compassion in satisfying the social needs of individual teachers. He has integrity in that he is "all of a piece" and therefore can function well in either situation. He is not *aloof,* nor are the rules and procedures which he sets up inflexible and impersonal. Nonetheless, the rules and regulations that he adheres to provide him with subtle direction and control for the teachers. He does not have to *emphasize production*; nor does he need to monitor the teachers' activities closely, because the teachers do, indeed, produce easily and freely. He does not do all the work himself because he has the ability to let appropriate leadership acts emerge from the teachers (low Production Emphasis). Withal, he is in full control of the situation, and he clearly provides leadership for the staff.

The Autonomous Climate

The distinguishing feature of this Organizational Climate is the almost complete freedom that the principal gives to teachers to provide their own structures-for-interaction so that they can find ways within the group for satisfying their social needs. As one might surmise, the scores lean slightly more toward social-needs satisfaction than toward task-achievement (relatively high scores on Esprit and Intimacy).

When the teachers are together in a task-oriented situation they are engaged in their work; they achieve their goals easily and quickly (low Disengagement). There are few minority pressure groups, but whatever stratification does exist among the group members does not prevent the group as a whole from working well together. The essential point is that the teachers do work well together and accomplish the tasks of the organization.

The teachers are not hindered by administrative paper work, and they do not gripe about the reports that they are required to submit. The principal has set up procedures and regulations to facilitate the teachers' task. A teacher does not have to run to the principal every time he needs supplies, books, projectors, and so on; adequate controls have been established to relieve the principal as well as the teachers of these details (low Hindrance). The morale of the teachers is high, but not as high as in the Open Climate. The high morale probably stems largely from the social-needs satisfaction which the teachers receive. (Esprit would probably be higher if greater task-accomplishment also occurred within the organization.)

The principal remains aloof from the teachers, for he runs the organization in a businesslike and a rather impersonal manner (high Aloofness). His leadership style favors the establishment of procedures and regulations which provide guidelines that the teachers can follow; he does not personally check to see that things are getting done. He does not force people to produce, nor does he say that "we should be working harder." Instead, he appears satisfied to let the teachers work at their own speed; he monitors their activities very little (low Production Emphasis). On the whole, he is considerate, and he attempts to satisfy the social needs of the teachers as well as most principals do (average Consideration).

The principal provides Thrust for the organization by setting an example and by working hard himself. He has the personal flexibility both to maintain control and to look out for the personal welfare of the teachers. He is genuine and flexible, but his range of administrative behavior, as compared to that of the principal in the Open Climate, is somewhat restricted.

The Controlled Climate

The Controlled Climate is marked, above everything else, by a press for achievement at the expense of social-needs satisfaction. Everyone works hard, and there is little time for friendly relations with others or for deviation from established controls and directives. This climate is overweighted toward task-achievement and away from social-needs satisfaction. Nonetheless, since morale is high (Esprit), this climate can be classified as more Opened than Closed.

The teachers are completely engaged in the task. They do not bicker, find fault, or differ with the principal's directives. They are there to get the job done, and they expect to be told personally just how to do it (low Disengagement). There is an excessive amount of paper work, routine reports, busy work, and general Hindrance which get in the way of the teachers' task-accomplishment. Few procedures have been set up to facilitate their work; in fact, paper work seems to be used to keep them busy (high Hindrance). Accordingly, teachers have little time to establish very friendly social relations with each other, and there is little feeling of camaraderie (low Intimacy). Teachers ordinarily work by themselves and are impersonal with each other. In fact, social isolation is common; there are few genuinely warm relations among the teachers. Esprit, however, is slightly above average. We infer that the job satisfaction found in this climate results primarily from task-accomplishment, not from social-needs satisfaction.

The principal is described as dominating and directive; he allows little flexibility within the organization, and he insists that everything be done "his" way (high Production Emphasis). He is somewhat aloof; he prefers to publish directives to indicate how each procedure is to be followed. These directives, of course, are. impersonal and are used to standardize the way in which teachers accomplish certain tasks. Essentially, the principal says, "My way of doing it is best and to hell with the way people feel." Means and ends have already been determined; the principal becomes dogmatic when members of the group do not conform to his views. He cares little about how people feel; the important thing is to get the job done, and in his way. Accordingly, he does not seek to satisfy the group's social needs (low Consideration). Nevertheless, he is trying to move the organization by working hard (average Thrust), and he personally sees to it that everything runs properly. He delegates few responsibilities; leadership acts emanate chiefly from himself, rather than from the group. (Surprisingly, it seems that many school faculties actually respond well to this type of militant behavior and apparently do obtain considerable job satisfaction within this type of climate.)

The Familiar Climate

The main feature of this climate is the conspicuously friendly manner of both the principal and the teachers. Social-needs satisfaction is extremely high, while, contrariwise, little is done to control or direct the group's activities toward goal achievement.

The teachers are disengaged and accomplish little in a task-oriented situation, primarily because the principal exerts little control in directing their activities. Also, there are too many people trying to tell others how things should be done (high Disengagement). The principal does not burden the teachers with routine reports; in fact, he makes it as easy as possible for them to work. Procedural helps are available (low Hindrance). The teachers have established personal friendships among themselves, and socially, at least, everyone is part of a big happy family (high Intimacy). Morale, or job satisfaction, is average, but it stems primarily from social-needs satisfaction. In short, the Esprit that is found in this climate is one-sided in that it stems almost entirely from social-needs satisfaction.

The behavioral theme of the principal is, essentially, "let's all be a nice happy family"; he evidently is reluctant to be anything other than considerate, lest he may, in his estimation, injure the "happy family" feeling (high Consideration). He wants everybody to know that he, too, is one of the group, that he is in no way different from anybody else. Yet his abdication of social control is accompanied, ironically enough, by high Disengagement on the part of the group.

The principal is not aloof and not impersonal and official in his manner. Few rules and regulations are established as guides to suggest to the teachers how things "should be done" (low Aloofness). The principal does not emphasize production, nor does he do much personally to insure that the teachers are performing their tasks correctly. No one works to full capacity, yet no one is ever "wrong"; also, the actions of members—at least in respect to task accomplishment—are not criticized (low Production Emphasis). In short, little is done either by direct or by indirect means to evaluate or direct the activities of the teachers. However, teachers do attribute Thrust to the principal. But, in this context, this probably means that they regard him as a "good guy" who is interested in their welfare and who "looks out for them."

The Paternal Climate

The Paternal Climate is characterized by the ineffective attempts of the principal to control the teachers as well as to satisfy their social needs. In our judgment, his behavior is nongenuine and is perceived by the teachers as nonmotivating. This climate is, of course, a partly Closed one.

The teachers do not work well together; they are split into factions. Group maintenance has not been established because of the principal's inability to control the activities of the teachers (high Disengagement). Few Hindrances burden the teachers in the form of routine reports, administrative duties, and committee requirements, mainly because the principal does a great deal of this busywork himself (low Hindrance). The teachers do not enjoy friendly relationships with each other (low Intimacy). Essentially, the teachers have given up trying; they let the principal take care of things as best he can. Obviously, low Esprit results when the teachers obtain inadequate satisfaction in respect to both task-accomplishment and social-needs.

The principal, on the other hand, is the very opposite of aloof; he is everywhere at once, checking, monitoring, and telling people how to do things. In fact, he is so non-aloof that he becomes intrusive. He *must* know everything that is going on. He is always emphasizing all the things that *should* be done (Production Emphasis), but somehow nothing *does* get done. The principal sets up such items as schedules and class changes, personally; he does not let the teachers perform any of these activities. His view is that "Daddy knows best."

The school and his duties within it are the principal's main interest in life; he derives only minimal social-needs satisfaction outside his professional role. He is considerate, but his Consideration appears to be a form of seductive oversolicitousness rather than a genuine concern for the social needs of others. In a sense, he uses this Consideration behavior to satisfy his own social-needs. Although he preserves an average degree of Thrust, as evidenced by his attempts to move the organization, he nonetheless fails to motivate the teachers, primarily because he, as a human being, does not provide an example, or an ideal, which the teachers care to emulate.

The Closed Climate

The Closed Climate marks a situation in which the group members obtain little satisfaction in respect to either task-achievement or social-needs. In short, the principal is ineffective in directing the activities of the teachers; at the same time, he is not inclined to look out for their personal welfare. This climate is the *most* closed and the least genuine climate that we have identified.

The teachers are disengaged and do not work well together; consequently, group achievement is minimal (high Disengagement). To secure some sense of achievement, the major outlet for the teachers is to complete a variety of reports and to attend to a host of "housekeeping" duties. The principal does not facilitate the task-accomplishment of the teachers (high Hindrance). Esprit is at a nadir, reflecting low job satisfaction in respect to both job satisfaction and social-needs satisfaction. The salient bright spot that appears to keep the teachers in the school is that they do obtain satisfaction from their friendly relations with other teachers (average *Intimacy*). (We would speculate that the turnover rate for teachers in this climate would be very high unless, of course, the teachers are too old to move readily to another job, or have been "locked into the system" by the attractions of a retirement system.)

The principal is highly aloof and impersonal in controlling and directing the activities of the teachers (high Aloofness). He emphasizes production and frequently says that "we should work harder." He sets up rules and regulations about how things should be done, and these rules are usually arbitrary (high Production Emphasis). But his words are hollow, because he, himself, possesses little Thrust and he does not motivate the teachers by setting a good personal example. Essentially, what he says and what he does are two different things. For this reason, he is not genuine in his actions. He is not concerned with the social needs of teachers; in fact, he can be depicted as inconsiderate (low Consideration). His cry of "let's work harder" actually means, "you work harder." He expects everyone else to take the initiative, yet he does not give them the freedom required to perform whatever leadership acts are necessary. Moreover, he, himself, does not provide adequate leadership for the group. For this reason the teachers view him as not genuine; indeed, they regard him as a "phony." This climate characterizes an organization for which the best prescription is radical surgery.

THE CLASSIFICATION OF THE 71 SCHOOLS WITH RESPECT TO ORGANIZATIONAL CLIMATE

We have now defined the six Organizational Climates of schools. Next we will explain how we classified the 71 schools in the sample with respect to these six Organizational Climates.

It will be recalled that when we initially had sought to categorize the school-profiles, we had chosen to deal with only those profiles which obtained a high loading on a single profile-factor. We did this in order to obtain an estimate of each prototype profile. Now, in order to classify those school-profiles which we temporarily had set aside, we compared each of these, in turn, with each of the six prototypic profiles. We used two methods in classifying these profiles. First, we noted on which factor each profile loaded most heavily. But since some of the profiles obtained high loadings on two or three factors, we decided that it would be wise to supplement this one basis of pertinence—the factor loading in respect to

TABLE 4.11

The Sample of 71 School Profiles
Grouped in Respect to the Six Organizational Climates

School Number	Disengagement	Hindrance	Esprit	Intimacy	Aloofness	Production Emphasis	Thrust	Consideration	Similarity Score
				OPEN CLIMATE					
69*	39	45	65	56	40	42	61	52	20
45*	46	45	69	50	38	42	58	54	20
6*	41	42	58	47	47	39	66	59	29
15	44	35	59	56	46	40	60	60	32
33*	42	40	59	43	43	48	60	66	33
12*	46	34	60	55	39	51	65	50	40
31	46	34	61	58	38	48	55	59	41
38	50	44	67	50	44	37	47	63	42
46	52	41	61	40	40	45	56	65	42
26*	44	54	69	46	46	37	58	46	44
50	47	41	47	47	41	47	69	62	45
64	45	45	58	53	31	61	60	47	50
4	36	64	57	50	37	48	59	51	50
60	42	56	56	32	44	50	60	60	54
70	33	53	62	59	39	48	48	58	54
9	33	46	64	40	52	56	59	49	55
41	34	63	56	58	42	42	47	58	62
Mean	42	46	60	49	41	45	58	56	

22*	38	41	56	61	60	36	58	51	14
25*	41	40	58	63	59	38	55	45	16
20*	36	39	57	58	63	43	56	49	22
16*	42	39	61	65	58	41	47	47	27
21*	42	44	44	61	65	37	50	57	33
23	44	32	57	53	61	41	59	53	35
24	41	46	49	53	70	52	52	37	57
19	44	52	56	71	49	43	45	39	60
18	56	31	58	56	62	51	43	48	64
Mean	42	40	55	60	60	42	51	46	

8*	34	64	50	43	50	63	52	43	26
32*	44	56	50	33	56	67	48	47	28
5*	42	63	58	33	53	61	54	46	29
28	33	49	63	39	54	59	53	50	35
7	53	58	49	31	58	61	51	41	39
66*	33	46	56	49	62	62	50	42	39
1	48	71	49	38	57	45	46	46	57
2	55	67	54	36	57	41	47	43	61
3	44	67	44	39	58	40	55	55	67
65	48	48	41	48	62	61	59	34	68
34	45	66	62	52	50	49	35	43	73
44	47	69	44	49	44	51	60	37	80
Mean	43	60	51	40	55	55	50	43	

TABLE 4.11 (Cont.)

School Number	Disen-gagement	Hindrance	Esprit	Intimacy	Aloof-ness	Production Emphasis	Thrust	Consideration	Similarity Score
FAMILIAR CLIMATE									
37*	59	46	51	58	40	33	50	62	19
13*	65	36	48	56	48	37	56	56	26
39*	67	45	56	53	45	36	43	56	35
55*	50	39	43	64	43	42	58	61	40
61	56	60	44	62	39	37	58	44	58
53	58	56	37	64	37	47	45	56	62
Mean	59	47	46	59	42	38	51	55	
PATERNAL CLIMATE									
51*	67	42	48	48	37	57	42	59	27
49*	72	44	44	44	44	56	44	53	28
27	73	49	44	49	40	46	50	48	34
62*	63	53	38	45	38	45	56	62	39
68*	61	43	48	48	33	61	60	47	40
71	68	41	41	54	41	61	44	50	41
54	52	41	54	47	33	62	48	62	50
52	47	53	46	50	33	51	52	69	54
57	53	62	47	31	42	60	51	54	55
59	47	66	47	53	31	56	51	49	61
48	48	48	42	61	36	67	52	46	61
42	45	45	50	35	45	68	56	56	63
Mean	58	49	46	47	38	58	51	55	

CLOSED CLIMATE

58*	70	51	36	48	51	56	42	46	27
56*	61	52	41	57	56	52	30	51	29
47*	60	62	38	59	54	47	43	36	34
63*	59	58	34	59	58	47	46	40	36
30	56	55	36	44	62	63	42	44	37
35	65	57	37	37	57	52	44	51	39
36*	70	45	45	51	50	57	36	47	42
14	62	46	46	46	55	66	42	37	43
67	63	61	43	62	47	42	40	43	44
10*	53	47	34	50	60	66	46	44	45
40	63	52	34	48	59	40	45	59	49
17	52	48	44	47	72	54	38	45	49
29	56	58	36	36	62	58	49	46	52
43	49	59	56	61	54	49	32	39	64
11	41	72	42	49	49	53	42	52	65
Mean	59	55	40	50	56	53	41	45	

* Those schools whose scores were averaged in order to depict the prototypic profiles shown in Table 4.10.

one of the factors—with a second basis for categorization: a profile-similarity score that allowed us to determine numerically to what extent each of the 71 school-profiles was congruent with the prototypic profile which characterized each of the six climates.

The similarity scores provided the simplest and quickest method for classification. We obtained each similarity score by computing the absolute difference between each subtest score in a school's profile and the corresponding score in the first prototypic profile, then in the second one, and so on. Thus we compared the scores of each school with those of each of the six prototypic profiles. In each instance we computed the sum of the absolute differences between the profile scores. A low sum indicates that the two profiles are highly similar, whereas a large sum shows that the profiles are dissimilar. We assigned each of the 71 schools to the set defined by that prototypic profile for which its profile-similarity score was lowest.

In Table 4.11 we have presented the profiles for the 71 schools, grouped in respect to profiles which are similar. The profile-similarity scores are shown in the last column, and the schools which depict each climate have been ranked in order from the lowest similarity score (indicating the profile most similar to each respective prototypic climate) to the highest similarity score.

THE THREE PROFILE-FACTORS

Having identified and named the six Organizational Climates, we now are ready to re-examine the factor pattern of the matrix and name the three profile-factors.

Before we examine the obtained factor loadings, let us first note what the "perfect" loadings would be in the "ideal" case. These loadings for the "pure" six climates are given in Table 4.12.

The actual loadings on the three factors, for each of the 71 schools, were given in Table 4.9, and the schools were grouped in respect to their Organizational Climates. Obviously, none of the schools in the sample secured factor loadings as clear-cut as those depicted in Table 4.12. Yet many of the schools approximated this ideal in that they obtained a high loading on only one of the

TABLE 4.12

FACTOR LOADINGS FOR EACH IDEAL CLIMATE

	Factor		
Climate	*I*	*II*	*III*
Open	1.00	.00	.00
Autonomous	.00	.00	1.00
Controlled	.00	—1.00	.00
Familiar	.00	1.00	.00
Paternal	.00	.00	—1.00
Closed	—1.00	.00	.00

three factors. But what about those schools whose pattern of factor loadings was not marked by a high loading on but a single factor?

It will be recalled that we had computed the prototype profile from those school-profiles which loaded most clearly on only one factor. The factor on which each school-profile loaded highest told us to which prototypic profile each school-profile was most similar (taking into account, of course, the sign of the loading). But few taxonomies have clear, razor-edged borders. How, then, should we explain instances in which a high loading on one profile-factor is accompanied by a high loading on a second profile-factor? If a given school-profile shows a substantial loading on a second as well as the first factor, then that school-profile is also similar to the prototypic profile characterized by the second factor. But this similarity is to a lesser degree than it is to the prototypic profile characterized by the first factor, the one on which the particular school-profile loads highest. To take an example, let us look at the factor loadings for School No. 45:

	I	*II*	*III*
School No. 45	.87	.25	—.02

Essentially, School No. 45's climate is an Open Climate (note the very high positive loading on Factor I). But this profile also shows a positive loading on Factor II, which indicates that School 45's profile is also similar, but to a lesser degree, to the profile which depicts the Familiar Climate. (The profile for a Familiar Climate obtains a high positive loading on Factor II.) Since this school's profile shows a nearly zero loading on Factor III, we also can conclude that those behaviors which typify both the Autonomous and the Paternal Climates are, for the most part, absent in this school. In short, School 45's climate is primarily Open, but it possesses, too, some of the characteristics found in the Familiar Climate.

In sum, the loadings which each school-profile secures on the three profile-factors tell us to what extent a school's climate is similar to each of the prototypic climates. In evaluating the climates it becomes clear to us that the "best" climate is the Open one. To determine how closely a given school's climate approximates the Open Climate, we need only compare the school's loadings on the three profile-factors with the "pure" instances illustrated in Table 4.12 and with the prototypic profiles given in Table 4.10. We can supplement this basis of comparison by also taking into account the similarity score provided by the difference between a specific school-profile and any one of the six prototypic profiles.

Now that we have described the types of behavior which occur in those schools whose profiles are similar, and have depicted each set of behaviors by a single construct (that is, the name of the Organizational Climate), we can proceed to use these constructs— the prototypic profiles for the six Organizational Climates—to identify the profile-factors.

It is difficult to select simple and appropriate names for those factors which seem to undergird specific test patterns, even when using the R technique of factor analysis. But there are two reasons why it is even more difficult to name factors which have been extracted by the Q technique. First, the identification of each factor must take into account the meaning of the subtests which compose the profiles, and, second, the identification must be reconciled with the fact that each of the three profile-factors is defined by two prototypic profiles which are precisely opposite to each other (the one loads positively on the factor; and the other, negatively). It is with full recognition of these limitations that we shall attempt to name the three profile-factors.

Let us look at Table 4.13, in which we present the factor *pattern* of the matrix that has been reported in Table 4.9. Note the climates which load highest on Factor I. The Open Climate obtains a high positive loading on this factor; conversely, the Closed Climate obtains a high negative loading on it.

To supplement the information given on the factor loadings *by school*, in Table 4.9, and the information given on the pattern of factor loadings, in Table 4.13, we present also, in Table 4.14, the results of an R technique three-factor varimax rotational solution for the subtest scores. The data from all three of these tables will provide the bases for the discussion which follows.

Now, let us describe how we have inferred what Factor I measures. By reviewing the way in which the Open and the Closed Climates differ, we can understand better what Factor I represents. The profile for the Open Climate scores high on the subtests of Esprit and Thrust, and low on Disengagement. These scores describe an energetic, lively organization which is moving toward its goals, but which is also providing satisfaction for the individuals' social needs. Leadership acts emerge easily and appropriately as they are required. The group is not preoccupied exclusively with either task-achievement or social-needs satisfaction; satisfaction on both counts seems to be obtained easily and almost effortlessly. Contrariwise, the Closed Climate is marked by low scores on

TABLE 4.13

THE PATTERN OF PROFILE-FACTOR LOADINGS FOR
EACH OF THE SIX ORGANIZATIONAL CLIMATES

	Factor		
Climate	*I*	*II*	*III*
Open	x*		
Autonomous			x
Controlled		x	
Familiar		x	
Paternal			x
Closed	x		

*The x indicates the factor on which each climate scores the highest loading.

TABLE 4.14

"R" Technique
Three-Factor Varimax Rotational Solution for
Subtest Scores, by School (N = 71)

| OCDQ Subtest | Profile Factors | | | h^2 |
	I	II	III	
1. Disengagement	—.86*	00	—.33	.85
2. Hindrance	—.13	.50	.34	.38
3. Esprit	.79	—.28	—.04	.71
4. Intimacy	—.07	—.85	.22	.77
5. Aloofness	.08	—.09	.80	.66
6. Production Emphasis	—.16	.76	.02	.61
7. Thrust	.64	.08	—.47	.64
8. Consideration	.02	—.07	—.85	.73
Factor Value	1.83	1.65	1.86	
% of Variance	.23	.21	.23	$\Sigma = 67\%$

* The italicized figures identify those loadings which most characteristically define the three major patterns of subtest scores.

Esprit and Thrust, and by a high score on Disengagement. There seems to be nothing going on in this organization. Although some attempts are being made to move the organization, they are met with apathy; they are not taken seriously by the group members. In short, morale is low, and the organization seems to be stagnant.

What, then, is Factor I measuring? In what way are the Open and Closed Climates related? The answer is obvious: the Open Climate is open in that the actions of the group members emerge freely and without constraint. But this can be stated in another way: the behavior of the group members is genuine, or authentic. Moreover, there is a balance between behavior which is oriented toward social control and behavior which satisfies social needs, and a further balance between the initiation of leadership acts by the principal and the emergence of such acts from the group. All of these conditions contribute to the openness of the climate; accordingly, we have named Factor I "Openness."

Now, let us examine Factor II, and note the behaviors that occur in the two opposite climates which load high on this factor: the Controlled and the Familiar. The Familiar Climate is highly personal, but undercontrolled. The members of this organization satisfy their social-needs but pay relatively little attention to social control in respect to task-accomplishment. Conversely, the opposite orientation is found in the Controlled Climate. The group's behavior is directed primarily toward task-accomplishment, and relatively little attention is given to behavior oriented toward social-needs satisfaction. In brief, social control and task-accomplishment are present, but are achieved apparently at the expense of some social-needs satisfaction.

The Esprit found in these two respective Organizational Climates is obtained in different ways: in the one case, by task-accomplishment; in the other, by social-needs satisfaction. Accordingly, Factor II pertains to the balance between these two orthogonal behaviors. However, both of the climates (the Controlled and the Familiar) are out of balance because one of the two major, requisite types of behavior is relatively weak. As a result, Esprit is not as high in either instance as it is in the Open Climate. We conclude that the behavior represented by a high loading on Factor II—whether positive or negative—is not as appropriate, or effective, as the behavior which distinguishes the Open Climate. In short, such behavior is not as "authentic." In the one climate there is a preoccupation with achievement; in the other, an over-concern with satisfying social-needs. Whenever one organizational requirement is stressed at the expense of the other, some degree of Openness or freedom in the behavior of the group members is lost, and to this extent the behavior within the group becomes less authentic. (The authenticity of behavior is indicated crudely by our best single index of perceived morale, Esprit.) In sum, Factor II pertains primarily to the style of organizational behavior *in respect to social-control versus social-needs satisfaction.*

Now, what is the axis of reference on which the Paternal Climate and the Autonomous Climate are aligned? Both obtain high loadings on Factor III, negatively and positively, respectively. Factor III can be construed as an index to the latitude within which the group members can initiate leadership acts. In the Autonomous Climate this latitude is wide, but the freedom that this latitude allows is not accompanied by sufficient direction and control from the principal. (In other words, the principal has not defined the structure, or the limits, within which the members can feel free to attempt leadership acts.) Under these circumstances some task-oriented leadership acts are not initiated, simply because the organization's immediate problems have not been defined clearly enough to allow the group members to decide what leadership acts would be most appropriate for solving those problems. For this reason the score on Esprit for the Autonomous Climate is not as high as the Esprit score in the Open Climate.

Contrariwise, the Paternal Climate is best characterized as one in which the principal constrains the emergence of leadership acts from the group and attempts to initiate most of these acts himself. In this instance the leadership skills within the group are not used to supplement the principal's own ability to initiate leadership acts. Consequently, some required leadership acts are not even attempted. The principal's personal disregard of the leadership potential within the group is accompanied by the low Esprit that we find in the Paternal Climate.

Consequently, for the group members to perceive the climate as authentic and for the leadership within the group to be construed as "reality-centered," leadership acts must be allowed to emerge from both sources—from the leader *and* from the group. But in a situation where the teachers and the principal are more greatly preoccupied with the source of attempted leadership acts than with their relevance and merit, the Organizational Climate is perceived by the teachers as being inauthentic and, hence, as not Open. In brief, Factor III pertains to the source of attempted leadership acts, whether they originate primarily from the group or from the leader.

In summary, we may say that from the profile analysis we have inferred three parameters which can be used to conceptualize the social interactions that take place within an organization:

1. *Authenticity:* The authenticity, or Openness, of the leader's *and* the group members' behavior.

2. *Satisfaction:* The group member's attainment of conjoint satisfaction in respect to task accomplishment *and* social needs.

3. *Leadership Initiation:* The latitude within which the group members, as well as the leader, can initiate leadership acts.

CRITIQUE

In brief, we constructed the OCDQ and identified eight dimensions of behavior within the domain tapped by this questionnaire. We analyzed the subtest profiles for 71 elementary schools and classified these profiles in respect to six Organizational Climates. And finally, by Q analysis, we extracted from the school-profiles three "higher order" factors which give us an alternative way of "understanding" what kinds of behavior, on the part of the principal and the teachers, are associated with the differences that we found in Organizational Climates.

At this point, we have left one vital thread dangling: the concept of authenticity. We will return to that. But first we must pause long enough to discuss several critical shortcomings and limitations of the present study.

Since there is not a longitude without a platitude, perhaps we can exercise our option by using up our quota of platitudes right now. The first piece of cant which we must utter is that this research effort has raised more new questions than it has answered. Of course! That is in the very "nature of the beast." The second obvious comment is that the present findings will need to be "cross-validated" on a broader and an independent sample of schools. The third apology is that in every research conducted under contract the investigators must contend with the realities of time, money, and the mobility of university personnel.[24] No matter how alluring the prospect may be to investigate new areas of inquiry which have been opened by the findings, the investigators must draw the line somewhere; they must report their findings to date, so that they can get critical feedback from their colleagues before a Lorelei song seduces them into further, and perhaps premature, digressions. These, then, are the conditions under which these findings have been reported. The cut-off point is arbitrary; it was dictated by the clock.[25]

In social science research, findings are seldom as tidy as the investigators would like them to be. Our situation provides no exception, yet our objective has been attained. We have found that it is feasible to dimensionalize the behaviors which define the Organizational Climate of elementary schools, and we have identified empirically six distinct Organizational Climates which make good sense, both practically and psychologically.

At this first stage, the overriding question was whether the Organizational Climate of schools could be mapped at all—no matter how crudely. This could be done.

Obviously, the Organizational Climate Description Questionnaire, despite all the revisions that we already have made in it, is not yet in perfect form. A few of the subtests do not contain enough items to provide measurements that are as dependable as we might desire. But this is no serious problem. Knowing, as we do now, what the eight major dimensions are, it will not be especially difficult to construct, for each of the subtests, additional items which will increase the dependability of these measures. Of course, a balance will have to be maintained between the length of the questionnaire and the tolerance of the teachers who are required to take it.

When the dependability of the subtest measures has been increased by the addition of more items, the next move will be to cross-validate the present dimensions by factoring similar data from an independent and larger sample of schools. A cross-validation study may show that the OCDQ will benefit from a few modifications. We do not know. Yet we surmise that the eight dimensions and the six climates which we have delineated here will survive the crucible of cross-validation.

We are certain that some readers have already objected to how we have used the term "validation" in the last paragraph. Or, throughout this entire report they may have wondered, "But what about validation?" We can only reply that at this point we have not been concerned about the relationship between the profile scores on the OCDQ and external criteria of a school's effectiveness. Our reluctance to deal with the criterion issue right now has been reinforced by strong and increasing evidence that many of the measures which have been used in education as purported indexes of a school's effectiveness, or of an administrator's effectiveness, do not justify the blind confidence that many of us have placed in them. The findings reported in the recent, monumental study of elementary school principals by Hemphill, Griffiths, and Fredricksen[26] show why we should be extremely cautious about the pitfalls of the criterion issue. Indeed, the "in-basket," simulated experience devised by Hemphill and his colleagues provides, in many respects, a far more useful and meaningful set of criteria for administrative performance than do some of the measures which heretofore have been used as alleged criteria. For example, ratings of principals by their superintendents have been revered for several decades. Yet serious questions can be raised about both the relevance and the dependability of such ratings.

Indeed, we are not quite sure against what criteria we should seek to check the climate scores. We cannot rule out the possibility that the climate-profiles may actually constitute a better criterion of a school's effectiveness than many measures that already have entered the field of educational administration and now masquerade as criteria. We simply do not know. But we also know that we cannot dismiss the criterion issue. Our point is clear: in the next phase of research with the OCDQ, when we seek to determine the relationship between the OCDQ scores and criteria, we must avoid the temptation of seizing upon certain criteria solely because they are lying around loose in the literature—or in the school's Central Office file. Instead, we must be ruthless in screening possible criteria and in determining which criteria, if any, are relevant to our purpose. Certainly, it would be perilous to ignore the findings of Hemphill and his colleagues.

However, we can suggest one type of criterion study that may prove relevant. Specifically, it would be useful to send a team of observers into a sample of elementary schools and have the team members do a case study of each school with the purpose of describing the school in respect to the OCDQ dimensions and the six climates that we have identified. Concomitantly, the OCDQ should be administered to the faculty of these same schools. Then a group of qualified judges should be asked to do a "blind matching" between the case reports and the OCDQ profiles.[27]

In the present phase of this research on the Organizational Climate of schools, we have failed to take into account another essential point: the probable curvilinearity of the relationship among the different variables. Throughout the present analysis we have made the assumption of linear relationships. Yet we know from studies such as those by Fleishman and Harris,[28] by

Triandis,[29] and by Urry[30] that the relationship between the Consideration and the Initiating Structure dimensions and various independent measures of group effectiveness, or productivity, can be understood far better when these relationships have been plotted curvilinearly rather than linearly. But we decided to handle the curvilinearity issue in another way. We knew that some of the OCDQ subtests tapped nonmonotonic functions. (For example, too much Intimacy as well as too little Intimacy can detract from the Openness of the Organizational Climate.) But we also knew that the method of profile analysis which we had used took this nonmonotonicity into account because this analysis dealt with the subtest *patterns*.

Obviously, the present data on the OCDQ cannot yet be used for normative purposes. We must not forget that the sample of 71 schools upon which the present findings are based is a fortuitous sample; it was not drawn at random from a clearly defined population. Accordingly, we can use this fortuitous sample for making estimates of the relationship among the subtests and for analyzing other *internal* relationships. We also can use these data if we should choose to estimate the relationship between these OCDQ scores and whatever measures we may select as external criteria. Furthermore, for the 71 schools within this particular sample we can compare the profile of any one school with the profile of any other—or with the profiles of all the other schools—in terms of its relative position *within this sample*. But we cannot state what the distribution of scores would be for a representative sample of elementary schools in the United States.

By converting the raw scores of the OCDQ into standard scores we have, in effect, forced upon the data the particular distribution that we have reported. There is nothing illegitimate in doing this. But it is imperative that we do not forget what we have done, imperative that we do not draw inferences from the data on the fallacious assumption that the sample has been drawn from a representative population and is, indeed, not merely fortuitous. Other samples may yield distributions of OCDQ scores which do not differ significantly from the distribution reported here. But we do not know; this is a question that must be checked empirically. To repeat, we can treat with reasonable confidence the *relationship* among the subtest scores and can compare, in relative terms, one profile with another. But we must remember that the anchor points for the true distribution of OCDQ scores have not yet been determined.

At this stage of the project, the prototypic profiles must be construed as only a relatively crude way of classifying the 71 schools in the present sample. Since the number of schools that were used to compute each prototypic profile was small (four to six schools), the subtest scores which we have obtained for each profile may vary as much as five points from the values at which these scores eventually will be stabilized when OCDQ data have been secured from additional and larger samples of schools. But the obvious unreliability of the prototypic profile scores does not disturb us because it is not severe enough to effect the basic *pattern of subtest scores* for the respective climates. However, this unreliability may force us to modify slightly our depictions of the six climates. Consequently, we are eager to use the OCDQ with additional samples of schools so that we can thereby determine the stability of the prototypic profiles.

Furthermore, in our vignettes of the six Organizational Climates, we have deliberately accentuated the distinctive features of each climate; hence, to some degree these descriptions have been "idealized." We have done this for three reasons: (1) to focus upon the salient characteristics of each climate so that we could more readily identify the three profile-factors, (2) to determine whether the six descriptions were "live" and recognizable, and (3) to judge whether the descriptions, *in toto*, were inclusive enough to cover most of the spectrum of leadership behavior and group interactions, as these have been reported in the research literature. Teachers and colleagues who have read these vignettes report that they are "live"— almost to the point of discomfiture. These readers claim that they "know" these climates, and "know" the characters in them only too well. We may have missed a few thin bands in the spectrum, but, on the whole, we seem to have covered the range.

One of the OCDQ dimensions, Consideration, is the same as one of the dimensions which has been identified previously in the Leader Behavior Description Questionnaire studies. But our findings on Consideration in the present study raise again a question which bothered us a few years ago when we were working with the Leader Behavior Description Questionnaire: have two or more facets of Consideration behavior been confounded within a single measure? We believe that there are certain kinds of behavior that can be described as Consideration which emerge from psychological weakness; the individual is impelled to be considerate to other people because he himself is so hungry for affection and approbation. Conversely, other kinds of Consideration seem to emerge from strength; the individual is considerate to others not because of his own poverty of love, but because of the freedom with which he can give love. The latter individual knows that the very act of giving love (Consideration) replenishes his own supply, whereas the former individual treats love as a medium of barter: he gives love only in order to buy some for himself. At the manifest and superficial level, the behavior of both individuals may appear to be the same. Yet we suspect that we are making a mistake when we interpret an individual's manifest behavior apart from the context of character in which it appears.[31]

We have noted a second, apparent split in the dimension of Consideration. Some administrators use a "spray-gun" approach in spreading consideration and affability in all directions. Like airline "stewardi" they behave as if they had attended Smile School. Other administrators appear to be much more discriminating; they focus their acts of consideration upon the specific requirements of a given individual at a given time. We do not imply that the polarity between that consideration which stems from weakness and that which is derived from strength coincides with the polarity between spray-gun consideration and focused consideration. We do not know. But we have a strong hunch that the research on Consideration which has been reported to date presents an utterly oversimplified picture of the variety of behaviors that are encompassed within this dimension. A more sophisticated way of measuring Consideration is sorely needed.

In interpreting the prototypic profiles, we have emphasized the impact of the behavior of the principal upon the climate which obtains in his school. There is no gainsaying the fact that such influence does operate and that it must be taken into account when we seek to understand the Organizational Climate of a particular school. But this is not a one-way street. The leader influences the behavior of the group members, but the group members also influence the behavior of the leader. However, since influence is an effect that takes place over time, it is impossible for us to make any inference about the direction of such influence on the basis of the present OCDQ measurements because measurements have been made at only a single slice in time.[32]

But we must be cautious in one other respect when we attempt to interpret the behavior of the principal. His behavior, in its effect upon the Organizational Climate of a school, should be construed *as a necessary but not a sufficient condition* which determines the school's climate. For example, if a principal behaves in a way such as is depicted in the sixth climate—the most Closed one—it is doubtful that the group members, entirely on their own, can do very much to change this climate. Indeed, their high Disengagement score suggests that they already "have given up."

But we also must take into account the converse of this situation. Suppose that a new principal has been assigned to an elementary school. He is young and intelligent, and he has had good experience and training. He possesses Thrust, and he is highly considerate. He moves into the school with every intention of maintaining an Open Climate such as he had maintained in the school from which he came. But what happens to him if the teachers are not prepared to deal with an Open Climate? Suppose that the teachers in this school have contended for the past ten years with a principal whose behavior typifies that which characterizes a Closed Climate. We must recognize the strong possibility that the very openness of the new principal's behavior presents the teachers with a severe psychological threat. When the members of a group have been deprived of freedom for a long period of time they seldom are quite ready to deal with it, especially if it be made available to them too abruptly. This, of course, is the issue which Fromm discussed in his classic analysis, *Escape from Freedom*.[33] It is for this same reason that the British Army established at the close of World War II special "decompression camps" for British soldiers who had been held as prisoners of war for several years in the Nazi compounds.[34] These camps were established because the Army psychiatrists recognized that a too abrupt shift from a Closed Climate to an Open Climate might prove psychologically traumatic to these soldiers. Additional supporting evidence for this view is provided by the experience of those men and women who survived Buchenwald and Dachau.[35]

Accordingly, our newly appointed principal should not be surprised when he discovers that his behavior constitutes a serious threat to the teachers. Because of the tenure system in public schools and because no public school has yet been known to have been put out of business as a result of poor teaching, it is the new principal who becomes "the patsy." The teachers channel their personal anxieties into a vengeful hostility focused upon him. In such situations it is common to hear the teachers say, "Principals may come, and principals may go, but we go on forever." Subjected to the teachers' hostile attack, the new principal is left with a narrow range of alternatives. He can, of course, resign. But he knows that a stay of only one year, or less, at a school will not look good on his résumé and may, indeed, jeopardize his career. Probably the superintendent of schools or some other official will tell the principal, "We agree with what you are trying to do. We are all for you, but you must remember that changes must be made very, very slowly. You are still a young man; you are too impatient. You have to remember to adjust to the local mores." Then, what happens? The principal is forced to backtrack from the position which he took initially. This provides positive reinforcement for the teachers who can then capitalize upon the principal's first compromise by pushing him into further compromises. Unfortunately, here is a situation where the group's inertia can immobilize a man who in other circumstances might prove to be a highly effective leader.

This type of problem occurs not only with principals but with superintendents of schools as well. Most of us probably know of at least one superintendency that is vacant at this moment, and we know, too, that any man, no matter how well qualified, who accepts the particular job will put his head under a guillotine. (Strangely enough, there never seems to be a dearth of willing victims.) The kindest thing that can be said about some administrative positions in the public schools is that the superintendent's job—or, in some instances, the principal's job—is untenable.

To reiterate, we recognize fully that in the present report we have not taken into account the effect which the group has upon the leader. The whole question of the direction of influence in a given climate at a given time remains to be explored.

Nor have we taken into account the extent to which the climate in a given elementary school is determined by the social matrix of the school system of which it is a part. School systems vary in respect to the degree of control that is exerted by the superintendent and the Central Office. In some systems the principal of each elementary school is permitted only a very limited range of discretion in how he may administer the school. In other systems the superintendent may encourage autonomy and freedom for all the principals in the system. It would be intriguing to analyze in depth the difference between two sets of school systems: one set in which the variance in Organizational Climates among all the elementary schools in the system is narrow, and a second set in which this variance is wide.

We surmise, too, that the organizational climate that we find in an elementary school may be related to such demographic factors as whether it is a new or old school; whether it is located in a wealthy suburb or in a deteriorated slum; and whether it is set in a metropolitan center, a village, or a rural area.

Other studies need to be done on the relationship between the Organizational Climate which characterizes the school and various biographical and personality measures of both the teachers and the principal. But biographical data will have to be handled in a much more sophisticated fashion than is customarily the case.[36]

Nor, in this day of reactionary societies and of zealous committees hunting for communists under every bed, can we ignore the relationship between the "political flavor" of a community and the Openness of climate that is allowed to exist in the elementary schools. During the McCarthy era many subtle restraints—and some that were anything but subtle—were imposed upon teachers; indeed, even the graduate schools of many universities did not escape unscathed. Accordingly, we have a hunch that how Open the climate of a school may be, will depend, at least in part, upon how much Openness the community itself considers "safe."

In short, the variance of the Organizational Climate of schools is undoubtedly associated with variance from a great many sources, only a few of which have been suggested here. The important point is that the OCDQ provides us with a tool that will permit us to determine what other variables do indeed co-vary with a school's Organizational Climate.

There is another pitfall of which we must be aware. Throughout this report we have stressed the point that the group members must be able to enjoy social-needs satisfaction *and* satisfaction from task-accomplishment. We have assumed that the principal source of social-needs satisfaction lies in the teacher's interactions with fellow teachers and the principal. But this, too, is an over-simplification. A school is not an assembly line; the teachers are working with children. Consequently, a teacher, especially in the elementary school, can achieve a major source of social-needs satisfaction through her close personal relationship with the children themselves. Indeed, this satisfaction may be sufficient to compensate her for many dissatisfactions which her membership in the school organization forces her to endure.

Next, we must emphasize as forcibly as we can a crucial point: the dimensions by which the Organizational Climates have been defined are descriptive, taxonomic, and phenotypic dimensions. Consequently, these descriptive dimensions do not *necessarily* correspond to the dimensions of behavior along which change can be induced in a school's Organizational Climate. This point is of extreme practical importance; it has bearing even upon the apparently simple matter of reporting the findings from the present study to those schools which have participated in this project. Specifically, suppose we report the OCDQ scores to the principal of School No. 11 (Table 4.10). This is the school whose profile depicts a climate more Closed than that found in any of the 70 other schools. What will the effect of this report be upon the principal or upon the teachers? For us to expect that the principal's knowledge of these scores will automatically result in an improvement in the school's climate would be rashly naïve. We would guess that the immediate impact upon the school of the knowledge of these scores would be a tendency for the climate to become even more Closed. Consequently, we must be extremely careful in how we use the information that is secured by means of the OCDQ. We must, for example, avoid the stupid inference that if Thrust is "good" then we ought to incorporate into our graduate training programs for principals an advanced seminar on Thrust. Such a plan would miss a central point: the subtests do not describe dimensions along which change can be induced by means of a direct frontal attack.

Yet, as we have already noted, we have at least one hunch about a possible genotypic dimension which may provide an avenue for change-induction: authenticity. But here, too, we must be cautious lest zealots degrade this concept into a slogan and post at strategic places in all schools, signs which, in bold type, urge one and all to "BE AUTHENTIC." We recall André Gide's incisive observation that no man can be sincere at the same time that he says he is sincere. Likewise do we surmise that the more a man *tries* to be authentic in his behavior, the less authentic will he be. There is no easy prescription to follow; nor will changes be made by the wave of a wand. The first step is to learn much more than we know now about the interpersonal conditions that make authentic behavior possible.

THE CONCEPT OF AUTHENTICITY

Research, as an activity, is fascinating for many reasons, but perhaps its most fascinating appeal lies in its element of *surprise* —surprise for the investigator who, in the course of a project, suddenly stumbles across a fundamental idea which he had completely failed to take in account when he started the project. Novelists often note that they have to change the plot with which they start because the characters "take over." Likewise, a novelist may say, while writing a story, that he does not know yet how it will turn out because he does not yet know *what the characters are going to do*. The research man often finds himself in the same position, although few social scientists like to admit to this point as freely as does Selye, who has sufficient greatness to allow him to confess to the many "romantic" aspects of research as a profession.[37]

We certainly were surprised at what happened to us, as investigators, during the course of the Organizational Climate study.

When we started, the word "authenticity" was not part of our professional vocabulary. But the more we worked with the Climate data, the more we scrutinized the behavior that differentiated Open from Closed climates. The more that we sought for explanations to account for the differences that we found, the more, too, did we find ourselves forced to contend with the concept of authenticity.

We were not always sure that we knew what we meant by the term. Indeed, even now we are not sure. Yet we found that the authenticity concept, fuzzy as it was, did give us a useful purchase on our findings.

As we looked at the schools in our sample, and as we reflected about other schools in which we had worked, we were struck by the vivid impression that what was going on in some schools was *for real,* while in other schools, the characters on stage seemed to have learned their parts by rote, without really understanding the meaning of their roles.[38] In the first situation the behavior of the teachers and the principal seemed to be genuine, or authentic, and the characters were three-dimensional. In the second situation the behavior of the group members seemed to be thin, two-dimensional, and stereotyped; we were reminded of papier-mâché characters acting out their roles in a puppet show. Something in the first situation made it possible for the characters to behave authentically —that is, "for real," or genuinely. The professional roles of individuals remained secondary to what the individuals, themselves, were as human beings. Within this climate there was enough latitude in the specification of roles to allow the role-incumbents to experiment with their roles—to work out ways of bringing their own individual style to their job and to their relations with confrères. In the language of the French existentialists, the incumbents were given the chance to *invent* themselves. Within the opposite climate the roles seemed to be overspecified. The individual appeared to use his professional role as a protective cloak, almost as if the cloak might serve to hide his inner emptiness and his lack of personal identity. (One gets the impression that these people are living their lives inside cellophane wrappers.) The role itself and the individual's status as a teacher or a principal appeared to constitute his essential sense of identity.[39] Furthermore, in these instances the individual used his role ritualistically, so that it became a device which kept others at a distance and thus precluded the establishment of authentic relationships.

These observations fitted neatly with the climate data, for the Open Climate appeared to reflect authentic behavior, whereas the Closed Climate reflected inauthentic behavior. The OCDQ subtests, and in particular those for Thrust and Esprit, provided indexes of this very quality of authenticity. Thrust represents the very combination of Initiating Structure in Interaction and Consideration which Argyris has described as "reality-centered leadership."

> Effective leadership depends upon a multitude of conditions. There is no one predetermined, correct way to behave as a leader. The choice of leadership pattern should be based upon an accurate diagnosis of the reality of the situation in which the leader is imbedded. If one must have a title for effective leadership, it might be called *reality-centered leadership*. Reality-centered leadership is not a predetermined set of "best ways to influence people." The only predisposition that is prescribed is that the leader ought to first diagnose what is reality and then to use the appropriate leadership pattern. In making his diagnosis, he must keep in mind that all individuals see reality through their own set of colored glasses. The reality he sees may not be the reality seen by others in their own private world. Reality diagnosis, therefore, requires self-awareness and the awareness of others. This leads us back again to the properties of personality. A reality-oriented leader must also keep in mind the worth of the organization. *No one can make a realistic appraisal if for some reason he weighs one factor in the situation as always being of minimal importance.*[40]

The principal who scores high on Thrust is not enslaved by a narrow definition of his role, nor does he seem to be preoccupied with his status. He is more intent on task-accomplishment, on getting the job done, and on moving the organization toward its goals. (Note, however, that he does this without sacrificing Consideration.) In a sense, he is willing to unfreeze the organization from one stage of its development (even if that stage be highly satisfying to the group members in terms—for example—of Esprit or Consideration). And he is ready to take the risk of change, confident that such change will result in a higher order of organizational development which, in turn, will permit a greater congruence between the social-needs satisfaction of individual group members and the specification of their roles. To take this risk and to gamble on the outcome of unfreezing the organization, the principal "must stand for something." He also must be open in letting his teachers and the school's patrons know what, indeed, he does stand for. In short, he must be authentic.

It was no accident, we saw then, that Argyris had described the behavior of the "reality-centered leader" as authentic. Argyris and we had reached the same point by different paths, but it was evident that we had focused on the same aspect of human behavior.

Contrast the Open principal's behavior with that of the principal in the Closed Climate. This principal's low Thrust, combined with moderately high Aloofness and Production Emphasis, suggests that he uses his role to keep people at a distance, to limit his "part" to a two-dimensional one, and to reinforce the present level of the organization's development (that is, he insists that nobody rock the boat). We would guess that he is afraid to let go, because letting go will expose his lack of the professional skills necessary for embracing change. Lacking professional competence, he must cling all the more tenaciously to his status. So he is compelled to "keep other people in their place," and to emphasize reiteratively that "we must move slowly and make changes very gradually." Because change represents so terrifying a threat to him, he clutters the organizational system with Hindrance. The result, as we can see in the prototypic profile for the Closed Climate, is high Disengagement and low Esprit.

We would guess that this man's strategy for diminishing Disengagement is to strive for even greater Production Emphasis, while he, at the same time, accentuates his own two-dimensionality. This strategy, of course, succeeds only in making the climate even more Closed than it was in the first place. The net result is that the teachers see through this principal; they know that he is a fraud and that authentic relationships with him are impossible.

In the same way that Thrust furnishes an index to the authenticity of the principal's behavior, so does Esprit provide an index to the authenticity of the group's behavior. Probably the best single index of authenticity which we can adduce from the present data is the combination of high OCDQ scores on both Thrust and Esprit.

As we have just noted, the present findings allow us to make inferences about possible indexes of authenticity. Yet ironically, when we started this project, we simply were not wise enough to incorporate into the design any *direct* measures of authenticity. Depending upon how we wish to view what has happened, we can say that we have been either blessed or damned by serendipity. We do not intend to disparage the worth of the present findings, and certainly we have no reason to apologize for what these findings reveal. But by the same token, we believe that the chief consequence of the present study is our identification of the pivotal importance of authenticity in organizational behavior.

Authenticity is a tricky concept; it does not lend itself readily to operational definition. Moreover, there is a central problem that complicates whatever attempt we may make to define this concept: the difference between (1) the authenticity of behavior as perceived by the participants in a given situation and (2) the authenticity of behavior as perceived by an outside observer who seeks to evaluate this authenticity against an essentially "absolute" standard, as compared to a relative one. This problem, of course, is another variation of the same issue that we encounter in the fields of mental hygiene and psychiatry when we seek to differentiate between "adjustment" and "positive mental health." For example, it is entirely possible that a patient can achieve a level of adjustment which allows him to cope with the world and to experience some measure of happiness, even though his level of functioning is still considerably below the standard which a team of competent psychiatrists and psychologists would construe as indicative of positive mental health. This is why psychiatrists refer to some patients as well-adjusted neurotics. This diagnosis points up the fact these are situations in which it is expedient to let a patient live with his symptoms, providing that they are not too acute and do not interfere too seriously with his daily functioning. Indeed, the symptoms may represent "frozen anxiety"; the psychotherapy required to unfreeze this anxiety in order to relieve the symptoms may confront the patient with an image of himself more hideous than he can bear. Consequently, under these circumstances, the therapist may decide that settling for adjustment entails a lesser risk for the patient than attempting to guide the patient toward full maturity.

Analogously, the participants in a given social situation may perceive (or believe) that their behavior vis-à-vis each other is entirely authentic. Yet a perspicacious outside observer can recognize immediately that the participants' behavior is outrageously phony. Each participant in such a situation can be likened to a man with extreme myopia who has not yet worn his first pair of glasses. Until such time as the correction for his visual defect allows him to see how the world "out there" actually looks, he must deal with many visual stimuli for which he possesses no authentic basis for judgment.

We know that when we start speaking in terms of an absolute standard of authenticity, many scientists will promptly bristle. Within the behavioral sciences, in particular, we have become so accustomed to the notion "that everything is relative" that even the slightest suggestion of an absolute standard is anathema to most of us. Yet in spite of the resistance which our suggestion may produce, we believe that future research efforts should be directed to the development of criteria for identifying authenticity in behavior, and that these criteria should be regarded as more analogous to standards for positive mental health than to those for adjustment.

In the past two decades the issue of adjustment and the problem of conformity in the American character have been discussed in a spate of books and articles. A few authors, particularly Fromm[41] and Lindner,[42] have raised serious questions about the leveling effect of conformity and the damage which man has suffered because of society's current emphasis upon adjustment. Accordingly, if the suggestion that we should differentiate between authenticity as perceived by the participants in the situation and authenticity as evaluated by an essentially absolute criterion should seem obtuse, we must counter this criticism by noting that the difficulty of dealing with the concept of authenticity does not diminish the urgency to deal with it promptly. This problem of authenticity transcends the specific area of the present research; indeed, it must be analyzed within the context of the major social changes that have taken place in America during the past 40 years. LaPiere, for example, has given us a penetrating analysis of these changes and has shown how Freudianism has had many damaging effects upon the American character.[43] Sykes deals with this same issue.[44] His book is uneven (it scarcely reaches the quality of LaPiere's work), yet he has many illuminating insights about the changing social scene.

There is a difference between how authenticity is perceived by the participants in a situation and how it is perceived by outside observers. Imagine, for instance, listening to two businessmen who, unbeknown to each other, have already gone into bankruptcy, but who, nonetheless, loudly boast about their financial success and put on an elaborate act to impress each other. In instances of this type we must be compassionate; we must realize that circumstances can create a situation so threatening to the participants that they simply cannot face up to the inauthenticity of their own behavior. To damn such people is both unkind and pointless; they are to be pitied. More than this, they need help.

But situations of this type are extremely serious, for they reinforce inauthentic behavior.[45] The individual's perception becomes increasingly selective so that he eventually either excludes or illegitimatizes any form of feedback that disagrees with the distorted image he holds of himself. Thus the selectivity of his perception provides a kind of tunnel vision which enables him to confirm the "rightness" of what he is doing. The problem often becomes even further complicated because those individuals whose behavior is inauthentic have a tendency to flock together to compose a cabal whose conspiracy is energized by an unvoiced agreement among the members that they will desist from exposing each other's inauthenticity. Consequently, the members of this coalition increasingly reinforce their respective inauthentic behavior. If an agent external to this coalition—for example, a newly appointed principal in an elementary school—should happen to see through the nonauthenticity of one member of this coalition and should try to persuade this member to change his behavior, the entire coalition becomes threatened. It tightens its ranks to support the member and quickly mobilizes its strength in opposition to the principal. In the same way that the vehemence and diffuseness of a neurotic's response is often completely out of proportion to the stimulus which presumably has triggered the response, so too is the coalition's response out of proportion to the stimulus of the principal's actions. But aside from the impasse which a cabal of this kind creates within the school, the reinforcement of inauthenticity must be examined in respect to an even more destructive effect: its impact upon the members of the cabal, each of whom ultimately becomes his own victim.[46] For, when such reinforcement of inauthentic behavior continues over a period of years, each victim reaches a point at which it becomes impossible for him to face up to the fraud that he is perpetrating. At times, the behavior of such coalitions makes us recognize, with a shiver, that the theme of Shirley Jackson's great short story *The Lottery*[47] is not as farfetched as we would like to believe.

And this brings us to a further complication in the concept of authenticity. To be authentic a man must first have something to be authentic about. Consequently, we surmise that none of us will significantly further our understanding of authenticity until we analyze carefully an important confusion that pervades our society: the confusion between the search for identity[48] and the search for status. For example, when a man uses his status as his chief source of identity his behavior inevitably becomes inauthentic. Furthermore, as long as he persists in using his status as a protective cloak, he also diminishes the likelihood that his behavior within the organization will ever approach authenticity. What happens is this: because he begins by being less than authentic, his colleagues respond in kind; their response, in turn, confirms his original, implicit assumption that he had better not be too open with them. And so the cycle continues and the breach widens.[49] Kubie, in an exquisite analysis, discusses the formidable resistances that are encountered when one attempts to help such a man reverse the direction of this degenerative spiral.[50]

Let us nurture no illusions: authenticity is not an easy concept to deal with. Yet fortunately, it has not been ignored in the literature. For example, Rinder and Campbell,[51] Seeman,[52] Erikson,[53] Argyris,[54] and Perlmutter[55] have all explored this problem of authenticity. Although each of these men started from a different part of the forest they all found that they were stalking the same deer. The several lines of inquiry have all converged on the same issue: authenticity.

Authenticity can be examined in respect to three major, conceptual frames of reference which are all interrelated:

1. The problem of the marginal man,
2. The problem of person-to-person relations in cross-cultural exchange, and
3. The crisis of identity.

It is a common observation that the marginal man has a tendency to overconform. The Negro who comes up from the South and achieves some success in moving to a lower middle-class status tends to overidentify with the white bourgeoisie.[56] The Jew who has only recently been "accepted" by his gentile neighbors and business or professional associates, tries to divert attention from his Jewness. He overconforms to the gentile norms and is not likely to differ with the group on important issues, because to differ on issues, or even in the expression of attitudes, might invite fresh and uncomfortable attention to the fact that he is a Jew. As a result, in the case of both the Negro and the Jew, the individual, in his effort to be accepted by a group that appears prestigious to him, denies something of himself and to this extent his behavior becomes inauthentic; he, indeed, is not himself. A famous rabbi struck at the core of this inauthenticity when he once told his congregation, "You can cut off your noses, but you can't cut off your Moses."

How does the marginal man concept apply to school personnel? Teaching can be construed as a marginal profession. The salaries of teachers are below those for other professions. For the most part, a teacher cannot be in business for himself, as can a physician, a lawyer, or an architect. He must practice his profession as a member of a community-supported organization (the school system), and in each community this organization exercises a monopoly. Hence, if the teacher is bound by personal and social ties to a given community, he cannot easily leave his job; he often must swallow his indignation and learn to adjust to the situation. Furthermore, a great many teachers were marginal students in their college or university, in that they had drifted down into a choice of teaching as a career only after unsuccessful attempts to make the grade in other departments on the campus. Finally, since teachers are recruited primarily from lower middle-class groups and, in recent years, have come in increasing numbers from the lower-class stratum, the marginality of their status is further accentuated.[57] Therefore, it is not surprising that teachers behave as do other marginal men. They are eager to overconform to what they think is expected of them. They fit themselves into a stereotype, and in so doing repress or repudiate parts of themselves. A recent study of the biographical characteristics of a nation-wide sample of elementary school principals shows that the portrait they present is that of "the good child."[58] Indeed, the portrait is that they are "too good to be true"—or, shall we say, to be authentic?

But we encounter another problem of marginality in the school: the marginality of the principal in his role as a leader—which marginality occurs, as Seeman[59] has pointed out, in all leadership roles in our society. Seeman's interviews with elementary school principals and school superintendents led him to conclude that the leadership behavior of principals can be examined profitably in respect to the more general problem of authentic versus inauthentic reactions to status. Indeed, Seeman's data suggest ways by which the authenticity of a principal's reaction to status can be measured. He notes that the authenticity problem in respect to a leader's behavior can be viewed as simply the special case of a more general sociological problem: the relation between status stereotypes and behavior.

The second conceptual framework deals with the problem of person-to-person relations in cross-cultural exchange. Perlmutter has used the concept of authenticity in his study of the experience of Americans living abroad and of foreign visitors living in this country.[60] He notes that most persons who go abroad exhibit a wish not only for *information* about the foreign culture but for a reciprocated interhuman experience with other persons of the foreign culture. Perlmutter describes this experience as an "authentic interpersonal relationship." Furthermore, he contrasts authentic experience with what occurs in other instances where the visitor engages in superficial, defensive encounters with members of the other culture and deals with members of his host country principally in terms of stereotypes. Indeed, Perlmutter describes those Americans abroad who do establish authentic relationships as people who are more *open*.

In describing the experience of Americans abroad Perlmutter also discusses "the crisis of identity." Specifically, when an American lives abroad for an extended period he finds that his answer to the question, "Who am I?" is closely linked to another question, "Who is the foreigner—who is the foreign, unexpressed me?" Some Americans abroad respond to this crisis by denying it and by keeping their perception of the foreigner as stereotyped as they can. (Note the similarity between this behavior and the behavior of principals described by Seeman as characterized by overconforming to the stereotype of the leader's role. In turn, this corresponds to the behavior of the principals in the Closed Climate.) Other Americans, however, use their foreign experience to reconstrue their own personal role-constructs[61]—or, if you will—to enrich their own sense of identity.

Let us illustrate this crisis of identity with two examples. First, consider the typical attitude toward masculinity held by American men. This attitude stresses sports, physical endurance, and a kind of rough-and-ready manner. On the other hand, gallantry toward women and interests of a literary, or aesthetic, nature are viewed as somewhat "sissified." Consequently, when the "typical" American visits France or Italy he may find himself disturbed by his discovery that Frenchmen and Italians, particularly those from a relatively high social class, are indeed gallant toward women, and also are vitally interested in art, literature, ballet, and the opera. Furthermore, these interests do not detract from the perception which these men hold of themselves as masculine.

There are two major ways in which our American visitors can respond to such an experience. If our visitor's attitude is essentially closed, he can reject this alternative view of masculinity; he can protect his own ego by stereotyping the men in his host country as "too feminine for my taste." Conversely, an American visitor whose attitude is more open may use the identical experience to question the tenability of the typical American concept of masculinity. As a result of his experience he may become more willing to recognize and accept "feminine" impulses within himself which he heretofore has repressed. By "opening" himself in this way, he enriches his sense of self-awareness.

As a second example of the crisis of identity, let us consider the difference between the typical American's attitude toward time and the attitude which Latin Americans and people of the Mediterranean culture display toward time. For example, when an American first visits Brazil, he may find himself disturbed by the Brazilian's attitude toward time and punctuality. When a Brazilian businessman arrives for an appointment an hour or more late, the American may feel that he has been insulted. Again, depending upon his openness or closedness toward a foreign culture, two major reactions are possible. The first reaction is to stereotype all Brazilians as unpunctual and, therefore, undependable. But an alternative reaction is possible. The American may begin to question his own attitudes toward time. He may note among his Brazilian hosts a kind of *joie de vivre* which he finds lacking in his own life, at home in North America. He may even reflect upon how many of his business associates have suffered from ulcers or coronaries, and he may be prompted to ask himself the tantalizing question, "Why am I killing myself?"

It is obvious, of course, that those visitors who use their foreign experience principally to reinforce the stereotypes which they have brought with them are analogous to the principals whom we find in the Closed Climate. Contrariwise, the American visitor abroad who uses his experience to expand his own concept of self is similar to those principals whom we find in the Open Climate.

If we view the entire profession of education as one subculture in our society, then we can look at the responses that members of this subculture make when they are confronted by members of other professional or public subcultures in America. Thus, when Dr. James Conant, Dr. Robert M. Hutchins, or Admiral Hyman Rickover criticizes public education, do the members of a given school system, or of a given college of education, respond to this criticism by stereotyping the critic, and by illegitimatizing his criticism? Or do the teachers, principals, and professors allow themselves to be open to the criticism so that they can perhaps enrich their own understanding of education by taking into account the critic's "axis of reference" as well as their own?

A schism between professors of education and professors in the liberal arts college is found on most American campuses. How do the professors of education respond to the allegations that the other professors make against them? Do the professors of education coalesce defensively, and thus encapsulate themselves? Or do they remain open enough to give themselves a chance of modifying their own behavior in respect to the criticism? It is not enough for professors of education to sing, with only a slight variation, Annie Oakley's song, "Anything you can do, I can do better—or, at least, as well." They must indeed show what they can do *in their behavior*.

Naturally, there are a few campuses where the schism we have noted does not occur. An outstanding example is the University of Chicago. The schism has been averted there principally because the research productivity of the department of education is so outstanding that no basis for invidious comparison exists. Because the quality of research is high within the department, the professors of education can deal with their colleagues in other departments authentically; they have no need to approach such encounters *defensively*. In short, the pattern of person-to-person interaction which Perlmutter finds in cross-cultural contacts can be found in the counterpart interactions between different departments on the same campus. We would also add that this is true between the teachers in a school and its patrons.

The third conceptual framework which can help us understand authenticity is that provided by Erikson[62] in his concept of the crisis of identity. We have already referred to this concept in discussing Perlmutter's work. To speak of the crisis of identity is another way of asking the familiar question, "Who am I?" or, "Who am I *really*?" What is the authentic me? The especial relevance of Erikson's approach for the present study of Organizational Climates is that much of Erikson's work has been concentrated on the child's *development* of identity, and that Erikson has, in particular, dealt with identity during the transitional period from adolescence to maturity. The differences in the child's behavior as he goes through succeeding stages in developing a sense of identity are not entirely dissimilar to the differences that characterize the behavior of the principal and the teachers as we move from the Closed to the Open Climate. Indeed, we suspect that the types of interpersonal interactions that occur between the principal and the teachers within each of the six Organizational Climates may have counterparts in the patterns of interpersonal reactions that occur between the parent and the child in different families, or in the same family at different stages in the child's development. Some adolescents never succeed in achieving genuine maturity. In like fashion some faculty groups never succeed in achieving an Open Climate. The conditions that retard an individual's development toward maturity may be psychologically analogous to those that prevent a faculty's climate from becoming Open.

These three general frameworks—the concept of marginality, the problem of person-to-person relationships in cross-cultural exchange, and the crisis of identity—are all useful in helping us to understand the concept of authenticity. Yet, useful as these approaches are, they all suffer from a lack of sufficient specificity for our purpose. At least, *at this time*, we have not been able to make these approaches sufficiently specific in their applicability to the concept of authenticity. However, despite this limitation, we believe that further work on the concept of authenticity will be forced to rely heavily on the three approaches that we have cited.

Even though we recognized the potential value of these three approaches, we still found ourselves searching for a more specific mechanism that might help us understand authenticity. We did not hope to find a mechanism whose variables had already been operationally defined. Nor did we expect to find variables already prefabricated for use in testing specific hypotheses about authenticity. Such expectations would have been too unrealistic—indeed, they were. But, guided by Erickson's emphasis upon the child's *development* of identity, we searched further into the literature of developmental psychology and found in the brilliant work of Schachtel a concept which seems to hold great promise for further research on authenticity. We refer to Schachtel's discussion of focal attention and the emergence of reality.[63] He traces the infant's development in learning how to apprehend the "reality" of the "object world":

> The child's exploration of the object world depends not only on the continued availability of the objects but also on the child's relative freedom from too strong need or anxiety tensions. The

emergence of the object world is inseparably linked to the temporary abeyance of needs. In the infant, this abeyance is brought about by the satisfaction of needs through the mothering one. But, in the course of development, it is also increasingly brought about by the child's capacity to delay need satisfaction. The more secure the infant or child feels in being able to depend on the mother for eventual need satisfaction—and, later, on his own capacity to satisfy his needs—the more adequately this capacity to delay need satisfaction is likely to develop. Focal attention is the instrument which plays a decisive role both in the development of the capacity for delay and in the grasp of reality, of the object world. Only by means of focal attention do distinct objects emerge from the impinging environment so that they can be perceived and understood as independent of human needs. This is possible only because the rest of the field is excluded for the duration of the act of focal attention—that is, the claim of all other needs and impulses for attention is delayed or abated.[64]

Schachtel then differentiates between his view and Freud's:

In contrast to Freud's view, I believe that thought has two ancestors rather than one—namely, motivating needs and a distinctively human capacity, the relatively autonomous capacity for object interest. Focal attention is the tool, the distinctively human equipment, by means of which the capacity for object interest can be realized. There is no proof that the wish for need satisfaction alone would ever lead to object perception and to object-oriented thought—that is, to a relatively objective view of reality. On the other hand, it can be shown that the more urgently need-driven perception and thought are, the less able they are to grasp and understand the object.[65]

Finally, we quote further from Schachtel's analysis of the relation between focal attention and the individual's achievement of a sense of identity:

The development of focal attention and the emergence of the object world presuppose relative freedom from basic need tension, so that the object can be perceived under many different aspects, rather than apprehended merely as something that will satisfy hunger or that arouses fear and has to be fled from.

And even after focal attention is fully developed and the environment is perceived as consisting of distinct objects, the need-driven (as opposed to the object-interested) perceiver or thinker will not see the object as fully in its own right as will the person who contemplates it in relative freedom from acute need tension. Curiosity, the desire for knowledge, the wish to orient oneself in the world one lives in—and finally the posing of man's eternal questions, "Who am I?" "What is this world around me?" "What can I hope for?" "What should I do?"—all these do not develop under the pressure of relentless need or of fear for one's life. They develop when man can pause to think, when the child is free to wonder and to explore. They are not, as Freud would have us believe, merely detours on the path to gratification of basic biological needs, any more than thought is only a substitute for hallucinatory wish fulfillment. They represent man's distinctive capacity to develop *interest*—the autonomous interest which alone permits the full encounter with the object. . . . The relation of autonomous interest to need-dominated interest is similar to the relation of love to sexual desire, and to neurotic need of the "love-object." Like love, autonomous object interest is potentially inexhaustible and lasting, while need-dominated interest subsides with the satisfaction of the need and revives only when the need tension, such as hunger or sexual desire, rises again. Moreover, while need satisfaction, according to Freud, is related to tension discharge, both love and object interest find their fulfillment not in a discharge of tension but, rather, in the maintenance of it, in sustained and ever renewed acts of relating to the beloved person or to the object of interest.[66]

Thus Schachtel shows that in order to develop the focal attention required for the apprehension of reality, the child must be at least temporarily free from need-driven interest. He must be able to count on the dependability of his mother (or a mother surrogate), and he must be able to experience an assurance of some stability in the structure of events around him. The teddy bear or the favorite rattle must *be there*. The story that his father reads to him each night before he falls asleep must be read night after night without a word being left out or changed. In brief, before the child can attend to the world with focal attention, he must be at least relatively free from anxiety-driven, need-dominated attention.

Likewise, in regard to the Organizational Climate of schools, the principal and the teachers are not able to deal with each other openly and to apprehend the school's tasks with focal attention unless the members' need-dominated attention is minimized. If, for example, the principal's personal need for affection causes him to lavish Consideration on the teachers, then his need-dominated attention prevents him from attending focally to the reality of the school's problems. Indeed, the OCDQ subtest of Thrust is probably an index of the principal's freedom from need-dominated attention. (Contrariwise, high Production Emphasis may represent a need-dominated attention which detracts from the reality-centeredness of his leadership. Argyris' reality-centered leadership thus refers to focal attention as opposed to need-dominated attention.) Furthermore, the factorial structure of the Thrust subtest shows that it contains both Consideration behavior and behavior which provides the teachers with a general structure of the field, including a definition of the limits within which leadership acts can be initiated. Thus Thrust would seem to serve as a counterpart within the group for the parents' behavior which Schachtel suggests is required by the child in order that he may apprehend reality focally. In similar fashion, the Esprit subtest would seem to reflect high focal attention as opposed to need-dominated attention.

Principals with high Thrust have the ability to satisfy the teachers in respect to task-achievement and social-needs; hence, the teachers' focal attention can be directed toward teaching. When teachers describe their principal as high in Thrust, they are saying that he is instrumental in satisfying their needs. Furthermore, high Esprit shows that the teachers have enjoyed satisfaction in their past achievement. But if the principal is described as low in Thrust, the teachers evidently by-pass the principal and seek satisfaction of their needs in their own way. This results in a diffuseness, in that different teachers follow different paths in search of this satisfaction. These individual searches are not always consonant with the goals of the organization; each teacher attempts to gain satisfaction in his own way, thus reducing the focal attention which he can direct to teaching itself.

The impact of Schachtel's argument is clear: the apprehension of reality—or, the authenticity of behavior—is inversely related to the stress of need-dominated attention. We would hold to this same argument in respect to the Organizational Climates: the greater the need-dominated attention among the faculty members, the less Open the climate.

It is important that we note five additional points about Schachtel's view. First, what Schachtel describes as focal attention is identical to what Fromm has described as "productive" thought. To put the matter in yet another way, to engage in focal attention is to do precisely what the artist does when he seeks to apprehend an object in all its reality and to *see* what is really "out there." To the artist this means that he sees what is "out there," uncluttered by any distortions produced by his own neurotic needs, and divested also of any socially induced sham that may interpose itself between the artist and what is "out there."

Second, when we speak of need-dominated attention we are not referring to any normal, or moderate, expression of any of the major human needs. The key word is "dominated," and the point is that a single need within the individual's psyche assumes overriding importance in commandeering the individual's attention, and in determining not alone those facets of the "out there" which the individual is driven to attend to, but also how those facets are seen, distorted, and interpreted. The individual's needs appear to have become so badly out of balance that his preoccupation with a single area of need becomes so demanding that he cannot, indeed, attend focally to what is actually "out there." In short, we are discussing *neurotic* needs.

And this brings us to a third point, one to which we have already alluded above in speaking of the artist. Whenever a single need dominates the individual's perception, he cannot attend focally to what is "out there." But in the sphere of social interactions, in particular, the individual's apprehension of reality is subjected to the risk of a further distortion induced not so much by something within himself as by a conspiracy of sham, created by the culture itself and interposed between the individual and what is "out there." This conspiracy of sham has been described in various ways. It is represented by the many cultural myths that every society perpetrates upon its members.[67] Such shams have also been described as Ritual Lies.[68] Consider, for example, how, in America, the myths about democracy make it extremely difficult for the typical American to see the appalling discrepancy between the Jeffersonian dream of democracy and today's actuality. And the myths that the USSR perpetuates about communism make it equally difficult for a Muscovite to discern the discrepancy between Marx's dream and the actuality of life in Soviet Russia today. Similarly, the advertiser's dictum that happiness consists in buying things retains its power even for the suburban husband whose every experience, dreary year after dreary year, has shown him that installment buying and a clutter of things have paved the road to his own enslavement. Ultimately, no matter how miserable and pointless his life becomes, he forces himself to believe that he *is* happy, because, having gone through all the prescribed rituals for happiness and success, he concludes that he now *must* be happy. Again, the American sentimentalization of Mother's Day retains its clammy grip even on those men whose entire lives have been stunted because they were cannibalized by their mothers when they were young. These few examples will have to suffice to illustrate the phenomena that we refer to as Ritual Lies.

Our point is simple, for in today's society we all are subjected to a bedlam of voices which persist in constantly telling us what is "out there"—what we should feel in any given circumstance: how to recognize happiness, success, love, or grief. Eventually, these culturally fabricated fictions get between the individual and his own direct experience of what is, indeed, "out there." And this is the crux of our third point, a point which takes us beyond Schachtel's position: the individual's focal attention is jeopardized not alone by neurotic needs within himself, but also by cultural myths which, in turn, are nurtured by the many neurotic twists of society itself. The neurosis of the individual and the neurosis of society—each feed the other. From this there follows an obvious yet critical implication: we cannot hope to understand authenticity within the organizational climate of a school unless we also understand those conditions in today's society which militate against human authenticity. Thus, in our effort to understand the concept of authenticity, we ultimately will have to examine the individual *and* his society, the organizational climate of the school *and* the social climate of the society within which the school operates.

As a fifth point, we must note another factor which militates against the individual's capacity for focal attention. This factor is the pace and the frenetic character of life in today's society. This is especially true, of course, in industrialized societies and in urban centers. The rarest of luxuries for a man today is silence. Equally rare is a sanctuary where he is free from being impinged upon by other people. Bombarded by incessant stimuli, the individual scarcely has the time or the energy to apprehend what is really "out there." At best, he has time to *notice* things, but not to *understand* them or apprehend them. Daily, he is stabbed by shrieking TV commercials, by importunate memos from the principal's office, by his wife's nagging insistence that they move to a larger ranch house in Futility Acres, by movie trailers that promise raunchier and raunchier sexual titillation, by the insolent demands of students in search of fresh, and possibly more perverse, "kicks." He becomes psychologically fragmented. His capacity for focal attention declines, and, rushing frenetically through each day, he finds himself snatching at superficials: noticing, but not understanding. An intensive, two-day, preschool conference briefs him on "Current Trends in Curriculum Development"; a magazine acquaints him with a condensed version of the newest best-selling novel; he "appreciates" a special version of the Minute Waltz, shortened—for more rapid listening—to twenty seconds; he listens to a five-minute news broadcast—punctuated by commercials—that presumes to give him "news in depth."

In passing, we should note that sensation and sensibility are at their height in the child; its thin, tender membrane of perception is constantly being stabbed by objects, words, and events that it does not understand.[69] Instead of understanding, the child "notices." But the child cannot act to any purpose about what he notices, and he cannot talk expressively about his experience. He lacks the words and the concepts required to give meaning to his experience. Consequently, the child passes a good part of his life in an attentive state of detachment. His attentiveness is the attentiveness only of "noticing." Essentially, he is outside the flow of experience and events, and, in this respect, he is dissociated. But the adult in a highly bureaucratized society is placed in a similar position to that of the child. The adult in a large organization is severely limited in the extent to which he can act to any purpose, and is also limited in his ability to talk expressively about what is happening to him. And herein lie the sources of his own sense of alienation both from society and from himself; as a "dissociated outsider," he cannot come to terms with his own experience—cannot understand it—he can only notice it.[70] In short, the pressures of our society diminish the individual's capacity for focal attention, and force him to regress to a childlike mode of apprehending experience. How frighteningly prophetic was Kafka's vision: in *The Trial*, for example, his hero, K, could not "understand"; he could only "notice."

To summarize, then, our comments about Schachtel's concept of focal attention and its pertinence for the concept of authenticity, we hypothesize that high need-dominated attention militates against authentic behavior. Yet we doubt that need-dominated attention, in itself, can suffice to explain inauthentic behavior. We believe that even as the individual's capacity to apprehend reality is diminished by high need-dominated attention, so too is it also diminished by the Ritual Lies of the culture that interpose themselves between the individual and "reality," and by the very pace of modern life, which prompts the individual to regress to a childlike mode of apprehension: to "notice," rather than to "understand," his experience.

And here it is necessary to pause again, to recapitulate what we have said in this section on the concept of authenticity. In brief, after we had identified the six Organizational Climates, we examined them and sought to understand what characteristics in the behavior of the teachers and principal would best account for the differences between the Open and the Closed Climates. We noted a difference in the *for realness* of the participants' behavior in these two climates. Furthermore, this attribute of *for realness,* or of authenticity in behavior, seemed, indeed, to define the first of the three higher-order factors which had emerged from our factor analysis of the climate profile-scores.

We have discussed the concept of authenticity as it pertains to Organizational Climate, and also have examined this concept within a broader context. We have noted that the literature in three areas, in particular, is highly pertinent to the issue of human authenticity:

the literature on the marginal man; the literature on person-to-person relations in cross-cultural exchange; and the literature on the crisis of identity. Yet, although the conceptual frames of reference furnished by the literature in these three respective areas does help us understand the issue of authenticity, all three approaches suffer from a lack of sufficient specificity for our purpose.

We then noted that Schachtel's distinction between need-dominated attention and focal attention seemed to give us a better purchase on the problem of authenticity. Specifically, we hypothesized that high need-dominated attention and authentic behavior were inversely related to each other. This inverse relationship certainly seems to apply to the Organizational Climates.

And finally, we emphasized that Schachtel's concept of focal attention could be used to account for only a portion of whatever inauthentic behavior we might find in a given situation. We observed how cultural myths and Ritual Lies interfered with the individual's capacity to apprehend reality, and hence with his ability to behave authentically. And we pointed out, too, how the very pace of modern society diminished the individual's capacity for focal attention. We concluded that we could not hope to understand the concept of authenticity without taking into account the forces within society itself that encourage inauthenticity. In short, to understand the issue of authenticity, we ultimately will have to examine the individual *and* his society, the Organizational Climate of the school *and* the social climate of the society within which the school is embedded.

THE HEURISTIC NATURE OF THE ORGANIZATIONAL CLIMATES

Before proceeding to suggest further avenues of research on the Organizational Climate of schools, it is advisable that we first review the general plan of the present research, and then discuss a few points of methodology. Briefly, what we have done in the present study is simple: we have proposed a way of describing differences in the Organizational Climates of elementary schools. We have devised *one* way of dimensionalizing the domain of Organizational Climate. The eight subtests that we have derived from the OCDQ, and the six Organizational Climates that we have identified by factoring the school-profiles on the subtest scores are all, in one sense, arbitrary. By naming the subtests and by naming the climates, we have, in effect, *invented* them. The six climates represent a taxonomy of climates, or a typology. It is impossible to demonstrate the "validity" of any taxonomy, or of any typology. The test of a typology must lie in its usefulness. What can be done with it that cannot be done without it? This is the heuristic test. Yet the heuristic test, when applied to classification solely for the sake of classification, proves barren. The crux of the test of any taxonomy is whether the categories defined by the classification schema can be converted into *variables* which are measurable and which also can be incorporated into specific hypotheses which are amenable to empirical testing. Hopefully, the testing of such hypotheses should, in turn, permit the investigator to build a nomological network which will support the *construct validity* of the major variables that undergird the taxonomy. Thus, suppose that the OCDQ is administered to a large sample of elementary schools. It is found that some of the schools secure profiles which closely resemble the prototypic profile of the Open Climate, whereas other schools secure profiles which closely resemble the prototypic profile of the Closed Climate. Invariably, some critic asks, "Well, are the schools that secure Open Climate scores on the OCDQ *really* Open? And the Closed Climate schools *really* Closed?" These questions are unanswerable. But more than this, they are irrelevant. Our concern is not with the actuality of any given Open Climate or of any given Closed Climate, but with the concept of Openness and the concept of Closedness. And since each concept is defined in terms of the other, we are dealing, in fact, with but a single concept: Openness versus Closedness.

But we have noted, too, that the scores on the higher-order factor of authenticity closely parallel the Openness-Closedness continuum. And the scores on the subtest of Esprit also tend to correlate with both authenticity and Openness. From this it is evident that we have been grappling with three concepts which are closely related: the Openness of the Organizational Climate, the scores on Esprit, and indexes of authenticity. Although we have noted the similarity among these three concepts, we have not been equally successful in delineating the differences among them. At this juncture the best that we can do on this score is to make a few guesses that we hope will be informed guesses. We already have noted the need for distinguishing between authenticity as perceived by the participants in a situation and authenticity as evaluated by external, essentially "absolute," criteria. We surmise—although we are by no means certain—that Esprit may be an index to authenticity *as perceived by the participants,* while Openness may be an index to authenticity as evaluated in a more independent way. But no matter what we may guess about the relationship among these three concepts—Openness, Esprit, and authenticity—the important task that lies ahead is to devise ways for defining each of these concepts operationally, and then differentiating them. The concept of constructive alternativism which has been developed by Kelly[71] gives us a lead on how we can attack this problem:

> We come now to a more difficult point. I must confess that I find this point hard to explain to my students and colleagues. The discussion usually starts with the innocent question, "Do you envision the personal construct as a dichotomy or as a continuum?" My answer is, "I envision it as a dichotomy." But when I give this answer trouble starts. It appears to my listeners that I have said that human behavior must conform only to stereotypes and that everything in the world is judged as either black or white—never in shades of gray. This, of course, is not true.
>
> I think I am beginning to understand what the root of the difficulty is. Most of us think about psychological matters concretely rather than abstractly. When we think of the form of human behavior we think of reflexes, of material learned, of decisions made, much as the child who, when he thinks of the mathematical value "four," thinks of "four apples," "four pieces of candy," "four pencils," or "four wheels."
>
> Perhaps if we step outside the field of psychology for a moment we can make sure we have recovered our ability to think abstractly. Let us step into the field of geography. Consider the geographical construct of "north versus south." This is a dichotomous construct, and it is abstract. As far as the construct itself is concerned, there are no "partial norths" or "partial souths" crammed in between "north" and "south."

However, it is a simple matter to use this dichotomous construct to create an array of objects ranged from north to south. All we have to do is to take advantage of the fact that the construct is abstract, and therefore readily available for use in a wide variety of circumstances. We may than apply it sequentially to the different objects we want to place in the array. But the array of objects we have thus set in order is not the construct; it is only one kind of concrete explication of the construct.[72]

It is in this sense that we refer to Openness versus Closedness in Organizational Climates as a dichotomy. We have used this dichotomous construct to create an array of climates ranged from Open to Closed. But we must reiterate Kelly's point: "But the array of objects we have thus set in order is not the construct; it is only one kind of concrete explication of the construct." In Kelly's terms, what we have done up to this point is to use a single axis of reference[73] as a basis for defining Openness versus Closedness. The six climates that we have delineated represent one concrete explication of the Open-Closed construct, but this explication by no means exhausts the alternatives by which we can explicate concretely this same construct. Accordingly, the similarities and the dissimilarities among the three concepts of Openness, Esprit, and authenticity can be checked empirically. In each instance we will need to devise several sets of indicators which we can then use as presumptive measures for each of these three constructs. *To such extent as subsequent research shows that the axes of reference of any two or more of these concepts do not coincide, we must conclude that the concepts are operationally different.* If the axes for two concepts do coincide, then the concepts are identical, and there is no longer justification for using two concepts—and two names—instead of one. But all judgments that we make on this score must be made empirically.

This is precisely the research task that lies ahead. The job is to devise ways of getting a better fix on the axis of reference by which Openness-Closedness is defined. Purely as illustrations of ways in which this job can be tackled, we list below nine sets of studies which we think will prove fruitful in understanding better the difference between Open and Closed Climates in schools.

1. Using the OCDQ, select two samples of elementary schools:

one composed of schools that score high on Openness; the other, of schools that score low on Openness. We would hypothesize that the principals and the teachers from these two sets of schools would differ in respect to concretism,[74] intraception, and ability to accept and deal with their own emotional impulses.[75] Specifically, we would expect that the faculty in the Open Climate would, on the whole, score lower in concretism, higher in intraception, and higher in the ability to accept and deal with their own emotional impulses.

We could administer to the two samples such an instrument as the Edwards Personal Preference Schedule.[76] Here we would expect that the faculty members in the Open Climate, as compared to those in the Closed Climate, would score higher on Achievement, Autonomy, Heterosexuality, and Intraception, and would score lower on Deference, Order, Dominance, Affiliation, and Abasement.

If it were possible to conduct a longitudinal study on these two samples of schools, we would further hypothesize that over the course of time the differences between the first and second testing of the measures and indexes which we have proposed would become more pronounced. In short, we suggest that there may exist an internal generative effect which tends to make an Open Climate become increasingly more Open while a Closed Climate becomes increasingly more Closed.

2. Again, let us deal with the same two samples of schools: the one characterizea ..ɔ ʊpen, the other as Closed. In keeping with Kelly's role-construct theory,[77] and in accord with Bieri's study of complexity-simplicity as a personality variable,[78] we would hypothesize that the principals and the teachers in each of these climates would differ on the complexity-simplicity variable. What we are suggesting here is that group membership within an Open Climate may tend to make it easier for individual members to develop a more complex and a more flexible set of axes of reference for their personal role-constructs. (Or perhaps it is the other way around: teachers with a more flexible set of axes of reference make an Open Climate possible.)

3. Dealing again with the same two samples of schools, we would hypothesize that the role definitions and the role expecta-

tions will be more highly specified in the Closed Climate than in the Open. This hypothesis can be tested, too, by using attitudinal-type questionnaires which tap the areas of role definition and role expectation.

4. Elsewhere, Halpin has discussed "muted language"[79] and the importance of "mixed messages." "Mixed messages" refer to the discrepancy between what a man says with his words and what he communicates with his voice, gestures, and bodily movements.[80] We believe that it is possible to devise methods by which we can determine the perceived congruence between the verbal and the nonverbal messages transmitted by an individual. We would hypothesize that we would find a greater congruence between these two types of messages within an Open Climate than within a Closed one.

5. Miller has devised a way of analyzing the written compositions of elementary school principals.[81] We suggest that a useful study could be conducted in comparing these indexes for a sample of principals drawn from Open Climates and a sample drawn from Closed Climates. It is possible that such a comparison of written compositions could be extended in a further way. Anyone who reads through the 232 compositions which Miller used in her study is struck by the banality of these compositions. They are saturated with pedagese, cant, and jargon. Moreover, they are highly redundant. On this score it might be worth while to compare the written compositions of principals and teachers from Open and Closed Climates. We would hypothesize that the faculties in the Closed Climates, in contrast to those in the Open Climates, would introduce into their compositions a higher percentage of clichés, slogans, and educational platitudes.[82]

6. Seeman's measures of status attitudes and the indexes he suggests for measuring inauthenticity in a leader's behavior could be used with samples of faculty groups from the Open and Closed Climates. In explaining why the concept of inauthenticity is being applied to leadership, Seeman notes, "The essence of inauthenticity in these terms is the use of irrelevant or inappropriate status references, that is, overreference to the fact of a given status incumbency."[83]

Concomitantly, one might also secure measures of the teachers' and the principals' perception of the marginality of their professional roles. Seeman suggests the hypothesis that:

> . . . good leaders are good, partially because they have wrestled effectively with the "marginality" of their position—that is, they have succeeded in placing their status and the stereotypes that go with it in a perspective which permits them to avoid some of the varieties of inauthenticity which are indicated here.[84]

Seeman does not provide an operational definition for "wrestling effectively with the marginality of their position." But he also states flatly that he has not clarified to his own satisfaction how this notion and such concepts as those of overreference and overconformity are to be explicated operationally. Difficult as the task of defining these concepts may be, it probably is not insurmountable.

Assuming that suitable indexes can be invented to measure a teacher's or a principal's attitudes toward the marginality of his professional role, we would hypothesize, along with Seeman, that the good leaders—that is, the principals in the Open Climates in contrast to those in the Closed, are less preoccupied with their marginality. We would surmise, too, that the leaders in the Open Climate also will be found to exhibit less status anxiety.

However, if we are to study status attitudes and attitudes toward marginality, we also will need to take into account the social and geographical setting of the school. For example, do such attitudes differ between a sample of suburban schools and a sample of city or village schools in which the status of the teacher is clearly above the status of the parents of the children whom she teaches?

7. We believe that useful information could be secured by comparing two samples of principals in respect to risk-taking. The principals from these two samples—the first composed of principals described as high on Thrust, and thus representing an Open Climate; the second composed of principals described as low on Thrust, and thus representing a Closed Climate—could be tested in a laboratory situation such as has been described by Scodel, Ratoosh, and Minas.[85] We would hypothesize that willingness to take risk is associated positively with Thrust.

8. Crutchfield reports a study[86] in which he has adapted Asch's technique with the autokinetic phenomenon for the testing of conformity in a sample of professional men. He found large and reliable differences among the men in their willingness to yield to group pressure. Furthermore, the correlations between these conformity scores and various personality variables are statistically significant. Crutchfield's findings are especially meaningful in respect to the Organizational Climate findings. Accordingly, we would hypothesize that the conformity measure that Crutchfield has devised will yield significant negative correlations with the Thrust scores by which the teachers describe the principal. Among the personality variables which Crutchfield used was Barron's[87] ego-strength scale which predicts response to psychotherapy. We would predict a positive correlation between this ego-strength measure and the OCDQ Thrust scores.

9. Finally, we need to comment on the possible relationship between the present OCDQ findings and Ryans' exceptionally comprehensive study of the characteristics of teachers.[88] One part of this study was the Teacher Characteristics Study which called for two observations of each teacher, the observations being made at different times by different observers. Ryans states:

> As a result of the direct observation and assessment of teacher classroom behavior and subsequent statistical analyses of the measurement data, several interdependent patterns of teacher behavior were suggested. Three in particular appeared to stand out in separate factor analyses of elementary and secondary teacher data:
> TCS Pattern X_O—warm, understanding, friendly vs. aloof, egocentric, restricted teacher behavior.
> TCS Pattern Y_O—responsible, businesslike, systematic vs. evading, unplanned, slipshod teacher behavior.
> TCS Pattern Z_O—stimulating, imaginative, surgent vs. dull, routine teacher behavior.
> It is of interest to observe that these behavior syndromes, TCS Patterns X_O, Y_O, and Z_O, are not entirely unique to the Teacher Characteristics Study. They are supported not only by rational analysis of the teaching process but also by reports of other factor analyses of teacher behavior data which have appeared in the literature during recent months.[89]

Among elementary school teachers, the Patterns X_0, Y_0, and Z_0 were highly intercorrelated, and each also seemed to be highly correlated with pupil behavior in teachers' classes.[90]

We must note, too, Ryans' report of the differences between two groups of teachers: one composed of teachers who had received assessments one standard deviation above the mean on all three patterns (X_0, Y_0, and Z_0); the other, of teachers who had received assessments one standard deviation or more below the mean.

> There was a general tendency for high teachers to: be extremely generous in appraisals of the behavior and motives of other persons; possess strong interest in reading and literary affairs; be interested in music, painting, and the arts in general; participate in social groups; enjoy pupil relationship; prefer nondirective (permissive) classroom procedures; manifest superior verbal intelligence; and be superior with respect to emotional adjustment. On the other hand, low teachers tended generally to: be restrictive and critical in their appraisals of other persons; prefer activities which did not involve close personal contacts; express less favorable opinions of pupils; manifest less high verbal intelligence; show less satisfactory emotional adjustment; and represent older age groups.[91]

Obviously, Ryans' study and the present one approach the study of teachers from different points of view. Nonetheless, the differences between his "high" and "low" teachers seem to correspond, at least in part, to the differences which we would expect to find between the behavior of teachers in Open and Closed Climates.

These nine areas of investigation should provide ways of getting a better fix on the concept of Openness-Closedness and the related concept of authenticity-inauthenticity. At this point, the specific type of studies that we have suggested is of less importance than the strategy upon which the total set of studies is based. In short, it is by this approach that we will be able to develop construct validity for the major concepts that we have introduced in the present research on the Organizational Climate of schools.

CONCLUSIONS AND IMPLICATIONS

In sum, we have devised the OCDQ and have delineated six Organizational Climates of schools. At the substantive level, what we have done on this score will, we hope, lead to an increased understanding of organizations. Furthermore, the techniques and the constructs which we have developed should prove applicable to organizations other than schools. We suspect that the six climates which we have delineated will also be found, for example, in industrial corporations, government agencies, and hospitals. The adaptation of the OCDQ to the requirements of organizations other than schools should not prove to be a difficult task.

Furthermore, we believe that the behavior defined by the OCDQ subtests and the differences among the six climates have direct pertinence for the study of Family Climates. Indeed, the three profile-factors which we have identified seem to be consistent with present knowledge from the field of child psychology and psychoanalysis about the kinds of parent-child relations that best promote psychologically healthy growth for the child.

But if we leave the substantive level, and for the moment disregard the detailed findings of the present research, then two conclusions stand out above all others. The first is the concept of Openness versus Closedness in respect to Organizational Climates; the second, the recognition that future research on Organizational Climates should take into account the issue of authenticity in behavior.

As we have noted throughout the present report, the concept of Openness versus Closedness in Organizational Climates is directly related to similar concepts about the openness or closedness of an individual's personality. The mechanisms which produce neurotic responses in the human individual appear to operate in much the same way within a group. Consequently, we believe that graduate training for school executives should include at least one course, or seminar, which will provide these administrators with insight into the behaviors that are associated with different Organizational Climates. Such a course should not be confined to the social psychology of groups, or to orthodox material on management;

it should include an introduction to those central concepts of psychoanalysis and clinical psychology which are as applicable to groups as they are to the individual patients.

But what implications does our concern about authenticity have for public education? We have noted that some elementary schools possess climates that are more Open than others and we have inferred that this Openness seems to be an index of greater authenticity on the part of the principal and the teachers alike.

Now, in conclusion, we are forced to ask a few embarrassing questions. How much of the lack of Openness and the lack of authenticity that we find in these elementary schools are associated not merely with the school itself, but with the essential nature of the teacher-training process in American education? To what extent should we be concerned about the pool from which candidates for degrees in education have been drawn? Is there evidence to suggest that those students who choose teaching as their profession possess personality characteristics which predispose them to the very kinds of behavior that characterize the Closed Climate?

A study by Guba, Jackson, and Bidwell[92] provides some evidence on this score. These investigators gave the Edwards Personal Preference Schedule to samples of teacher-trainees and veteran teachers. Guba and his colleagues note:

> The findings showed that the needs most characteristic of this group of teachers were high deference, order, and endurance and low heterosexuality, dominance, and exhibition. Marked variations, however, were found among subgroups divided by sex, teaching level, and years of experience. The six needs may probably be taken as representative of an emergent occupational pattern found most prominently among what will be termed the "veteran teachers," that is, teachers of ten or more years of experience. Conspicuous by their absence are such needs as achievement, intraception, and nurturance, which might have been expected for a teacher group. Interestingly, the characteristics seem to fit the cultural stereotype of the teacher as sexually impotent, obsequious, eternally patient, painstakingly demanding, and socially inept.

.   .   .   .   .   .

. . . One might hypothesize that the deferent, orderly, enduring teacher is a boon to the administrator, an asset to someone who is concerned with the effective functioning of a social institution. Yet these very attributes might be linked with a rather negative self-image. One is reminded here of the stereotype of the office clerk whose services are highly valued yet who is so self-deprecating that he is afraid to ask his boss for a raise. It might also be conjectured that the data reflect a real change in satisfaction, effectiveness, and confidence as the teacher realizes more and more how far from ideal everyday teaching practices and school procedures really are.[93]

Obviously, Guba, Jackson, and Bidwell's findings suggest that the candidates who select teaching as a career are not those who are likely to facilitate Openness in the Organizational Climate of their schools.

Furthermore, when we look at the attitudes of college students toward courses in education, the picture is not encouraging. When we hear students on our campuses refer to courses in education as "Mickey Mouse courses," what does this say about the authenticity of the programs that we now provide for prospective teachers? We have repeatedly listened to highly intelligent students who have started to follow a teaching career but who, after a few courses in education, have declared, "I quit. I can't stand any more of that pap."

When we find correlations of chance order between the number of graduate courses which elementary principals have taken and several criteria of the principals' effectiveness[94] in their jobs, what does this tell us about the "for realness" of current graduate programs in educational administration?

We can ask similar questions about the effect of the customary method for certificating teachers and administrators. If a teacher's certification and, indeed, his subsequent promotions depend upon a sheer count of how many courses he has taken in prescribed areas, what effect does this procedure have in reinforcing inauthentic behavior among school personnel?

And what do the recruiting procedures of many schools tell an intelligent, prospective teacher? Recently, a principal in St. Louis County spoke to a group of student teachers and blandly stated,

"What we want as teachers in our school are highly creative young men and women who know how to conform." Two young women in the audience retched. Consider, too, the case of a highly qualified and extremely intelligent young lady who recently visited the Dade County Schools in Florida to inquire about a teaching position. Her sole encounter was with a brusque flunkey who handed the young lady a sheaf of forms thicker than a CIA dossier, replete, of course, with a loyalty oath and other queries. The girl never went back; she is working, instead, in a business office. One gets the impression that the recruiting procedures of many schools are deliberately designed to discourage "authentic" human beings, and to encourage only docile drones.

But above everything else, we must remember the purpose of our schools: they exist for our children. We know, too, that children interiorize their value-systems through a process of identifying with those adults in their immediate environment who provide ego-ideals that the children can respect. But what happens when the range of available ego-ideals is constricted? Or more pointedly, what is the price that a Closed, inauthentic climate exacts from the children themselves?

To conclude, then, we believe that the OCDQ provides a useful technique for describing the Organizational Climate of schools, and that further research with it is warranted. But an even stronger conclusion emerges from our experience with the present study. We believe that one of the most important areas to be investigated is that of authenticity. The three questions for which we must seek answers are these: what are the conditions within the profession of education which reinforce authenticity of behavior? What are the conditions which reinforce inauthenticity? What changes are needed in the profession—in the recruiting and training of teaching candidates, and in the administration of schools— to increase the likelihood that the profession as a whole will become more authentic?

Long-range programmatic research in this area will be complex and will demand a great deal of stamina from the investigators. They probably will be crucified by the members of the very profession which they are trying to help. But no matter. The almost insurmountable difficulty of the problem is not sufficient reason for postponing our attack upon it.

NOTES FOR CHAPTER 4

1. The material presented in this chapter is an abridgment of the findings reported by Andrew W. Halpin and Don B. Croft in *The Organizational Climate of Schools* (Chicago: Midwest Administration Center, University of Chicago, 1963). It has been reproduced here with the permission of the publisher and with the consent of Dr. Luvern L. Cunningham, Director of the Midwest Administration Center. I also want to acknowledge the characteristic generosity of my colleague, Mr. Don B. Croft, who has graciously allowed me to abridge our monograph for inclusion in this book.

The research described here was conducted under Contract Number SAE 543 (8639) with the United States Office of Education, Department of Health, Education, and Welfare. I had prepared the original proposal for this research during the winter of 1958-1959, when I was teaching at the University of Chicago and was a member of the Midwest Administration Center there.

When I moved to the University of Utah in March 1959, Dean Roald F. Campbell of the University of Chicago, who at that time, was the Director of the Midwest Administration Center, most graciously encouraged me to take the contract with me to the University of Utah. The contract was consummated at the University of Utah in September 1959, and I directed the research in my capacity as director of the Bureau of Educational Research. Mr. Croft became my colleague at that time. A mimeographed, final report for the project was submitted to the Office of Education in August 1962. I presented a brief report of the findings to the February 1963 meeting, in Chicago, of the American Educational Research Association. Shortly after that meeting, a synopsis of the findings was published. (Andrew W. Halpin and Don B. Croft, "The Organizational Climate of Schools," *Administrator's Notebook*, **11**, No. 7 (March 1963), pp. 1-4.

In August of 1963, the report was published in monograph form —as noted above—by the Midwest Administration Center. The published version differs in only minor details from the original, mimeographed report submitted to the Office of Education; Dean Roald F. Campbell wisely extirpated a few of my digressions and blue-penciled several of my more uninhibited passages of crimson prose. The research completed at the University of Utah and reported here had been only the first, exploratory phase of what had been conceived of originally as a much more extensive research program.

Accordingly, the material in the present chapter must be viewed in this light; it is an interim report, and nothing more. However, circumstances beyond the control of either Don B. Croft or myself have prevented us from continuing with the further research that we had planned (written December 1964). Fortunately, several other investigators have picked up the loose strands and have moved ahead with further research on the Organizational Climates.

To complete this brief historical note, perhaps I should add one further point. I first discussed the idea of a study of "The Organizational Climate of Schools" at a meeting of the CPEA held on the campus of The Ohio State University in the spring of 1954. At that time I outlined the general plan of the present study. Ironically enough, nobody picked up the idea. The task was still waiting to be done when Don B. Croft and I tackled it in September 1959.

2. During the period from 1950 to 1955, John K. Hemphill, then a member of the Personnel Research Board at The Ohio State University, directed a research project, under contract with the United States Air Force. These investigations, *Studies in Aircrew Composition,* were part of The Ohio State Leadership Studies. The findings of these studies have been summarized in a set of Technical Reports submitted to the Air Force. Most of the original work on the LBDQ (see Ch. 3 of this book) had been done under this Air Force contract and as part of the aircrew composition studies. In particular, one study in this series was especially relevant to the present investigation: Carl H. Rush, Jr., *Group Dimensions of Aircrews* (Columbus, Ohio: The Ohio State University Research Foundation, 1953).

3. John K. Hemphill and Charles M. Westie, "The Measurement of Group Dimensions," *Journal of Psychology,* **29**, No. 29, (1950), pp. 325-342.

4. Stanley A. Muliak used the OCDQ with a sample of nurses. He factored the items and found that they held up even better than in our original school sample. His factoring revealed higher loadings and greater consistency than were found in our original study. His report has not yet been published. (At present, Muliak is in the Department of Psychology at the University of Utah.)

5. The term "ordinality" is used here with the meaning applied to it by general semanticists. See, for example, Alfred Korzybski, *Science and Sanity* (Lakeville, Conn.: The International Non-Aristotelian Library Publishing Company, 1933). For a more popular treatment of semantics, see Wendell Johnson, *People in Quandaries* (New York: Harpers & Brothers, 1946).

6. It is instructive, for example, to compare the type of categories used by Graff and Street, in examining the performance of educational administrators (Orin B. Graff and Calvin M. Street, *Improving Competence in Educational Administration* [New York: Harpers & Brothers, 1956]), with the type of categories used by Hemphill and his colleagues, in dealing with the same domain. (John K. Hemphill *et al., Administrative Performance and Personality.* New York: Bureau of Publications, Teachers College, Columbia University, 1962.) The Graff and Street effort is methodologically primitive. Contrariwise, Hemphill *et al.* derive their categories of principals' performance empirically.

7. An *eigenvalue* represents the sum of the squared factor loadings for each unrotated factor when the communalities of the variables are one; it thus crudely indicates the importance of the factor. See Harry H. Harman, *Modern Factor Analysis* (Chicago: University of Chicago Press, 1960), p. 157.

8. One can sometimes push a solution to the point where what emerges is simply one large, general factor. Such a factor meets the requirement of "fewness" of higher-order concepts, but whatever "explanation" we may derive from a single, general factor is likely to give us far less *information* than we might receive from alternative "explanations" based upon either a two-factor or a three-factor solution.

9. For a discussion of communality as an index of reliability, see Benjamin Fruchter, *Introduction to Factor Analysis* (New York: D. Van Nostrand Co., Inc. 1954), p. 47. The communality represents a lower bound, or a highly conservative, estimate of the reliability.

10. Henry F. Kaiser, "Comments on Communalities and the Number of Factors," p. 37. Paper read May 14, 1960, at an informal conference on "The Communality Problem in Factor Analysis," held at Washington University, St. Louis, and sponsored by Professor Philip DuBois.

11. The *eigenvalue* of .97 for the third factor in the unrotated factor matrix, Table 4.6, obviously is close enough to 1.00 to permit us to use the three-factor solution.

12. William C. Schutz, *FIRO: A Three-Dimensional Theory of Interpersonal Behavior* (New York: Rinehart & Company, Inc., 1958).

13. Stanley A. Muliak, "A Factor Analytic Investigation of the Equivalence of Personality Factors and Semantic Factors," Ph.D. dissertation, University of Utah, 1963.

14. Charles E. Osgood, George C. Succi, and Percy T. Tannenbaum,

The Measurement of Meaning (Urbana, Ill.: University of Illinois Press, 1957).

15. The Q technique is used to factor-analyze a matrix of inter-correlations among profile scores (to correlate the profile scores of individuals or, as in the present instance, of individual schools). The factor loadings for each school indicate the degree to which the school-profile possesses the attribute measured by each factor. We could have used the R technique of factor analysis, which describes the factors in terms of the subtests, and could have then computed the factor scores for each school. Instead, we chose to use a Q factor analysis because the statistical computations required by this method are far less laborious than those demanded by the R technique.

16. Where scores have been standardized both ipsatively and normatively, we can expect to obtain transposable factors when we factor-analyze with both the R technique and the Q technique. Broverman discusses the results of applying both techniques to the same data. See Donald M. Broverman, *Psychological Review,* **68** (January 1961), pp. 68-80.

17. An exciting exposition of the limitations of the R technique of factor analysis in adequately controlling the confounding of inter-individual and intraindividual sources of variance is presented by Donald M. Broverman, "Normative and Ipsative Measurement in Psychology," *Psychological Review,* **69** (July 1962), pp. 295-305.

18. We also computed an R technique factor analysis of the school profile-scores and found that three factors accounted for the major portion of the common variance of the test battery. The three-factor rotational solution for this matrix is presented in Table 4.14.

19. We temporarily put aside those school-profiles which were marked by high loadings on two or more factors.

20. The term "prototypic" implies nothing exemplary; it merely describes the central tendency of the scores within each of the six sets for those schools which secured high loadings on but a single profile-factor.

21. Kurt Lewin, *A Dynamic Theory of Personality* (New York: McGraw-Hill Book, Inc., 1935), pp. 194-238.

22. At this stage of the analysis we used the scores on the Esprit subtest as a basis for ranking the six climates. We chose Esprit because it was the best index to openness that we had available at this point. However, as we will point out at the end of this section, we later found that the teachers' perception of Openness does not necessarily coincide with our evaluation (as research investigators) of

Openness. We discovered later that the pattern of profile-factor loadings provides a better index of openness than do the scores on the single subtest of Esprit.

23. We use the term "genuine" in much the same way as Argyris uses the concept of authenticity. Argyris states, "Authentic relationships are, therefore, those relationships in which an individual enhances his sense of self- and other-awareness and acceptance in such a way that others can do the same" (Chris Argyris, *Interpersonal Competence and Organizational Effectiveness,* [Homewood, Illinois: The Dorsey Press, Inc., 1962], p. 21). Likewise, Perlmutter discusses authentic relationships and uses the terms "genuineness" and "authentic" almost interchangeably (Howard V. Perlmutter, "Person to Person: A Psychological Analysis of Cross-Cultural Relationships," mimeographed, Menninger Foundation, October 1959. Presented at Yale University, New Haven, Connecticut).

Metaphorically we can differentiate between the "nongenuine" person and the "genuine" one by saying that the nongenuine person seems to be two-dimensional, and hence "thin"; however, the genuine person strikes us as three-dimensional and as a person with depth. The concept of genuineness has not as yet been pinned down in precise operational terms, but this is not sufficient reason for dismissing it from our consideration. The words that we use for describing this particular quality of human experience are not, in themselves, important. Essentially this quality of genuineness is what the theologian, Buber, refers to in discussing "I-Thou" relationships (Martin Buber, *I and Thou,* 2nd ed. [New York: Charles Scribner's Sons, 1958]). We will discuss the concept of authenticity later in the present chapter.

24. Specifically, Halpin left the University of Utah in August 1962 to join the faculty of the Graduate Institute of Education at Washington University, St. Louis. At the same time, Croft left the Bureau of Educational Research and became consultant at the Computer Center, University of Utah.

25. Deadlines required that the analysis of the data be completed by June 1962.

26. John K. Hemphill, Daniel E. Griffiths, and Norman Fredericksen, *Administrative Performance and Personality* (New York: Bureau of Publications, Teachers College, Columbia University, 1962).

27. Such a study would be similar to one done with the Consideration and Initiating Structure dimensions of the LBDQ, as part of a Staff Associate Project at the University of Chicago. See *Observation*

of Administrator Behavior, Report of 1958-1959, Staff Associate Project (Chicago: The Midwest Administration Center, University of Chicago, 1959).

28. Edwin A. Fleishman and Edwin F. Harris, "Patterns of Leadership Behavior Related to Employee Grievances and Turnover," *Personnel Psychology,* **15**, No. 1 (Spring 1962), pp. 43-56.

29. Harry C. Triandis, "A Critique and Experimental Design for the Study of the Relationship Between Productivity and Job Satisfaction," *Psychological Bulletin,* **56**, No. 4 (July 1959), pp. 309-312.

30. Vern W. Urry, *Employee Perceived Supervisory Behavior, Attitude Toward Supervision, and Performance* (Master's Thesis, Department of Psychology, University of Utah, June 1962).

31. For a discussion of this issue, see, for example, Erich Fromm, *Man for Himself* (New York: Rinehart & Company, Inc., 1947), particularly pp. 54 ff.

32. See Ch. 2, particularly the discussion about the need for having two or more measures at different points in time, before being able to make dependable statements about organizational change or statements about intraorganizational effects.

33. Erich Fromm, *Escape From Freedom* (New York: Rinehart & Bros., 1941).

34. Adam Curle, "Transitional Communities and Social Re-Connection: A Follow-up Study of the Civil Resettlement of British Prisoners of War," *Human Relations,* **1**, No. 1 (1947), pp. 42-68, and No. 2, pp. 240-288.

35. See, for example, Bruno Bettelheim, *The Informed Heart: Autonomy in a Mass Age* (New York: The Free Press of Glencoe, 1960).

36. For an analysis of the biographical characteristics of principals, see Andrew W. Halpin and Don B. Croft, "The Biographical Characteristics of Elementary-School Principals," unpublished report to the Cooperative Research Branch, United States Office of Education, Contract #214(6905), (Bureau of Educational Research, University of Utah, 1960). The authors suggest ways in which biographical information can be used to check on the degree of the respondent's self-deception.

37. Hans Selye, *From Dream to Discovery: On Being a Scientist* (New York: McGraw-Hill Book Co., Inc., 1964).

38. This superficial learning of a role is nicely illustrated by an incident which took place before World War II in a suburban school system in Westchester County, New York. A new superintendent of schools had recently been appointed. But his predecessor, Dr. Q.,

before he was fired, had left his mark on the system. This incident took place during what can be described as the "later orange-crate Renaissance" in progressive education. Dr. Q., who had recently acquired his Ed. D. from Columbia, had decided to make the school system "progressive." It was evident that the elementary school principals were not sympathetic with Dr. Q's views and that they suffered no grief when he was fired. One day, about six months after the new superintendent had been appointed, the school psychologist asked one of the principals, Miss B., for an appointment that afternoon. She said that she could not make it and that she was sorry; then she added, "When Dr. Q. was here, the principals and a group of teachers thought that we had better learn something about progressive education. So we have been going down to T.C. two afternoons a week for the past year. *We figured that we had better learn the vocabulary.*" And this is precisely what had happened. They had "learned the vocabulary," but they also had remained innocent of any understanding of Dewey's ideas.

39. We use the term "role" here in very much the same sense as Jung used the concept of "persona"—drawing from the original Greek meaning: the mask worn by an actor. Jung noted: "The persona . . . is the individual's system of adaptation to, or the manner he assumes in dealing with, the world. Every calling or profession, for example, has its own characteristic persona. . . . Only, the danger is that [people] become identical with their personas—the professor with his text-book, the tenor with his voice. . . . *One could say, with a little exaggeration, that the persona is that which in reality one is not, but which oneself as well as others think one is*" (Carl G. Jung, *The Archetypes and the Collective Unconscious, Collected Works,* Vol. IX, Part 1 [New York: Bollingen Foundation, 1959], pp. 122 ff. Italics mine).

40. Chris Argyris, *Personality and Organization* (New York: Harper & Brothers, 1957), p. 207. Italics mine.

41. Erich Fromm, *Man for Himself.*

42. Robert Lindner, *Prescription for Rebellion* (New York: Rinehart & Company, Inc., 1952).

43. Richard La Piere, *The Freudian Ethic* (New York: Duell, Sloan and Pearce, 1959).

44. Gerald Sykes, *The Hidden Remnant* (New York: Harper & Brothers, 1962).

45. Nor is this reinforcement of inauthenticity confined to the field of education. Some evidence suggests that a similar reinforcement of inauthenticity occurs in our country's program for promoting better

international relations. See, for example, William J. Lederer, *A Nation of Sheep* (New York: W. W. Norton & Company, Inc., 1961). Obviously, we know that in daily, social intercourse some degree of inauthenticity is required to lubricate the social machinery. A guest, for example, does not tell his hostess that the roast was overcooked and that the wine she has served is fit only for barbarians. Yet we contend that, in a program of professional training, where standards presumably are important, it is unethical not to tell the student that "his roast is overcooked." But if the professor's taste buds have atrophied and if he knows nothing about cooking, how can he possibly tell the student anything authentic?

46. The theme about the power of corruption—the corruptor corrupted—seems to have escaped the attention of psychologists and other social scientists. But it has never escaped the attention of novelists and poets. For a recent example, see Richard Condon, *An Infinity of Mirrors* (New York: Random House, 1964).

47. Shirley Jackson, *The Lottery* (New York: Avon Book Division, The Hearst Corporation, 1949).

48. See for example, Allen Wheelis, *The Quest for Identity* (New York: W. W. Norton & Company, Inc., 1958), and Maurice Stein, Arthur J. Fidich, and David Manning White (eds.), *Identity and Anxiety: Survival of the Person in Mass Society* (New York: The Free Press of Glencoe, 1960).

49. One notes how often this degenerative cycle occurs as a consequence of a man accepting an administrative job for which he is not yet qualified. His striving for status tempts him into a trap since he is forced, from the very outset, to operate at a deficit. So he tries to bluff. And in most cases, as the demands upon him increase, especially after the honeymoon in the new job is over, he finds himself operating at a steadily mounting deficit. So he bluffs even more. By now, his bluffing has become so habitual that he "believes" himself. (See Wendell Johnson, *Your Most Enchanted Listener* [New York: Harper & Brothers, 1956].)

Finally, when his fraud becomes so evident that most of his associates see through it, he is either forced into a dead-end position in the organization or is persuaded to move to a new job. But because he lacks the courage to step down—to accept a lower salary or a lower status for a period during which he can try to make up for the deficit in his competence—he usually repeats the same pattern and takes a new job where he again gets into the same box. And again he must endure the same crucifying experience. Tragedies of this kind can be seen in almost every organization. Because these tragedies have such devastating effects upon both the victims and their families, we believe that social scientists have a moral obligation to give high priority to research in this specific area.

50. Lawrence S. Kubie, "The Eagle and the Ostrich," *Archives of General Psychiatry,* 5 (August 1961), pp. 109-119.

51. Irwin D. Rinder and Donald T. Campbell, "Varieties of Inauthenticity," *Phylon,* 13 (December 1952), pp. 270-275.

52. Melvin Seeman, *Social Status and Leadership: The Case of the School Executive* (Columbus, Ohio: Bureau of Educational Research and Service, Monograph No. 35, The Ohio State University, 1960). See also Melvin Seeman, "The Meaning of Inauthenticity," unpublished paper.

53. Erik H. Erikson, "The Problem of Ego Identity," in Stein, Fidich, and White (eds.), *Identity and Anxiety.*

54. Chris Argyris, *Interpersonal Competence and Organizational Effectiveness* (Homewood, Ill.: The Dorsey Press, Inc., 1962).

55. Howard V. Perlmutter, "Person to Person: A Psychological Analysis of Cross-Cultural Relationships," mimeographed, Menninger Foundation, Topeka, Kansas, October 1959.

56. A poignant example of the overconforming behavior of the Negro is illustrated by an incident that took place in an office in a Midwestern city. The three secretaries in the office were young Negro women who had recently come up from the South and had moved successfully into middle-class status. These were intelligent, competent women. In overconforming to middle-class "white" expectations they had eschewed *Ebony* but avidly read *American Home* and *The Reader's Digest.* One of the psychologists asked the girls whether they were going to a Louis Armstrong performance which was scheduled for that evening. "Oh, no, Mrs. H., we wouldn't go to hear *him.*" The girls were aghast at the very idea that Mrs. H. had thought that they would go to hear Louis. Mrs. H. inquired further to find out which "popular" musicians the girls liked. For whom had they rejected the jazz that was both their own racial heritage and perhaps America's greatest single contribution to culture? They had rejected jazz in favor of the elephantine cadences of a popular TV band leader, and the slimy arpeggios of an equally popular nightclub "pianist."

57. Robert J. Havinghurst and Bernice L. Neugarten, *Society and Education* (Boston: Allyn and Bacon, Inc., 1957), p. 359.

58. Halpin and Croft, "The Biographical Characteristics of Elementary-School Principals."

59. Seeman, *Social Status and Leadership.*

60. Perlmutter, "Person to Person."

61. The concept of personal role-construct is used here in the sense in which it has been defined by George A. Kelly, *The Psychology of Personal Constructs,* Vols. I and II (New York: W. W. Norton & Company, Inc., 1955).

62. Erikson, "The Problem of Ego Identity," in Stein, Vidich, and White (eds.), *Identity and Anxiety.*

63. Ernest G. Schachtel, *Metamorphosis* (New York: Basic Books, Inc., 1959).

64. *Ibid.,* pp. 265-266.

65. *Ibid.,* p. 268.

66. *Ibid.,* pp. 273-275.

67. See, for example, Henry A. Murray (ed.), *Myth and Mythmaking* (New York: George Braziller, Inc., 1960). For a very special yet highly important example of how those myths that get between the individual and reality are developed, see Eric Hoffer, *The True Believer* (New York: Harper & Brothers, 1951). Hoffer discusses the nature of mass movements. Yet his points are apposite for the field of public education, because in many respects teachers, as members of a profession, resemble "the true believers" whom Hoffer describes. Hoffer develops his themes further in a later book, *The Ordeal of Change* (New York: Harper & Brothers, 1963).

In a discussion of the myths that political leaders fabricate for the masses, the Italian novelist, Ignazio Silone, reaches conclusions startlingly similar to Hoffer's. See Ignazio Silone, *The School for Dictators* (New York: Atheneum Publishers, 1963). This book was first published in 1939, at about the time when the Nazis invaded Poland. In the 1963 edition, Silone revised the book and dealt more fully and more insistently with the conditioning of political forms in present-day mass society. It is doubtful that Silone and Hoffer were familiar with each other's work; since each approaches his topic from a drastically different vantage, the similarity of their conclusions therefore becomes especially impressive.

To get a sampling of the ways in which the advertising field creates its own set of myths and Ritual Lies, see Herbert M. McLuhan, *The Mechanical Bride* (New York: Vanguard Press, 1951). This savage book bristles with ideas.

68. For a discussion of Ritual Lies, see, for example, Margaret Halsey, *The Pseudo-Ethic* (New York: Simon & Schuster, 1963).

69. For this point, I am indebted to the observation of Mary

McCarthy, *On the Contrary* (New York: Farrar, Straus and Cudahy, 1961), pp. 277 ff. Her discussion of the reasons why the literature of the twentieth century is so greatly dominated by the novel of sensibility (Proust, Joyce) and the novel of sensation (Hemingway, Farrell, Bellow, Chandler) is particularly relevant to our concern about authenticity.

70. This, of course, is the plight of the character who passes as the hero in modern fiction. Camus' *Stranger* and Lawrence Durrell's Darley *(The Alexandria Quartet)* are examples of "heroes" to whom things happen, but who, themselves, can only *notice* what happens. These happenings are described as discrete sensory impressions, as if they were the tiny points on a Seurat canvas, or the nuances of color that flicker across a painting by Monet. But these impressions are the *disjecta membra* of consciousness passing across a primitive perceptual screen.

The modern American novel, in particular, is marked by the presence in the central role of a character who can be best described as a "non-hero." Not alone is he no longer master of his fate; he no longer even knows who he is. Of course, this describes the very problem of human authenticity. Nor should we be surprised to find that here again the novelist has preceded the social scientist in noting a central problem of the human condition.

This is not the place to discuss the theme of human authenticity in modern drama. Suffice it to note that Ibsen's *Peer Gynt* describes in Peer, the "dissociated outsider," that authenticity is a persistent theme in almost all the plays of Luigi Pirandello, and that, today, Edward Albee has focused on the same issue—especially in *The American Dream.*

71. Kelly, *The Psychology of Personal Constructs.*

72. From George A. Kelly, "A Mathematical Approach to Psychology," prepared at invitation of the Moscow Psychological Society (USSR) and read at Moscow, April 10, 1961, pp. 12-13.

73. Here we use the term "axis of reference" as Kelly uses it. (See Kelly, *The Psychology of Personal Constructs,* Vol. I, Ch. 3.) Axis of reference within this context does not correspond precisely to the axis concept in factor analysis.

74. We use this term in the sense in which it was introduced by Goldstein. See Kurt Goldstein and Martin Scheerer, "Abstract and Concrete Behavior: An Experimental Study with Special Tests," *Psychological Monographs,* **53**, No. 2 (1941).

75. This ability, of course, could be tested by an index such as the Rorschach *Erlebnistyp,* or by other analyses of the M and C scores.

76. Allen L. Edwards, *Edwards Personal Preference Schedule* (New York: The Psychological Corporation, 1957 rev.).

77. Kelly, *The Psychology of Personal Constructs.*

78. James Bieri, "Complexity-Simplicity as a Personality Variable in Cognitive and Preferential Behavior," in Donald W. Fiske and Salvatore R. Maddi (eds.), *Functions of Varied Experience* (Homewood, Ill.: Dorsey, 1961). The intellectual antecedents for Bieri's study include the work of such men as Kelly, Lewin, and Piaget.

79. See Ch. 5.

80. A provocative example of "muted cues" can be seen in the case of a certain well-known educational psychologist whose comments on most subjects are knowledgeable and insightful. But whenever the conversation turns to one of his two *bêtes noirs*—criticism, in any form, of teacher-training methods, or of the quality of students in colleges of education—his behavior suddenly changes. His voice reaches a higher pitch and loses timbre. What comes out sounds like a prerecorded "commercial." One is suddenly reminded of the image of an excommunicated Catholic who, after an injection of sodium amytal, proceeds to recite by rote, fragments from the catechism which he had memorized as a child.

81. Marcella M. Miller, *A Psychological Analysis of Written Compositions of Elementary-School Principals,* unpublished M.A. thesis, Department of Educational Psychology, University of Utah, June 1961.

82. A similar comparison could be made through the content analysis of taped interviews obtained from these principals and teachers.

83. Seeman, *Social Status and Leadership,* p. 103.

84. *Ibid.,* p. 104. This skill in placing one's status in perspective is illustrated by a remark which Adlai Stevenson made shortly after he conceded the election to Dwight Eisenhower. He was asked to give a speech to a group at the Democratic headquarters. His opening line was, "A funny thing happened to me today when I was on my way to the White House."

85. Alvin Scodel, Philburn Ratoosh, and J. Sayer Minas, "Some Personality Correlates of Decision Making Under Conditions of Risk," *Behavioral Science,* 4 (1959), pp. 19-28.

86. Richard S. Crutchfield, "Conformity and Character," *The American Psychologist,* **10**, No. 5 (May 1955), pp. 191-198.

87. Frank Barron, "An Ego-Strength Scale Which Predicts Response to Psychotherapy," *Journal of Consulting Psychology,* **17** (1953), pp. 327-333.

88. David G. Ryans, *Characteristics of Teachers: Their Description, Comparison, and Appraisal* (Washington, D.C.: American Council on Education, 1960).

89. The similarity between the three TCS factors and the three OCDQ *test* factors is evident.

90. Ryans, *Characteristics of Teachers,* p. 382.

91. *Ibid.,* pp. 397-398

92. Egon G. Guba, Philip W. Jackson, and Charles E. Bidwell, "Occupational Choice and the Teaching Career," *Educational Research Bulletin,* **38**, No. 1 (January 14, 1959), pp. 1-13 and 27.

93. *Ibid.,* pp. 4 and 27.

94. Hemphill, Griffiths, and Fredericksen, *Administrative Performance and Personality.*

PART THREE

Words and Actions

5

The Eloquence of Behavior[1]

Communication embraces a broader terrain than most of us attribute to it. Since language is, phylogenetically, one of man's most distinctive characteristics, we sometimes slip into the error of thinking that all communication must be *verbal* communication. To persist in this narrow view of communication is folly. Yet few executive training programs escape such folly; they ignore the entire range of nonverbal communication, the "muted language" in which human beings speak to each other more eloquently than with words. Spoken and written language can be compared to blowing the trumpet with its throat open, and nonverbal language to music played with a mute in the bell. In the first instance the notes sound out sharp and clear; in the second, they may be more muffled but certainly are no less evocative. (Anyone who has listened to the muted trumpet of Louis Armstrong or Jonah Jones can testify to this.)

My point is perhaps old-fashioned, but shockingly simple: actions speak louder than words. To choose a homey theme such as this, one whose very expression has been distilled into a cliché, is to invite embarrassment. Yet I must run this risk, for, in this instance as in many others, the triteness with which an idea is expressed does not reflect upon the viability of the original observation. In short, we cannot categorically dismiss an idea solely because the mode of expressing it has been worn thin.

In examining the adage that "actions speak louder than words," we should key our inquiry to action; specifically, we must alert ourselves to the subtle ways in which nonverbal behavior speaks more eloquently than our most emphatic words.

Unfortunately, the very nature of higher education forces all of us to place great store by the *word*, whether oral or written. What passes as education often consists of little more than having students regurgitate to the professor the same words that he has given them—untouched in the process by human thought. But the language of words is only a fragment of the language we use in communicating with each other. We talk with eyes and hands, with gestures, with our posture, with various motions of our body. Arthur Ogden has stated the issue succinctly:

> Frowns, smiles, blushes, quivering skin, dwindling pupils, bristling hair, knitted brows—these gestures, only partially under our control, make up the repertoire of facial utterance. We call it a language, but that is only courtesy. It voices no concepts, submits no reasons. But it endlessly publishes the shifts of attention, the entreaties and alarms, of the inner life. We often misunderstand it, but we dare not disregard it. . . .
>
> Glances and gestures, they tell us, the meaningful changes of the human face, are socializing agencies that start their work at birth. They give us our first intimations that we are not alone in the world. They open to us the delightful and hazardous prospect of shared existence. They reveal the presence of other beings, compounded like ourselves of opaque flesh through which run currents of feeling and intention that are not accessible to our sight. Equipped with a knowledge that we can never make complete, we learn to be accommodating and apprehensive.
>
> It is custom, usages, collective goals, and joint undertakings that lighten our apprehension. When we are engaged in an enterprise with someone else, we are least likely to misunderstand his looks. Context enables us to read with more confidence.[2]

THE USE OF *TIME* AS A CUE

We also speak by the way we use time and space in dealing with others. In America we have strict attitudes about time: time itself is valuable and should not be wasted. Furthermore, we ascribe a tangibility to time and consider it a commodity that can be bought, sold, saved, spent, wasted, lost, made up, and measured. This attitude contrasts to attitudes toward time encountered, for example, in Latin America or in Arabia. The American executive seems especially enslaved by his attitudes toward time. Indeed, he is to the extent that the amount of time he allots to a subordinate, and the point in the day when the time is allotted, tells the subordinate—in muted language, of course—something about his status and the urgency, to the superior, of the issue under consideration. Thus, a ten-minute appointment has a significance different from a 30-minute appointment. The appointment a principal makes with a teacher for 3:30 in the afternoon, immediately after classes have been dismissed, connotes greater consideration than one set for 4:30, which tells the teacher that she can keep herself busy with other things until the principal can get around to her. To set an appointment ten minutes before the expiration of a teacher's free period is different from saying, "Let's have lunch together, and talk it over."

Witness the case of a dean who prided himself on the consideration he showed to his faculty, but who called a faculty meeting late in the afternoon of the Wednesday before Thanksgiving. Technically he was within his rights, for at this university the professors were expected to follow a schedule which ran from at least 9 A.M. to 5 P.M. But leaving the campus early on the day before a holiday was a common and condoned practice. Many of the professors had been hoping to get an early start for out-of-town trips, but everyone knew that the dean planned to spend most of the weekend at his desk; he was too ambitious a man to waste sentiment on Thanksgiving. At the faculty meeting—which dealt with no issues which would have suffered from postponement—the dean's characteristic facial expression of beaming, patriarchal benevolence for all his staff was perceived for what it indeed was: a mask. Nothing he might say about the wonderful cooperation he had with his staff could stifle what his muted language shrieked—by "cooperation" he meant that the staff should "coo" while he "operated."

When a meeting is scheduled, whether between two or more people, who waits for whom and for how long says important things about relationships to the people concerned. Most organizations or cultures develop informal tolerance ranges for lateness; to keep a person waiting beyond the tolerance limit is a subtle way of insulting him. However, the handling of promptness and lateness can vary with the subculture and with the functions of the meeting. Thus military officers are likely to arrive a few minutes ahead of the appointed time, whereas professors usually arrive from five to ten minutes after the set time. In the social sphere, only a yokel will arrive at a cocktail party at the stipulated time; whereas good manners require a guest to arrive at a dinner party not more than ten minutes late.

Bruno Bettelheim refers to the "remote control" factor when he speaks of the effects of the "distance in time":

> Consciously or unconsciously, distance in time is used by the boss in our society who lets an inferior wait before seeing him. This impresses the person with the boss' power and his own inferiority. Conversely, seeing the inferior immediately helps to establish direct, personal contact on a friendly, equal footing. This example also shows the inner forces at work: the waiting person becomes tense and anxious as time passes. He cannot deal with the accumulating anxiety about seeing the manager, his feeling of impotence grows and weakens his position. Only the very secure person (or someone who does not care about the outcome of the meeting) can stand the tension without getting anxious, and then insecure.[3]

THE USE OF *SPACE* AS A CUE

The use of space also communicates a person's attitudes toward others. At a conference table, does the executive invariably seat himself at what is clearly the head of the table? When he has two or more of his immediate associates with him in a conference with the members of a subordinate group in the organization, do he and his associates align themselves in formidable array on one side of the table, so that the physical arrangement itself emphasizes to the members of the subordinate group that they are supplicants before the judges of a high court? In a conference room where a table has been set, the chair farthest from the door is usually associated with higher status; the wise executive will avoid earmarking this chair for his exclusive use. Where office space permits, a sensitive executive will keep a small table, with chairs, in addition to his desk; he meets visitors at this table, with the chairs arranged so as to diminish social distance.[4]

We communicate, too, by the distance at which we stand or sit when talking to others. A neutral distance between persons for communicating information of nonpersonal matter is about 4½ to 5 feet. For personal matter, 20 to 30 inches is a neutral distance. On the other hand, the range of 5½ feet to 8 feet is a public distance; to keep a conferee at this distance is to discourage completely any discussion of personal matters. In short, the physical distance you set controls the content of the discussion.

The use of space and of other muted cues is remarkably communicative in the social relations between women and men. Watch particularly how a woman, when first meeting a man, uses space as a nonverbal cue. For the purpose of ordinary social conversation let us assume that there is a neutral distance at which a woman would normally stand in relation to a man. Let us assume, too, that there is a range of tolerance on either side of this predicated point. Now, in some cases that we observe, the woman appears to be straining her back against the rear edge of this margin; she keeeps the man at as great a distance as she can, within the normal standard of good manners. Yet we note another woman who pushes the edge of the front margin; she stands a little closer—the closeness may be a difference of no more than 3 or 4 inches. But by this difference, she says that she is ready to be friendly, that she is willing to come closer. This is in contrast to the first woman who, by bracing herself against the margin of the tolerance range, declares that she is poised to flee if the man should try to get too friendly.

Observe not merely the distance which a woman places between herself and a man whom she has just met, but also the angle at which she holds her body. Note especially the "orientation" of her shoulders, and whether her posture appears unduly rigid. The shoulders braced rigidly horizontal, with the body held strictly erect implies a formal attitude, perhaps a slight resistance. But the woman who allows her shoulders to slope, with one placed a little further forward than the other, suggests receptiveness. A woman cannot place her shoulders in this position gracefully without relaxing her body—which in turn, suggests a potentiality for "yieldingness."

Think too of the statues of women sculptured during the Classical Period in Greece—for example, the famous Venus de Milo.

Note the lines around her mouth. They are relaxed, suggesting that despite the medium of stone, this is a woman who was willing to be kissed. Contrast this with the tight-lipped expression of the mouths of so many of the predatory women we see every day. Their mouths are not able to relax enough to let pure laughter emerge. Their smile often resembles a grimace. Their laughter is tinny and forced; they turn it on or off like water from a faucet. When such laughter is abruptly shut off, no traces of pleasure remain on the woman's face. But genuine laughter must come from inside; the person must laugh with her eyes as well as with her mouth. Genuine laughter recedes: it does not simply stop short.

MIXED MESSAGES

Muted language often reinforces the verbal messages we receive, but sometimes the opposite occurs, and we find ourselves confronted by "mixed" messages. Where reinforcement occurs, we usually are comfortable with our message "intake." But when we find ourselves in a situation where we seem to be receiving absolutely contradictory messages from the same person, we are puzzled and uncomfortable. His words say one thing, but through some strange intuition we feel that his behavior says just the opposite. Under such circumstances which message are we to believe?

Consider a few homely examples. You meet John Anderson for the first time in his office by appointment. You arrive on time; his secretary says that he is busy but that he will see you in a few minutes. He is alone in his office, and as you wait in the outer office you note from the receptionist's switchboard that no lights are glowing, indicating that Anderson is not on the phone. Yet you wait fifteeen minutes until he buzzes his secretary to have her usher you into his office. He is seated behind a large mahogany desk, and across the desk, directly opposite him is a visitor's chair. He reaches across the desk to shake hands with you, declares that he is happy to meet you, and asks, "What can I do for you, Mr. X?" In shaking your hand, his handclasp is firm enough, but you feel that his forearm is locked at the elbow, that at the same time he is saying how pleased he is to meet you, his hand and his arm are almost pushing you away from him and are subtly reminding you that he wants you to keep your distance. This is emphasized by the obvious status symbol of the impressive mahogany desk, and by the fact that he uses this symbol physically as a barrier which he keeps interposed between you, his visitor, and himself. You begin now to realize more fully the significance of the fifteen-minute wait in the outer office and the fact that instead of coming to the door himself, he buzzed his secretary to bring you in. The omission of any apology for keeping you waiting fits with the rest of the picture. Here is a man infatuated by the sense of his own importance, a man who will insist upon keeping status lines clear and who will see to it that you "know your place." His voice is hearty, he says all the proper things, and he assures you of his cooperation. Yet at least twice during the course of your short conversation he interrupts you before you have quite finished your sentence. During your 20-minute visit his phone rings three times. He excuses himself on each occasion with a deprecatory gesture, as if trying to say, "You know how these things are." But because his expression shows no concern for you, the intended apology in his gesture does not come through. What comes through instead is, "See what a busy, important man I am. You should be grateful to me for even seeing you, for letting you nibble at the crumbs of my time which I'm throwing to you." And when your conversation is finished, Anderson stands—but still behind his barricade, smiles at you, perhaps a bit too unctuously, and tells you, "Feel free to drop in any time at all. I'm always glad to help the cause of education." You notice his stealthy glance at his watch, and the slight tightening of the corners of his mouth—betraying his impatience and fear lest you commit the blunder of trying to prolong the interview after he has decided to terminate it.

What good are this man's words, if his behavior violates everything he says? This example may seem slightly exaggerated, but is it really? Or does it seem exaggerated only because it is too close for comfort? In greater or lesser degree, we have all found ourselves in similar situations. But sometimes the cues from the muted language of others are so subtle that we do not immediately catch the discrepancy between what these others say and what their behavior tells us they believe. The contradiction between open language and muted language occurs because human beings are just as adept in using words to hide meaning as in using them to explicate meaning. The problem is confounded by the ironic fact that the man who uses words for obfuscation is frequently trapped in the net of his own deception, so that he himself no longer knows what he actually feels or believes.

One of the keenest observers of the discrepancy between words and behavior was the distinguished French littérateur André Gide. In a devastating remark about an associate, Gide once said, "He talks about himself with great modesty, but constantly." Oblique to Gide's thrust, but equally incisive, is Albert Einstein's appraisal of a mediocre colleague: "He has no right to be so humble; he is not great enough."

A few more illustrations of mixed messages will, no doubt, invoke to memory many others.

In his classes Professor Holiday stresses the value of education, scholarship, and integrity. Yet in neither class nor conference has he once referred to any primary-source research in his field which has been published within the past five years. What his lectures lack in substance is made up for by amusing anecdotes and auto-biography. When he speaks about colleagues in his own depart-ment, he is quick to use a knowing glance, a shrug of the shoulder, or a deprecatory gesture with his hand, while he adds with a simper, "Yes, Cooper is a good man, a good man indeed." His courses are shallow and disorganized, his own distasteful struggle with research terminated with his doctorate, and his students can confer with him only if they, too, can spare time for the golf course. To be properly catalogued, Professor Holiday's courses should be assigned to a new department: the Department of Hypocrisy.

Mr. Martin, superintendent of schools in the suburban town of East Futility, announces to his visitor at a faculty meeting, "In our school we have a democratic administration. Our curriculum and, in fact, all of our school policies are determined by group decision. We really are one happy family." He smiles benevolently at the group, and a few of the teachers sheepishly smile back. Mr. Martin sits at a desk mounted on a dais, and he paces the faculty through the tight agenda which he has prepared. He interrupts group members before they have finished talking. While some teachers are speaking, he nods approval; when others speak, the small muscles at the side of his lips tighten, and he drums his fingers against the desk. When a topic is introduced for discussion, he firmly states his own opinion at the outset and, oddly enough, those teachers whom he first invites to express their reactions—the same ones on whom he has previously bestowed his smiles—unanimously agree with his judgment. At one point where a few teachers voice objection to the regulations he has inaugurated on lunchroom duty and where other group members rush quick support to this opposition, he suggests that this is a matter on which the faculty should not decide hastily. He appoints a subcommittee with himself as chairman, which will report back to the larger group next month. When the meeting is over, the teachers file quietly out of the room; no one speaks to the superintendent. As he escorts his visitor from the meeting, he explains in his best stentorian tone, "The only way to keep a faculty happy is to allow complete freedom of expression."

Sonia, a luscious coed whose slinky walk could have inspired the idea of fluid drive, complains that all men are alike and are all after the same thing. None of them respects her intellect. But how can they keep their mind on her intellect when the sultry timbre of her voice when she says no more than "Hello" to a man—any man—makes Delilah sound like a fish wife? Which part of the mixed message is the man to believe: her words which protest with vigor both her virtue and her intellect, or her voice which promises intimacy and sensual delights.

Tom Young and his wife, Yvonne, present to friends the image of a happily married young couple. Tom is attentive to Yvonne, and he repeatedly tells her how much he loves her and respects her. He has stocked her kitchen with so many appliances that it looks like a radar station. He tells her not to worry her pretty little head about household finances or other matters of business, yet he instructs her how to cast her vote in the local elections. Yvonne earned her own Phi Beta Kappa key; Tom, aided by persuasion from the Scholastic Standards Committee, quit college to become a partner in his father's business. Tom and Yvonne once came close to an outright quarrel when Yvonne suggested a career of her own. Tom blanched, and his lips became thin. With his voice pitched much higher than usual, he said, "I won't allow *my* wife to work. What would people think? Your place is in the home." His voice then softened and with calculated patience he explained to her how much he loved her, how much he respected her individuality, how much he wanted her to bear children for *him*. Yvonne is attractive and has a flair for striking clothes. Tom devours the covetous glances which Yvonne receives when they attend the country club dances. He gazes at her with the same possessive admiration that he usually reserves for his new Buick. How should Yvonne handle the mixed messages she receives from Tom? His words vehemently declare that he loves her and respects her individuality as a human being. But in his behavior he treats her as if she were a second-class citizen. How soon will she tire of being used as a decoration? How soon, despite her husband's protestations of love, will she come to realize that her husband wants neither a wife nor a partner, but a socially sanctioned concubine? And Tom, poor man, will never understand; his own frantic faith in words has enchanted him into believing that he does indeed respect and love his wife.

Ken Cowan, a middle-management executive, has just returned to his home office after attending a Group Development and Leadership Training Institute at the State University. He is enthusiastic about what he has learned and he wants to inject a fresh dose of "human relations" into the company's local office. He starts calling his associates by their first names, he uses an "open" plan in arranging desks so as to diminish the social distance between employees and himself during conferences, and he introduces an in-service management development program based upon the group dynamics approach. But Ken's company is hierarchically organized, and channels of command are clearly stipulated; in fact, the central office controls policies for all the branches. Ken's salary is more than $4,000 above that of any of his associates in the local branch. According to company policy, Ken has sole local jurisdiction over all hiring, firing, and promoting for his branch. Ken is loquacious to his employees about developing a team spirit, and he conscientiously tries to substitute "we" for "I" in his talks with the workers. But when a prolonged strike in the major local industry causes a slow-down in the branch sales and two of the salesmen have to be fired, it is Ken who fires them. And there is no "we" and no "team" spirit about it. As one of the salesmen remarks, "When someone stabs you in the back, it doesn't matter whether he calls you by your first name or your last." How should employees in such a situation read Ken's mixed messages? When the realities of the organization make a mockery of Ken's words, how can his employees, or even Ken himself, view his Group Development lessons with anything but cynicism?

Consider another case where the unreflective use of a technique produced an effect diametrically opposite to what the executive intended. The executive, the president of a publishing firm, had just returned from a five-week vacation, and was visiting the various editorial offices, making pleasant talk with the employees, displaying jovial camaraderie, and, in general, spreading his benevolence and good will. He noted an extremely conspicuous but attractive collage that one of the editors had constructed on the wall above his desk. The executive made what he considered appropriate noises about the editor's artistic talents, and the recipient of the praise smiled feebly. He and the woman editor who shared the same office saw nothing to be gained by telling the executive that the same collage had been on the wall for six months, that his present effusion about the collage served only to underscore how much he had ignored both editors for the past half year.

Once, upon leaving a conference she had just completed with the same president, the woman editor fumed, "What annoys me most is when someone asks me questions and then doesn't bother to listen to my answers!" This is another instance in which open and muted language may disagree. If you ask a person a question, then you explicitly lead him to believe that you would like to have an answer and that he has your sanction to answer freely. But if you patently do not listen to what he has to say, if the drumming of your fingers on your desk, or your wandering, distraught gaze shows that you have asked the question in the first place only to hear yourself talk, then how can you expect the other person to believe—either now or later—that you respect his judgment?

Professor Holiday, the playboy; Mr. Martin, the martinet manipulating people in the name of "democracy"; Sonia, the coed with too much allure for her own comfort; Tom Young, the husband who confuses possessiveness with love; the astigmatic publisher; and Ken Cowan, the executive who ritualistically applies "human relations" gimmicks within a formal organization for which they were never intended—each of these people is baffled to discover that others do not really understand him. But in each instance the brutal truth is that others *do* understand him; they understand what his behavior says, not what he says with his words. The words become a "cover"; unfortunately, these words are likely to deceive the speaker more than the listener.

To say that the words become a cover does not mean that these people are knowingly insincere. For example, the executive Ken Cowan is a good man caught in the jungle of business; he hopes that soft words will dull the edge of the naked power which he often must wield. And in America where formality is mistaken for stuffiness and where "togetherness" becomes a national slogan, it is easy for Ken to impute to the language and the techniques of group dynamics greater potency than they possess.

So, too, with the young husband, Tom Young, who has traded his soul for a mess of cottage. He is not knowingly insincere to his wife, Yvonne. Love has many faces, and few of us are ever privileged to know the meaning of mature love, love which liberates the loved one. Tom has never achieved this understanding; yet he speaks the words of love as kind of a ritual. Why? Probably because at some time in his courtship he found himself in a situation with Yvonne where he felt that he *should* declare the three words of the magic formula. Both Tom and Yvonne had seen too many movies, had watched too much TV, had sung too many popular songs dripping with sentiment. It became altogether too simple for them to let nature copy art. But their mistake was that they chose a low form of art to copy; they chose "art" forms which reduce human beings to puppets and which compress complex emotions into slogans. Tom, like so many other men, let the words escape his lips before the feeling they declared was indeed present. Then he hoped that by incanting these same words often enough he could bring to pass the emotion that the words purported to describe. One wonders how many couples there are who are married not because each loves the other, but because each said words of love to the other under circumstances where he or she felt that the words were expected. One word led to another and soon each person became a prisoner of the other's expectations. Too late the husband and the wife learn that no torrent of words can make up for a poverty of genuine emotion; too late do they discover that one must learn to read the total behavior of others and not be sidetracked by the ritualistic use of words. No, Tom is not insincere; he has simply allowed himself to say what he thought was expected, instead of what he actually felt.

MUTED CUES IN WRITTEN LANGUAGE

Up to this point, for the sake of simplicity we have discussed muted language as if it occurred only in person-to-person situations and in nonwritten form. Obviously, this is not the case, for we all have had the experience of being so repelled by the tone of a letter that we have categorically rejected its intended content. Many executives belatedly discover that their writing style transmits a muted message which says more to the recipient than the actually intended message. The letters of some men have verve and can reveal across a continent the warmth and spontaneity of their personality. The letters of other men are stiff, dogmatic, and insensitive to the feelings of the recipient. When we read a letter, the emotional tone comes through faster than the substantive content.

The executive who is addicted to rules and regulations exposes his contempt for the human individual in letters that are bloated with bureaucratic jargon. Heavy reliance on the third person and the neuter gender and the persistent use of the passive voice reflect impersonality ("It has been decided that . . ."). The repetitive use of stale clichés as substitutes for thought bespeaks either laziness or shallowness. Regrettably, few executives realize that a pompous style and poor manners in writing can create attitudes just as antagonistic as those aroused by poor manners in face-to-face meetings. In face-to-face relations even a boor—if he's perceptive enough—can catch some feedback from his listeners, can modify his behavior before he has done irreparable damage. But in a letter or memo, a gauche remark is imprisoned in print and can haunt the writer for years to come.

Many letters or reports written by administrators can be described best not as muted language but, more pathetically, as mutilated language. Our schools and especially our colleges of education may be partially responsible for what Shaw's Henry Higgins called "the cold-blooded murder of the English tongue." Books on education, and especially those on educational administration, ooze with verbal slush. After repeated exposure to this deadly fare a reader is no longer able to distinguish between a slogan and an idea. And then to compound the felony, the professors insist that the graduate student, in preparing a thesis or dissertation, follow a manual of style that perpetuates the use of the inert, passive voice. Fortunately, a few major universities are trying to get away from this, by recognizing that the dogged use of the third person does not automatically produce the objectivity ascribed to it. Perhaps we should listen to the plea of Dr. W. Furness Thompson, Vice President in charge of Research and Development for Smith, Kline, and French Laboratories, in his sparkling article, "Why Don't the Scientists Admit They're Human?"[5] Thompson urges us to report scientific findings in a lively fashion, to avoid the pretentiousness of a spurious objectivity.

Listen, too, to the wise words of the literary critic, Lionel Trilling:

> A Specter haunts our culture—it is that people will eventually be unable to say, "They fell in love and married," let alone understand the language of *Romeo and Juliet,* but will as a matter of course say, "Their libidinal impulses being reciprocal, they activated their individual erotic drives and integrated them within the same frame of reference."
>
> Now this is not the language of abstract thought or of any kind of thought. It is the language which is developing from the peculiar status which we in our culture have given to abstract thought. There can be no doubt whatever that it constitutes a threat to the emotions and thus to life itself.[6]

When we stoop to this language of nonthought, we reveal to others our intellectual sterility. Trilling's example is extreme, but not far removed from the "baffle-gab" perpetrated every day by harassed executives.

Bureaucratic language is weasel language, constructed for men who want to pass the buck and evade personal responsibility; it is the language of the faceless "They." If you have a feeling of warmth toward other human beings, why suffocate it under a pile of bureaucratic cant? However, the bureaucratic style is ideally suited to three types of people. It is perfect for the fellow who is so mean that he would steal the straw from his mother's kennel. In his case, he had best stick to jargon and use it as a cover for his own meanness. Second, gobbledygook is a handy solution for the person who has neither the time, capacity, nor predilection to think. Finally, bureaucratic prose is perfect for the "faceless ones" who have long since renounced any desire to develop their own individuality. If you fall into any of these categories, then continue to write in a dull, impersonal, plodding style. But if you still belong to the human race, let your own humanness shine through your writing.

NONVERBAL CUES AS A "COVER"

In the examples we have cited thus far, the words have been used as a "cover" for nonverbal communications which belie the words. But nonverbal communication can also be used as a cover. Consider the inexorable smile of the airline stewardess. (It would do my heart good if I could just once see a stewardess snarl at a passenger.) And reflect, too, upon the unctuous affability which the automobile salesman sprays upon a potential customer. And in advertisements and TV commercials, the housewife is so happy over her new detergent that one knows that, if her husband were to give her two bottles of the detergent for Christmas, she would respond as though she had received an ounce of Sortilége. Smiles and hearty laughter (often canned) have become so commercialized that a sensitive human being cannot help but feel suspicious when he encounters any form of promiscuous amiability.

The distinguished French philosopher, Jacques Maritain, has commented on the American smile:

The yearning to make life tolerable is best revealed, it seems to me, in the American smile.

You meet on American streets smiling faces, which plunge you into a stream of quite general and anonymous good feeling. Of course, there is an immense part of illusion, of ritually accepted illusion, in the universal benignancy thus displayed. I had a dentist in a small town whose nurses were so well trained that you were dazzled by their radiant smiles and their unshakeable optimism. Finally you came to think, in a kind of daydream, that the fact of dying in the midst of these happy smiles and angel wings of these white, immaculate uniforms, would be a pure pleasure, a moment of no consequence. Relax, take it easy, it's nothing. Thereafter you would enjoy the cleanness and happiness of the funeral home, and the chattering of your friends around your embalmed corpse. . . .

I left this dentist, in order to protect within my mind the Christian idea of death.[7]

MUTED CUES IN THE STYLE OF SPEECH

The language of behavior also includes the *style* in which we speak. A man's style of speaking can tell others that he is alive with ideas, or that he is an accomplished bore. Some men, whenever they open their mouths, spew forth a verbal hemorrhage; they seem convinced that the sheer amount of words, any words, will compensate for a dearth of ideas. This flow of words often immobilizes the listener who may be too polite to interrupt the torrent. But the net result is that the speaker fails to communicate what he thinks he is communicating; he has sought no feedback from his listener, and the sheer flow of words would make such feedback exceptionally difficult even if it had been sought. Other speakers invariably talk *at* people, not *with* them. This, too, precludes dependable feedback to the speaker.

This brings us back to a point which we mentioned earlier: that we learn who we are by communicating and that we will benefit from more, not less, communication with others. But this idea will be polluted if we should make the mistake of confusing the volume of words or actions expressed with the amount of meaning transmitted.

There is no direct relationship between the number of words used and the number of ideas expressed. If you doubt this, a quick glimpse at a typical textbook in education will convince you. The difficulty which many students experience in reading some textbooks—and not alone those in education—is that they get the constant feeling that "they've been there before." The reader finds that he can anticipate every cliché which the author perpetrates. He can even anticipate the systematic use of strong qualifying adverbs such as "truly," "really," and "very." Many writers forget that if they cry "wolf" often enough, and always in the same predictable fashion, their message will lose its impact. An astute editor of a distinguished university press remarked to me after she had spent a few weeks wading through the soggy prose of a few textbooks in education, "I think that most of the books in education could be published under the same title: *Everybody to the Barricades!*"

We often find a counterpart to this kind of writing in some of the conversation to which we are subjected. This is typified by the person who speaks in italics, who resorts to exaggerated gestures, and egregiously describes everything in superlatives. If everything is "fantastic" or "simply fabulous," these expressions soon lose their meaning. The person who uses these devices profusely reveals to others the essential poverty of his ideas. Live, vital ideas do not require histrionics for presentation.

Now this brings to focus a crucial fact about communication: that the more probable the message, the less information does it give. For example, if I say "Good morning" to a colleague and he replies with the most probable answer, "Good morning," his answer is socially pleasant but contributes little information to me. But suppose I say "Good morning" and he snaps, "What's good about it?" His answer may not be as socially comfortable as the more prosaic reply, but it certainly does give me more information about how he feels.

Much of our social conversation seldom rises above the level of the soap opera; it is disgustingly predictable. Everybody is friendly in the blandest way possible. The moment that a guest's reply is not the most probable or the most commonplace answer, the hostess or another guest quickly changes the conversation to another topic. After a while, you cannot distinguish one such soirée from another; the company may be different, but the substance—and I use the term loosely—of the dialogue is precisely the same.

The axiom that the greater the probability of a message, the less the amount of information communicated, can help us identify the members of a certain specie in our midst. A typical member is the man whose every utterance is predictable, who unerringly chooses the stale image and the lame bromide, who elaborates the obvious and leaves nothing unsaid, whose cadence of speech or writing follows the undeviating rhythm of blah, blah, blah, thud— blah, blah, blah, thud. He telegraphs his every tortured point three sentences before he personally delivers it by hand. The ratio of words uttered to information conveyed is high. And there is no "surprise" in anything he says. He is a bore.

By conceptualizing the bore as one whose response is invariably the most probable, or the most predictable, we discover that there are other than verbal bores. The girl-on-the-make who raises her plucked eyebrows and widens her big blue eyes at every innocuous remark that a man makes to her is also a bore. Because she fails to distinguish between stimuli, her response is highly predictable and soon becomes commonplace. Her style, like that of the verbal bore, is rigid because she has so limited a repertoire of available responses. If she were *not* to wig-wag her hips at every eligible male, that *would* be "information."

COMMUNICATION AND SELF-DISCOVERY

It should be clear from these illustrations that communication is a much more complicated affair than most of us imagine. Yet to be fully human we must communicate not less, but more; to fail to communicate to others is to become psychotic. By communication we not only learn to understand others, but, what is more important, we discover who we are. Yet we can make this self-discovery only if we are fully aware of what it is we are communicating to others—and indeed to ourselves. We cannot afford to deceive ourselves, through our own words, into believing that we are other than what we are. For when we do, we will be the only victims of this deception; those with whom we deal will "read" what we really are from a host of nonverbal cues and will discount our words whenever they run counter to our behavior. In brief, we must "listen" to our own behavior and must resist the temptation to talk one game and live another. To "read" the behavior of others and to "read" our own behavior, we must learn to distinguish the phony from the real, the shadow from the substance. We must become skilled in detecting phoniness in others and in the very culture which surrounds us. But we also must have guts enough to recognize phoniness in ourselves. How, for example, can a student respect himself or dare to discover who he is, if he discourses on honesty and the virtues of the Christian life in his church on Sunday, and cribs on a quiz on Monday? We praise integrity as a Christian virtue. But what does integrity mean except that a person is whole, that he is all of a piece, that his words, his deeds, and his feelings reflect a unity?

Until recently, little effort had been made at any university in the country to include in the training for educational administrators a set of systematic experiences to develop in these administrators an explicit awareness of the subtleties of nonverbal communication. This is a serious omission, for a man cannot be a successful administrator unless he is highly skilled in "reading" muted language, and is also sensitive to the nuances of meaning which he transmits to others through his own muted language. Many men learn these skills through experience on the job, but although on-the-job experience can prove to be a good teacher, it can also be a very expensive teacher—at times, it can even cost a superintendent his job.

How, then, can we sensitize ourselves to the eloquence of our own behavior? How can we use communication to discover who we are? Here is an old-fashioned suggestion, one which in our time sounds almost obscene: READ! Read good literature. Shut down the TV more often and become acquainted again with the exquisite joy of quiet, and time to think. Once in a while, we should try to surround ourselves with silence. Once we learn not to be afraid of quiet, then we need no longer feel compelled to fill precious time with words that are nothing more than "noise." We have spoken of discriminating between the phony and the real, between enduring ethical values and the cheap and tawdry titil-lations which devour so much of our time, between integrity and expediency. But these discriminations are the precise objectives of a liberal education; these are the marks of the educated man. The university presents to every student the opportunity to learn how to make better discriminations in these areas. But unless a student uses his four years for the purpose of becoming an educated man, and not solely for the crass purpose of "getting ahead," he cheats himself.

Now I know full well that to speak of "the educated man" is to sound Victorian; universities today are perceived mainly as ex-press elevators to better jobs, better marriages, and better social status. The student who declares that he is here to be educated, to become a cultured man is regarded by his peers as quaint—as a "square." Yet, I submit that this is the student who stands the best chance of using his four years profitably—to advance in the discovery of himself.

Through what courses will the young man or woman learn how to understand his own behavior, how to read the behavior of others? Will it be through the practical courses? the how-to-do-it routines? Certainly not. He will acquire his greatest stature as a human being through the humanities and through the social sciences.

When we define our task, as we have done, in the form of the question, "How can we teach human beings to be more sensitive to the wide range of messages which they are continuously re-ceiving from their fellows?" what else have we done but define one of the salient purposes of literature? The administrator is working with human beings, and his job puts him in a position of economic power over others; it behooves him to understand the human heart, to understand—if you will—the ineffable ambiguity of the human condition. But this understanding is precisely what the poet, the playwright, the short-story writer, and the novelist seek to achieve. Through the eyes of these writers, we as ad-ministrators can freshen our insights into our own personal prob-lems and the problems of those with whom we work. A competent novelist shapes his characters by what they do, not just by what they say. In this shaping he explicates for us the myriad muted cues through which man communicates with man. The perennial acrimony between colleges of education and liberal arts colleges has perhaps blinded us to the genuine and unique contribution which courses in literature can make to the training of better administrators. Lest this suggestion be conceived as the impractical proposal of an academician, let us note that a dramatic, successful experiment along this line has been conducted by the Bell Telephone Company of Pennsylvania.[8] The organization granted to 17 of its middle-level managers a ten-month's leave of absence with full salary to attend a special institute at the University of Pennsylvania in which they received a far richer diet of liberal education than undergraduate literature majors receive in most universities. Significantly, one of the experiences which these executives later reported as most useful to them in their jobs was their study of James Joyce's *Ulysses*. The company was delighted with the results of the experiment. Those who may be skeptical about this approach should also examine the book, *Toward the Liberally Educated Executive*,[9] sponsored by The Fund for Adult Education.

Literature will help a person understand muted language; it also will give him a respect for language and this will teach him how to communicate clearly. Listen to Peter Drucker, professor of management at New York University and an industrial consultant to a number of large American corporations:

> It can be said with little exaggeration that of the common college courses being taught today the ones most nearly "vocational" as preparation for management are the writing of poetry and of short stories. For these two courses teach a man how to express himself, teach him words and their meaning and, above all, give him practice in writing. It can also be said that nothing would help so much to prepare young men for management as a revival of the honorable practice of the oral defense of one's "thesis"—only it should be made a frequent, normal, continuing part of college work rather than something that happens once, at the end of formal schooling.[10]

Similarly, in other areas of the humanities, philosophy will introduce the student to issues which have tormented men in all times and will help destroy some of his own "provincialism in time."

Anthropology will allow him to examine the "givens" of his own culture from a fresh perspective. Foreign languages will open for him an understanding of cultures other than his own. Psychology, especially as exemplified in the work of men such as Freud and Fromm, will reveal to him the significance of much of his own behavior which has heretofore escaped his notice.

And at this point I hear a "practical" young man mutter, "There's the old line again. These academic guys just don't dig what business wants." That, of course, depends upon the business he wants to enter. If he goes into a small or mediocre business, a liberal education may not have great market-value for him. But if he aspires to top management in a national organization, perhaps he had better revise his sights. Witness again the success of Bell Telephone of Pennsylvania's program; the assigned readings include Homer, Virgil, Dante, Goethe, Tolstoy, T. S. Eliot, James Joyce, Freud, MacLeish, Riesman, and dozens of others. And what is the rationale behind the program? Simply the recognition that a top-notch executive must know how to communicate clearly, must be aware of what his own behavior says to others, and must be able to read the behavior of others.

Similarly, in the field of education, the training of school administrators has undergone drastic changes in the past decade. In current doctoral programs at major universities, the candidate is urged to include in his program courses in anthropology, psychology, economics, industrial relations, and sociology. Much time is spent on the sociology of organizations. The student is made to realize that the most indispensable skill of an administrator is his ability to diagnose social situations, to "read" the behavior of others. In a few recent instances, professors of administration have boldly attacked the task of teaching the student how to "read" his own behavior, especially his nonverbal behavior.

Perhaps I should add in passing that those of us who have been responsible for training executives, whether in industry, government, or education, are appalled by one glaring flaw in most of the candidates: they are culturally illiterate. They have been so frantic in their race to get ahead of the next fellow, and have been so intent upon climbing one rung higher on the status-ladder, that they have not taken the time to become complete human beings.

Having answered the muttered criticism of the "practical" young man, let me hasten to note that to choose a liberal arts program because it will help one to get ahead in business is to choose it for the wrong reason; the ends will contaminate the means. Such a program must be chosen because one wants to be an educated man and to share the thoughts and feelings of cultured men of all ages. The moment a man measures his education in terms of dollars and cents or according to what it contributes to his getting ahead, he betrays his ignorance of the meaning of education. I have referred to certain business advantages of liberal education, but these advantages are by-products. The student's choice should be based upon the intrinsic merit of a broad education and should be calculated in terms of what this education will do to increase one's stature as a sentient human being. In short, I ask you to resist what T. S. Eliot has described:

> The last temptation is the greatest treason:
> To do the right deed for the wrong reason.[11]

So we return to the recommendation with which we started: the most immediate step which a person can take toward understanding his own behavior and that of others is to balance the applied, technical, and professional courses which he takes with a rich liberal arts program.

At a much more specific level we can recommend two excellent books which deal with the issue of nonverbal communication. The first one is by Jurgen Ruesch and Weldon Kees and is entitled *Non-Verbal Communication*.[12] It is composed mainly of photographs with explanatory text. The photographs pungently illustrate how we communicate to each other nonverbally. Several of the more provocative pictures show how even the arrangement of furniture in our homes and specific items of decor tell things about us. The senior author of this book, Jurgen Ruesch, is a psychiatrist; the junior author, Weldon Kees, now deceased, is a poet. The second book is *The Silent Language* by Edward T. Hall,[13] an anthropologist who is now president of Overseas Training and Research, Incorporated, a concern which trains and advises the personnel of American corporations with extensive foreign interests.

One or two attempts have been made to use films for training purposes. For example, the Veterans Administration has used one film on *Non-Verbal Communication* for training psychiatrists. Scenes are presented with and without the sound track in operation, and the student is asked to see how much of the situation he can read without the sound. When the same scenes are played again using the sound, the student must then note to what extent the words of the patient either reinforce or contradict what the patient is saying with his body and gestures. Interviews recorded on tape are also useful devices for teaching students how to read nuances of behavior from changes in tone of voice, changes in pace, and the change in the speaker's style according to the status of the person to whom he is speaking. For the most part, however, not much has been done with audio-visual materials in training students how to "read" behavior.

I would now summarize in six points what has been said:

1. We communicate to others with all of our behavior.

2. What people say is not always in accord with what they communicate nonverbally. I have illustrated this with a few examples and have shown how style itself conveys a message.

3. There is no direct relationship between the volume of communication and the amount of information transmitted; the least probable message is likely to convey the most meaning.

4. I have suggested that we gain in stature as human beings to such extent as we become sensitive to what we do indeed communicate.

5. We should avoid the trap of being enchanted by our own words, deeds, and feelings; we should conscientiously try to prevent our words, deeds, and feelings from becoming disassociated from each other. We should not let "words get into our eyes."

6. The best means for sensitizing ourselves to the various facets of communication is through a liberal arts program.

CHALLENGE

I shall conclude with two final warnings:

The first is concerned with the use of clichés. There are several ways in which all of us tend to use clichés as a form of resistance;

having acknowledged a platitude, having indeed mouthed it many times, we feel relieved of responsibility for *acting* on the idea that lies at the core of the expression.[14]

This trick of rendering an idea impotent by indicating it as a cliché, and, in fact, by deliberately transforming it into a cliché, appeals especially to those who pride themselves on being "intellectual" or "educated." Thus, in complaining about his physical symptoms, the well-educated neurotic is quick to declare to his friends at the espresso bar or at the "art" theatre, "I'm sure it's all psychosomatic." Having admitted his shortcomings, then, at this empty, verbal level, our man is now less inclined to explore the emotional tangles which have produced his symptoms. *Having confessed, he need not act*—that is, change his behavior in accord with the inevitable implications of his confession. For example, the pseudo-intellectual believes that once having acknowledged that behavior speaks louder than words, he need not *act*—he need not examine the discrepancy between what he *says* and what he *does*. Many of us, I fear, would just as soon not know, for on this score ignorance seems more comforting than truth. Yet this is a false comfort, a comfort of delusion; ultimately, we are all judged by what we communicate to others through our total behavior, both verbal and nonverbal.

Second, I believe that each of us will benefit from an increased awareness of what we say to others with our behavior. But a personal improvement program along this line is not altogether easy. Many of us will prefer the solace of self-deception, for to discover who we are, to see ourselves as others see us, may prove too traumatic. When a man tries to become all of a piece, tries to make his words, his deeds, and his feelings reflect the same unity, he discovers that there are fewer and fewer personal shortcomings that he can condone. If he cheats, he knows that he is a cheat. If he exploits others, he knows that he has sinned. If he betrays his integrity, he knows that he and he alone is responsible.

The journey of self-discovery can be frightening and harrowing. Yet the man who refuses to take this journey confines his life to a ritual of self-deception; he becomes one of "the hollow men," one of the many non-persons who, trancelike, "notice" life but never live it.

NOTES FOR CHAPTER 5

1. This chapter combines the essence of two papers: "The Eloquence of Behavior," delivered as a Thursday Lecture at the University of Utah, October 29, 1959; and "Muted Language," *The School Review,* **68,** No. 1 (Spring 1960), pp. 85-104. The latter paper was first presented, June 24, 1959, at the University of Utah. The sections from "Muted Language" are reprinted here with the permission of *The School Review.* A short excerpt of this chapter has been published, under the same title, in *Trans-action,* **1,** No. 2 (January 1964), pp. 23-24. This excerpt is reprinted here by permission of *Trans-action,* a publication of the Community Leadership Project, Washington University, St. Louis, Missouri.

2. Arthur Ogden, "Looks and Glances," *Harper's Bazaar* (June 1961), pp. 84, 109-110.

3. Bruno Bettelheim, *The Informed Heart: Autonomy in a Mass Age* (New York: The Free Press of Glencoe, 1960), pp. 87-88.

4. If this discussion of tables seems picayune, please recall how much time of the opening sessions of the 1959 Geneva Conference was devoted to the seating of the East German delegates. The size of the table—whether it should be square or round—and its placement in relation to the main conference table became explosive issues of protocol.

5. W. Furness Thompson, "Why Don't the Scientists Admit They're Human?" *Saturday Review,* **40,** No. 36 (September 7, 1957), pp. 44-46. Also see Sheridan Baker, "Scholarly Style, or the Lack Thereof," *AAUP Bulletin,* **42,** No. 3 (Autumn 1956), pp. 464-470.

6. Lionel Trilling, *The Liberal Imagination* (New York: The Viking Press, 1950), p. 285.

7. Jacques Maritain, *Reflections on America* (New York: Charles Scribner's Sons, 1958), p. 91.

8. Digby Baltzell, "Bell Telephone's Experiment in Education," *Harper's Magazine,* **210,** No. 1258 (March 1955), pp. 73-77.

9. Robert A. Goldwin (ed.), and Charles A. Nelson (consultant), *Toward the Liberally Educated Executive* (White Plains, N.Y.: The Fund for Adult Education, 1957).

10. Peter F. Drucker, *The Practice of Management* (New York: Harper & Brothers, 1954), p. 375.

11. Thomas S. Eliot, *Murder in the Cathedral* (New York: Harcourt, Brace & World, Inc., 1935), p. 44. Reprinted by permission both of the American publisher and of Faber and Faber, Ltd., London.

12. Jurgen Ruesch and Weldon Kees, *Non-Verbal Communication: Notes on the Visual Perception of Human Relations* (Berkeley and Los Angeles: University of California Press, 1956).

13. Edward T. Hall, *The Silent Language* (Garden City, N.Y.: Doubleday & Company, 1959).

14. For a probing discussion of this point, see Martin H. Stein, "The Cliché: A Phenomenon of Resistance," *Journal of the American Psychoanalytic Association,* 6, No. 2 (April 1958), pp. 263-277.

PART FOUR

Beyond Glyphs and Graphs

6

Ways of Knowing[1]

My thesis is simple: there is more than one gate to the kingdom of knowledge. Each gate opens upon a different vista, but no one vista exhausts the realm of "reality"—whatever that may be. Therefore, it is important to understand what each vista can and cannot yield. To expect returns through one way of knowing which can be achieved only through another is to invite frustration and disillusion. Yet obvious though this thesis may be, its implications are violated every day—ironically, by our universities as well as by the man on the street. Each purveyor of knowledge in academe claims that his brand of knowledge is more spectacular and more dependable. All human knowledge is partial, and as human beings none of us is so rich in understanding that he can afford to ignore any of the several gates to the kingdom of knowledge.

But what has this to do with educational administration? To answer this question we must examine briefly the quiet revolution which has been taking place in university programs for training school administrators. Before World War II the training for educational administrators was composed principally of substantive information about the presumed content of the field: courses in educational philosophy, curriculum, finance, buildings, and personnel. What was taught about administration consisted of maxims, exhortations, and several innocuous variations on the theme of the Golden Rule. The material was speculative rather than theoretical in the true sense of the term; empirical research on administration was slighted, and contributions from the behavioral sciences and personnel research in industry were zealously ignored.

With the development of the NCPEA, CPEA, and UCEA programs,[2] professors of educational administration discovered that they could identify a profession of administration as administration. Despite certain content differences, such areas as educational administration, business administration, public administration, and hospital administration, did, in fact, share a significant common core. Attention was directed to the social and human skills of the administrator and to the sociology of the organizations in which he operated. The postwar period also saw a surge of interdisciplinary research in the social sciences; at several major universities, professors of educational administration participated in this movement. With the recognition that skills and attitudes were as important to an executive as factual knowledge, various forms of internship were incorporated into the training programs for school administrators. The professors sought help from psychologists and sociologists and discovered that, without the support of an explicit theoretical framework, their discipline could easily degenerate into a jumble of inert facts.[3]

QUALMS ABOUT THE ROLE OF THEORY

This emphasis on theory holds great promise. Yet many superintendents get the feeling that an important piece is missing. They ask, "If analytical theory is supposed to be so good for us, why do we feel so uncomfortable in its presence?" The administrator's doubt is justified; there is indeed something missing. The fault is that the scientist's theoretical models of administration are too rational, too tidy, too aseptic. They remind us of the photographs in magazines devoted to home decorating—the glossy pictures of dramatic and pristine living room interiors. (The rooms are beautiful, but they have never been lived in. Nor are the rooms pictured as inhabited by human beings, except perhaps for a vacuous but poised fashion model.) The superintendent distrusts such tidiness in administrative theory and senses intuitively that the theoretical-analytical approach has ignored much that is reality. This is why I think we had better examine afresh our present perspectives in educational administration. We had better be sure that the current slant on administrative theory is taking us where we want to go. We will discover, I hope, that we do not have to ignore any recent work, but that we may have to distribute our intellectual load more judiciously.

In the first place, there does not exist today, either in education or in industry, a single well-developed theory of administration that is worth getting excited about. Recent hue and cry on this subject have created a completely false impression; many superintendents and professors of education have been led to believe that our knowledge in this area is more secure than it actually is. Accordingly, I think it is wise for us to check our present bearings. We might just as well start with the theme "Administrative Theory as a Guide to Action."[4] Translated into question form, this becomes "How can administrative theory be applied by the superintendent?" I think that when we pose the question in this form, we invite confusion. This is the wrong question, or at least it is a premature question at this juncture. It would be better to ask, "How can the practitioner use the social scientists' findings to sharpen his analysis of the social situations with which he must deal?" There are some social science research findings which can prove useful to the practitioner. There are also a few ways of thinking about social and organizational phenomena which will help him discern the similarities and differences between day-to-day administrative situations, and thus will enable him to make wiser decisions. And there are ways, too, by which the practitioner and the scientist can each freshen the other's observations. An exchange of ideas in these domains should prove exceedingly fruitful. We should examine together the chasm which now separates administrative theory from actual practice. We should discern how deep and how wide the chasm is, and determine where it can be bridged safely.

CLINICAL *AND* ANALYTICAL SCIENCE

We will be in a better position to leap when we have first developed a more balanced attack, by the scientists themselves, upon the problems of educational administration. Much of the present difficulty stems from the fact that the scientists who have chosen to work in this field represent, for the most part, a parochial view of science. They are social scientists who are intent upon aping the more prestigious physical scientists in building highly abstract, theoretical models. These men have castigated the role of clinical science. They have disregarded the advice which Homans gave us a decade ago:

> It is high time we knew the difference between clinical and analytical science. Clinical science is what a doctor uses at his patient's beside. There, the doctor cannot afford to leave out of account anything in the patient's condition that he can see or test. He cannot leave it out either in itself or in its relation to the whole picture of a sick human being. It may be the clue to the complex. Of course the doctor has some general theories at the back of his mind, theories of the connections between a limited number of physiological factors: what the others will do when one is changed. These doctrines may turn out to be useful, but he cannot, at the outset, let them master his thinking. They may not take into consideration, and so may prevent his noticing, the crucial fact in the case before him.
>
> *In action we must always be clinical.* An analytical science is for understanding but not for action, at least not directly. It picks out a few of the factors at work in particular situations and describes systematically the relations between these factors. Only by cutting down the number of factors considered can it achieve this systematic description. It is general, but it is abstract. As soon as he left friction out of account, Galileo's science became analytical. To return to our medical illustration, a description of particular cases of anemia is clinical science, whereas a theory of blood chemistry is analytical. When progress is rapid, clinical and analytical science help one another. The clinicians tell the analysts what the latter have left out. The analysts need the most brutal reminders because they are always so charmed with their pictures they mistake them for the real thing. On the other hand, the analysts' generalizations often suggest where the clinicians should look more closely. Both the clinician and the analyst are needed. We ought to be sick and tired of boasts that one is better than the other.[5]

At the present stage of our knowledge in educational administration, the clinically oriented scientist has as much to give us as the analytically oriented man. I do not intend to fall into the same trap that Homans warned us against: we need both orientations. But right now I think we need to pay greater heed to the clinical orientation, if only as an antidote against too heavy and too premature a dose of analytical science.

The key to the issue lies in Homans' observation, "In action we must always be clinical." Yet even this observation falls short of the mark and it has remained for Erikson, a distinguished psychoanalyst, to spot the crucial difference between people and things which most social scientists have missed completely—a difference which forces the clinician to adopt a personal attitude unlike that of the theoretically oriented scientist. Erikson admits that we can learn about the nature of things as we find out what one can do *with* them. But people are not things, ". . . the true nature of man reveals itself only in the attempt to do something *for* him."[6] But the moment you attempt to do things *for* other human beings, you must assume moral responsibility for what you do. And this is the very responsibility which the analytical scientist has refused to accept.

The clinician's concern about doing things for human beings coincides with the administrator's. It is precisely for this reason that I believe the clinical approach offers hope for greater *rapprochement* between practitioner and scientist. A clinical orientation should prove especially salutary at this time because it will reaffirm an obvious yet often forgotten point which applies to science as well as to all other forms of knowledge-seeking: the quality and the relevance of our knowledge are determined by the freshness of our observation. (And note that such observation need not be devoid of feeling or emotion.) In graduate courses on research we have made such an ado about the nature of scientific evidence and the use of statistical inference that we have blinded our students to the essential issue: without fresh, viable observation all the machinations of research methodology become an empty and self-deceiving ritual. There is no virtue in demonstrating that one can count or that one can compute Pearsonian correlation coefficients on the items he has counted; the trick is to know what things are worth counting in the first place. And no course in research methodology can teach us this. This skill can be acquired only through direct experience with the phenomena we are seeking to understand, and can be matured only by developing within ourselves—as human instruments—the capacity to view with unfettered perception the world around us. This capacity to "see" what is "out there" is imperative for both the scientist and the practitioner. In fact, the superintendent who is highly skilled in sizing up a complex social situation, in observing precisely what is taking place in his school system, exhibits the very essence of scientific method. The heart of the method, I repeat, is the freshness of observation, irrespective of whatever ritual is subsequently performed upon these observations. Yet by emphasizing such rituals and by stressing the parochial aspect of the analytical orientation in science, we have foolishly accentuated a false difference between the social scientist and the superintendent. This has not been wise strategy.

THREE WAYS OF KNOWING

But Victorian sighs and even Freudian confessionals are futile. The immediate issue is how we can most constructively alter our course. Since the form of our questions determines our answers, perhaps we should begin by asking questions different from those which have guided our recent strategy. Let us therefore examine more carefully how the administrator learns to "know" his job. After we have identified the major "ways of knowing" which the administrator employs, we will be in a better position to try to answer the question which I consider crucial for administrator and scientist alike: "How can the practitioner and the scientist help each other increase the freshness and the viability of their observations of organizations and of group members within these organizations?"

What are the chief ways of knowing which an administrator uses? How does he learn to know his job? I believe he relies on three major ways of knowing, ways which correspond to the three levels of culture defined by the anthropologist Edward T. Hall[7]: the formal, the informal, and the technical. Hall maintains that social learning takes place through a combination of inputs from all three levels.

Formal activities are taught by precept and by admonition. The father corrects his son by saying, "Good boys don't do that," and the tone of his voice declares that what his son is doing is unthinkable. The ranch hand yells at the dude, "Hey, not the right side of the horse, the left side! Remember, never approach a horse from the right!" The boss snarls, "Damn it, Jones, if you ever skip channels again, I'll fire you on the spot." Formal patterns are almost always invoked when a mistake is made and someone corrects it. The correction is usually made with personal vehemence and emotion, or through the cold and impersonal authority of an institution but with the clear understanding that a violation will be promptly punished. Formal learning teaches us the rules of the game as these rules have been defined by a particular culture. The details of formal learning are *binary*, of a yes-no, right-wrong character. You either break a taboo or you do not. You rifle your colleague's desk or you do not. You make a pass at your secretary or you do not.

Informal learning is acquired mainly through imitation. The content of this learning is not explicit, but whereas formal learning is preoccupied with the limits of a role or with the rules of the game, informal learning deals with the details and nuances of the role and with the techniques of one-upmanship within the rules of the game. You find a model, and then you try to copy it. "Mother," asks the preadolescent girl, "how does a woman get a man to marry her?" "Well, darling, it's a little hard to describe, but as you get older you'll find out." The daughter correctly translates this reply. "Don't ask questions, look around and see what people do." The earnest graduate student in educational administration says to the superintendent in whose school he has been working, "You know, Dr. Great, I admire the way you work with the board of education. I sure hope I'll be able to do as well. How do you do it? How can I learn to handle a board the way you do?" And Dr. Great, slightly stunned, replies, "Thank you, Jim. But I can't answer your question. I suppose I 'play it by ear.' The only thing I can tell you is to watch. And, Jim, if you do discover how I do it, would you please let me know?"

Technical learning is transmitted in explicit terms from the teacher to the student, either orally or in writing. It usually is preceded by a logical analysis of a body of content which is then organized into a coherent outline form for purposes of presentation. This is how most of our learning in school takes place. When a student asks how he can best understand the administrative process and Professor Getzels replies by describing his formulation of administration, we have an instance of technical learning about administration.

The Interplay Among the Three Ways of Knowing

Now let us look at an example of the interplay among these three modes—the formal, the informal, and the technical—from the standpoint of the learner, or the standpoint of the "knower." Let us examine what happens when a beginner learns to shoot pool. His teacher will probably sketch the rules of the game. These are formal stipulations; the boy can be said to "know" how to play pool to such extent as he can recite these rules (for example, rules about the order of play, scoring, "scratching"). But he quickly discovers a few more formal stipulations: "For Pete's sake, Jack, lift your cue. You're not digging potatoes. If you try to hit the cue ball like that you'll rip the felt into shreds." "Jack, will you please shut up when I'm trying to plan a shot. When the other fellow is shooting don't talk to him."

As the boy progresses he watches other players and, using them as models, he consciously or unconsciously imitates their handling of the cue-stick. He notices that Don spreads his fingers to provide a firm bridge, and that Harry's body is relaxed, not stiff, when he makes his shot. In the case of his most accurate shots he discovers with delight that at the very moment the cue hits the cue-ball— and even before the ball moves—his stroke "feels right." He cannot explicate a lot of his learning at this stage. Yet with his body itself he "knows" when he is in process of making a clean shot and he "knows," too, when he is going to muff. He "knows" not with his frontal lobes but with his fingers, his arm, his shoulder. This informal knowing is not the same as his formal knowing (his knowing, for example, about the rules of the game).

Eventually, dismayed by his opponent's skill in banking the balls and in maneuvering the cue-ball into advantageous position for the next shot, the boy decides to do some reading on the subject, to learn the principles of physics which apply to the control of the cue-ball. He comes to know technically why "right-hand English" produces results different from those which ensue when he delivers a sharp "draw-shot." He tries to apply these principles in his play. In this way the theory, in the sense of a theoretical model of how solids respond to forces applied to them, gives him a way of interpreting the results of his direct experience in play. The theory freshens his observations about his direct experience. But by the same token his direct experience forces him to analyze why the theory does not seem to work in every instance, makes him aware of the extraneous variables that the pure form of the theory was not obliged to take into account—variables such as random sources of friction, the worn cushion right below the side pocket, and the cue-stick that is slightly warped. He finds that he often has to "correct" the theory in terms of the particular table on which he is playing. At the techical level what the boy knows about the principles governing the motions of the balls constitutes another aspect of his knowing how to play pool.

To repeat, then, the boy knows the rules of the game, knows when a shot "feels right," and knows the technical principles governing the balls' motion. But though we use the same word to describe each of these "knowings," they are not quite the same; respectively they represent formal, informal, and technical knowing. Of course these modes are interrelated, and the demarcations between them are not always sharply etched. But it is important that we keep these three categories straight. For example, any attempt to *prove* a formal knowing by the same scientific methods which apply to the technical mode of knowing is as pointless as trying to use the laws of physical motion either to prove or to disprove the fact that the bishop in chess moves on the diagonal.

Just as these three modes of knowing operate in what the pool player knows, so do they apply to how a superintendent knows his job. At the formal level the superintendent knows the rules of the game. These are given by the culture. Some rules are historical accidents, some have been devised only after careful planning, while some have literally been drawn from mythology. The scientist can help identify these rules by showing that they exist or do not exist, but he can never *prove* that these rules are either true or false. They simply *exist*. In short, these rules represent an order of phenomena different from that with which the theoretically oriented scientist is equipped to deal.

The superintendent, or any other administrator, knows many things at the informal level in much the same way as a man knows that he loves his wife. He does not love her because of technical or rational reasons or because he is following a set of rules which tell him that he loves her; he simply loves her. Similarly on the job, the superintendent knows that he feels at ease with some influential members of the community yet also knows that there is an invisible screen between himself and certain other figures in the community power structure. After a faculty meeting which seems placid enough on the surface, he still knows that something went wrong—the butterflies halfway down his esophagus and his desperate yen for a double martini before dinner give him a genuine piece of "knowledge," but a piece which he can't quite put into words. He does not derive this knowing from a rational Q.E.D., but this does not make it none the less real.

However, I believe that the superintendent can train himself to become a better "human instrument," can learn to be more acutely aware of subtle cues, and can improve the richness and the quality of what he knows on a direct intuitive basis. And in doing this he can freshen his observation of the world around him, and can then share these observations with the scientist. From these raw data the scientist may then devise new hypothetical models which will agree more closely with the reality of the superintendent's direct experience. The superintendent's observations in this regard are guided by the clinical orientation in science. At this level of informal knowing the administrator and the scientist can help each other in sharpening their observations. The scientist can be especially helpful in devising a language of greater precision for describing the practitioner's observations so that the fruits of the practitioner's experience can be communicated more effectively to new trainees in administration. But at this level of knowing the wise scientist will be wary about introducing theoretical models prematurely.

Finally, at the technical level, the superintendent knows many things about administration. In addition to substantive information about bond issues, bus routing, curriculum changes, and the care and feeding of board members, he knows many things about the nature of administration because he is familiar with much technical research on the sociology of organizations and the behavior of executives. For example, he knows the work of Chester Barnard,[8] certain theoretical formulations of administration such as those devised by Getzels and Guba,[9] and perhaps about the leadership behavior dimensions of Consideration and Initiating Structure.[10] Each of these three ways of knowing is derived from a different context and is associated with a different purpose. The way of knowing and the human purpose of the "knower" must be treated conjointly. The logic of rationality which is applicable in the case of one human purpose cannot be applied willy-nilly to all other purposes. Nevertheless, what a man knows is derived inextricably from all three sources.

WAYS OF KNOWING AND REALNESS

There is one foolish notion that should be discarded now: the belief that different ways of knowing can be ranked according to the realness of the data with which they deal. When confronted with different "knowings" the naïve person is tempted to ask, "Which is more real?" "Which is *really* the truth?" This question is just as rhetorical, just as futile today as it once was in the mouth of Pontius Pilate. Here indeed is the pivot of my thesis: the reality of the scientific way of knowing is no more nor less real than any *other* way of knowing. The theoretically oriented scientist can make accurate predictions about uniformities in human behavior, but the very fact that he is dealing with a probability model makes his predictions those of an entirely different order from those made by either the clinically oriented scientist, the superintendent operating within the complex milieu of his job, or the poet and the playwright. We fall into a trap the moment we assume that one type of knowing is better than another. The most we can say is that each knowing differs from the other but that the complete human being—to be completely human—must be sensitive to his full heritage of knowing.

Let me illustrate the point about the realness of knowledge with a few lines by the poet, John Ciardi:

> There is no poetry for the practical man. There is poetry only for the mankind of the man who spends a certain amount of his life turning the mechanical wheel. But let him spend too much of his life at the mechanics of practicality and either he must become something less than a man, or his very mechanical efficiency will become impaired by the frustrations stored up in his irrational human personality. An ulcer, gentlemen, is an unkissed imagination taking its revenge for having been jilted. It is an unwritten poem, a neglected music, an unpainted watercolor, an undanced dance. It is a declaration from the mankind of the man that a clear spring of joy has not been tapped, and that it must break through, muddily, on its own.[11]

Is Ciardi's knowledge any less real than what you will find in a text on psychosomatic medicine? Is his knowledge any less real than a corpus of knowledge which I, as a scientist, can pin to a cross with nails made of means and standard deviations?

Sam Striver, an up-and-coming superintendent of a rapidly growing suburban community, conscientiously reads thick sociological monographs on suburbia but is oblivious to the short stories of John Cheever![12] Yet I am not convinced that the sociologists' jaded statistics are any more real or will be any more useful to Sam than Cheever's compassionate insight into the hearts of suburbanites.

A PATHWAY TO FRESHER OBSERVATION

Thus I have returned to the question which I raised before discussing the informal, formal, and technical modes of knowing: "How can the practitioner and the scientist help each other increase the freshness and the viability of their observations of organizations and group members within these organizations?" The first step is for the scientist to rid himself of the prejudice that his skill in constructing theoretical models is somehow more respectable than skill in the direct observation of human events.[13] Never let us underestimate the consummate skill needed for the direct observation of human behavior. Both skills are needed, and neither is less respectable than the other.

But if the scientist has been blinded by the myths of his professional prestige system, so too has the superintendent been blinded by the dry dust of words which has billowed between him and the sentient human beings with whom he must work and *for* whom he must be responsible. Here is a quotation in which the Swedish novelist Frank Heller appraises Benito Mussolini; unfortunately, this analysis applies to many administrators:

> If he did not become great it was because he let himself be drugged by a poison which is more dangerous than opium and hashish—by words. He talked so much and so often that at length he took his own words for reality and lost his contact with the real world. But reality is like God: it does not permit itself to be mocked.[14]

Consider, for example, how educators have polluted the word "democracy" in an attempt to apply a political concept to formal organizations which, by necessity, are based upon a rationale different from that which undergirds political institutions. Note, too, how administrators continue to use the fictitious distinction between line and staff as if staff personnel never do, in fact, carry the same force of authority as line personnel. In both these examples the words have been cut loose from their anchors in experience.

If we are to freshen our observations of organizational life, we somehow must rid ourselves of clichés, slogans, and meaningless words. Ironically, the less aware a superintendent is of the emptiness of his clichés, the more vehemently does he seem to brandish them. This hypnosis by words is one source of "the arrogance of the practical man" who knows what *he* knows and is having no part of anyone else's way of knowing. But he is not alone in arrogance; for totally different reasons, the theoretically oriented scientist flees from the reality of direct intuitive and observational experience. Deprived of the knowledge such direct experience can furnish, he becomes arrogant about the theoretical models he has constructed.

I conclude with the plea for a more tolerant, a more catholic view of various ways of knowing. I suggest that the crux of all science, of all practice, and of all wisdom lies in a careful, sensitive observation of what is indeed "out there." But it is easy to be blinded, whether by the slogans of the practitioners' work-a-day world or by the jargon of the scientists' never-never land.[15] How, then, can we break through? How can we learn to see what is "out there"? How can we learn to work more effectively with other human beings? How can we better understand the human heart? How can we sensitize ourselves to a wider range of knowing?

Here I shall perform the *coup de grâce* which I suppose will alienate me from the camps of both superintendents and scientists. In reiteration of my leitmotiv I suggest that if we are to learn how to observe—how to see what is "out there"—we had better avail ourselves of a rich heritage which superintendents and scientists alike have studiously ignored: the heritage of the humanities. For what else is the function of the poet, the playwright, and the novelist than to examine and describe the perplexing enigma of the human condition? Who other than the creative artist is better equipped to describe man "in the round"? But the man of letters has been discredited by the market place. To such extent that we as educators have adopted the standards of the market place we, too, have discredited him. The voices of the market place have pleaded for increased technical specialization, and the universities have responded with all the determination of an ambitious sales-man eager to give the customer precisely what he wants. This has resulted in a fragmentation of subject-matter areas in our univer-sities and, in turn, has led to intolerance among the disciplines about the ways of knowing peculiar to each area. Our society has given increasing rewards to men in the practical arts and the sciences. But the training in both areas has been incomplete. There was a time when a Ph.D. meant precisely that—a Doctor of Philosophy. A man who held the degree was expected to be con-versant with philosophy and with the humanities as well as with his specialty. I suggest that, without this broader education, the practical man and the scientist alike are poorly equipped to bring to their observations the freshness and the perspective which their disciplines demand. Fortunately this view of the role of the humanities in freshening our observation of the human condition is now gradually being recognized in business and industry. The most conspicuous example is the training program conducted by the Bell Telephone Company of Pennsylvania[16] (see Chapter 5). A recent evaluation of this program, after its first six years, shows that it does, indeed, achieve its objectives.[17] Similarly, Peter Drucker, professor of management at New York University, has noted the inestimable value of courses in creative writing for sharpening the observational skills of executives.[18]

With but few exceptions such as Joseph Wood Krutch and Lewis Mumford, the Renaissance Man has disappeared from our civilization—and we have suffered for it. Perhaps it is time that we, as educators, develop a new twentieth-century Renaissance Man, for without the wisdom of the humanities, I believe that the parochial ways of knowing so endemic to practitioner and scientist alike will prove increasingly crippling. We need a reaffirmation of intellectual tolerance, a recognition that "knowledge" about human beings, whether as individuals or as members of formal organizations cannot be secured cheaply and certainly not through the blandishments of a single discipline. Nor does this imply that we must retreat to a position of sloppy relativity in which each of us feels entitled to what he knows without responsibility for cross-checking his knowing with the knowing of others.

My plea is for a more balanced appreciation of various ways of knowing. In the present context we have touched upon only a few; we have not referred to knowing through faith or to the role of myth in our knowing.[19] Nor have we examined the "no-knowledge" of the East as advocated, for example, in Taoist philosophy.[20]

We must remember that it is impossible to appeal to a neutral principle to determine the rationality of competing systems. There must be intellectual tolerance. No matter what any of us may say, and no matter how infatuated we may become with our own sense of righteousness, we will achieve greater wisdom if we are gracious enough to temper our convictions with the admonition once given to Horatio: ". . . there are more things in heaven and earth . . . than are dreamt of in your philosophy."

NOTES FOR CHAPTER 6

1. From Roald F. Campbell and James M. Lipham (eds.), *Administrative Theory as a Guide to Action* (Chicago: Midwest Administration Center, University of Chicago, 1960), pp. 3-20. Reprinted by permission of the publishers. Delivered to the second seminar of the University Council for Educational Administration sponsored by the Midwest Administration Center, University of Chicago, in November 1959. Since that date, several authors have dealt with the theme of this chapter in greater detail than was appropriate for the audience to whom this paper was originally addressed. Two treatments of this theme should be especially noted: Jerome S. Bruner, *On Knowing: Essays for the Left Hand* (Cambridge, Mass.: Belknap Press of Harvard University Press, 1962); and "The Limitations of a Scientific Philosophy," Ch. 1 in Sir Herbert Read, *The Forms of Things Unknown* (New York: Horizon Press, 1960). But note, too, that the point of view presented here invites violent attack from many social scientists. For example, Jacob W. Getzels, certainly one of the most eminent educational psychologists in America, has written an exquisite indictment of the present chapter. See Jacob W. Getzels, "Theory and Practice in Educational Administration: An Old Question Revisited," Ch. 3 in Campbell and Lipham (eds.), *op. cit.*, pp. 37-39, in particular.

2. National Conference of Professors of Educational Administration, Cooperative Program in Educational Administration, and University Council for Educational Administration. For the relationship among these organizations, see Ch. 1.

3. Two books in particular serve as markers in the transition from the "old" to the "new" approach in graduate programs for educational administrators. The first is Roald F. Campbell and Russell T. Gregg (eds.), *Administrative Behavior in Education* (New York: Harper & Brothers, 1957); the second, Andrew W. Halpin (ed.), *Administrative Theory in Education* (Chicago: Midwest Administration Center, University of Chicago, 1958). The idea for the present conference came from the same thrust which produced these two books.

4. See note 1.

5. George C. Homans, *The Human Group* (New York: Harcourt, Brace & World, Inc., 1950), p. 15. Italics mine.

6. Erik H. Erikson, "The Nature of Clinical Evidence," *Daedalus,* **77** (Fall 1958), p. 87.

7. Edward T. Hall, *The Silent Language* (Garden City, N.Y.: Doubleday & Company, 1959). In the following section I have drawn freely from this book.

8. Chester I. Barnard, *The Functions of the Executive* (Cambridge, Mass.: Harvard University Press, 1938).

9. Jacob W. Getzels and Egon G. Guba, "Social Behavior and the Administrative Process," *The School Review,* **65** (Winter 1957), pp. 423-442.

10. See Ch. 3.

11. John Ciardi, "An Ulcer, Gentlemen, Is an Unwritten Poem," in Robert A. Goldwin and Charles A. Nelson (eds.), *Toward the Liberally Educated Executive* (White Plains, N.Y.: The Fund for Adult Education, 1957), pp. 54-55.

12. For example, John Cheever, *The Housebreaker of Shady Hill* (New York: Harper & Brothers, 1958).

13. The argument against this prejudice has been developed most perspicaciously by the French psychiatrist, Pierre Janet. See Elton Mayo, *Some Notes on the Psychology of Pierre Janet* (Cambridge, Mass.: Harvard University Press, 1958), especially pp. 99-101. If it is difficult to "see" human behavior, it is sometimes no less difficult to "see" physical events. For a superb example of how even a trained observer can fail to "see" what is "out there" when his vision has been distorted by his own preconception, examine the paintings and chromoliths of the Colorado River canyons made by artists who traveled through this region during the 1857-1880 period. Then compare these paintings with the meticulous observations of the explorer, John Wesley Powell. The paintings are reproduced in Wallace Stegner, *Beyond the 100th Meridian* (Boston: Houghton Mifflin Co., 1954), between pp. 92-93. Recall, too, the French public's first shocked reaction to the early impressionists because these artists saw "out there" colors and lines which the public had never before seen.

14. Frank Heller, *Twilight of the Gladiators,* trans. by Llewellyn Jones (New York: G. P. Putnam's Sons, 1944), p. 82.

15. As I read the work of some of my colleagues in the social sciences, I am reminded of Samuel Johnson's comment on Thomas Gray, whom he admired only for *The Elegy:* "He was dull in a new way, and that made many people think him GREAT."

16. See Ch. 1.

17. Morris S. Viteles, " 'Human Relations' and the 'Humanities' in the Education of Business Leaders: Evaluation of a Program of

Humanistic Studies for Executives," *Personnel Psychology,* **12** (Spring 1959), pp. 1-28.

18. See Ch. 1.

19. See, for example, the Spring 1959 issue of *Daedalus,* **82**, No. 2. The whole issue is devoted to the topic of "Myth and Myth-Making."

20. See, for example, Ch. 9 in R.G.H. Siu, *The Tao of Science* (New York: John Wiley & Sons, Inc., 1959). Note the dramatic insight of the book's subtitle: "An Essay on Western Knowledge and Eastern Wisdom."

7

A Rationale for Training
Research Workers[1]

In our time, science has gained tremendous prestige—but for the wrong reason. What we in America seem to have responded to most avidly have been the technological, and even the gimmicky, aspects of "science." Our zeal has been accompanied by only a remote understanding of the essential ideas that undergird all critical and creative inquiry. In the same way that we in America have bureaucratized corporate, governmental, and university life, we have also sought to bureaucratize research. The increasing federal and foundation aid to social science and educational research that has stimulated the research scene since World War II has been accompanied by several attendant evils, not the least of which is the virulent, contagious disease that now ravages many of our campuses: "projectitis." To have a research proposal approved by most fund-granting agencies, the investigator must stress design and must indicate what data will be gathered. Data are treated as so many units of production, almost as if they were automobiles on a production line. We have come to revere technique; I fear that, at times, substance has been sacrificed to method. We are guilty of what Lord Dunsany once described as the tendency to place technique above inspiration. He noted that if this notion were to spread we would have the diamond cutters valuing their tools more highly than the diamonds, with the result that, as long as they cut them in accordance with the rules of the craft, they would then cease to care whether they cut diamonds or glass, and finally would cease to know.

Far too many of us who aspire to be scientists miss the point that the foundation of creative inquiry lies in observation, in identifying what is "out there." I grant that such observation never can be random and always is more fertile when it has been guided by an explicitly stated theoretical formulation. But we must start with observation; all our techniques—including the clinical and the statistical—are just that: techniques. Yet no technique, no matter how elaborate, can pull important generalizations from raw data that are, themselves, not viable. We sometimes are in such a hurry to count things that we fail to take enough time to decide whether or not what we do count is, indeed, worth counting. This defect arises out of a misguided effort in education and the behavioral sciences to mimic the more prestigious physical and biological sciences. But the prestige of these older sciences has been earned not so much by the use of quantitative methods as through insightful, patient observation. As Feibleman has noted: "A scientist is not one who can see better but one who can watch more intensely."[2]

However rich any set of observations may be, they are useless to science and to mankind unless the investigator can communicate his findings to others. Thus J. Z. Young, professor of anatomy at the University of London, states, "Science consists in exact description of one's observations to other people."[3]

In other than a face-to-face situation there are only three languages by which one can communicate a description of events or experience to other people: by words, by numbers, or by pictures.[4] Irrespective of which of these three channels the scientist uses he must recognize that his language becomes an integral part of his behavior as a scientist, that his language is not merely an appendage to his "scientific" activity. Without endorsing to the hilt the Whorfian hypothesis, we must, nonetheless, accept Whorf's major conclusion that the language in which each of us is acculturated cuts up our perception of events and experiences in specific and limiting ways.[5] Indeed, the greatest benefit any one of us can derive from command of one or more foreign languages is the inexorable realization that language itself structures our experience, that our concept of reality is restricted in part by the very words that imprison us.

Since the structure of our language can distort our reporting of experience, and even can interfere with our apprehension of experience, I believe that the first unit in a course in research methods in education—or for that matter, in any of the social sciences—should be devoted to the topic "Language and Events." In an introductory course on research methods that I teach, I start the students with readings from Wendell Johnson's *People in Quandaries*[6] and Young's *Doubt and Certainty in Science*. I encourage the most competent students to acquaint themselves, too, with Cassirer's penetrating essay on "Science,"[7] and also to go directly to Korzybski.[8] I repeat Korzybski's theme: "Words are to events as maps are to territories."

Let it be noted, too, that in this course we also remind the students that words are man made; because a word exists we have no guarantee that there exists "out there" a "thing" that corresponds to the word.

Some of the logical positivists—even, for that matter, Percy Bridgman himself—have, to some extent, recanted. Bridgman, for example, is no longer as unreservedly enthusiastic about the value of operational definitions[9] as he was when he first discussed such definitions in *The Logic of Modern Physics*.[10] Yet at the present stage of our knowledge in educational research, I would rather see students err in the direction of insisting upon operational definitions than have them submit to the enticement of the vague, exhortatory slogans which characterize so much pap that masquerades as "research" in education.

Scientific advancement consists in finding ways of conceptualizing anew our experience. This means that one endeavor of science must be to define our experience in new terms—new language, unfettered by previous concepts and stereotypes. If man can make words, he also can unmake them. Or to state the point differently, man can eliminate from his vocabulary those words and concepts that create greater confusion than they are worth.

Having started the research methods course with a discussion of general semantics and having illustrated the advantages of using operational definitions, we next explicate the role of theory in research. We emphasize that theory must deal with "is's" not "ought's," and note why the models that we use can never be declared as either valid or invalid. The question of validity is irrelevant; the only relevant test is an heuristic one. Models are "as if" statements that we use to generate "if . . . then" statements which we can, then, test empirically.

Just before the curtain falls on Act I of the course, I deliver what usually turns out to be a telling blow: I suggest that language itself can be construed best as a theoretical model—an "as if" statement about experience and events. Furthermore, this "as if" statement must be subjected to continual revision.

The map can never be the same as the territory; the map is an abstraction designed for a specific purpose. Thus the language-map of the poet is not the same as the language-map of the scientist. This, of course, does not mean that one map is better than the other, only that each map is different from the other. To ask whether a map is "true" is silly; the relevant question is whether a given map is useful for a specific purpose at a specific time and at a given stage in our knowledge. This point of view comes as a distinct shock to many students who, for a long time, have enjoyed the spurious security that faith in the *word* seems to have afforded them. To illustrate how words can get between us and our experience, let me quote from Harold Taylor's excellent book, *Art and the Intellect:*

> The trouble is that most kinds of education are devoted to teaching students how not to be themselves, but instead how to cover up, how to gain enough knowledge, for example, in a survey course in Western civilization so that no one will ever know that you haven't read any of the authors or that you haven't ever really understood the works of art you were asked to observe. The usual kind of education—that is, the kind that is divided into courses, condensed into textbooks, put out in three lectures a week, tested by examinations, and rewarded by three academic credits a throw—is designed to give answers to questions which nobody asked and to inhibit the student in discovering his own truth and insight. The lectures and the texts do all that sort of thing for you. They provide a way in which the student can cover up his true self by finding a vocabulary acceptable to most people and a set of facts which are generally known among people generally considered to be generally educated.

Once this skill of covering up has been acquired, the student may never be called upon to say what he really thinks or feels at any point in his education or later life. This is what makes bores, and produces college graduates who are ignorant and dull, but successful and plausible.[11]

What I have been saying is simple: no man or woman can presume to do research unless he first becomes knowledgeable about the relation between language and events. Yet it is on this very point that most textbooks and courses in educational research have failed. Those authors start the student with techniques and "cook-book" recipes and assume—erroneously, I believe—that the student already understands the pitfalls of language and the essential nature of theory in science. Furthermore, the premature introduction of the student to technique tends to cripple his skill in observation. We already have too many scientists who choose their research topics not in terms of the importance of the domain but because techniques for measurement in the particular domain they choose happen to be available.

Such a situation recalls the story of the policeman who one evening discovered a drunk fumbling his way around a lamppost, evidently searching for something. The policeman asked the drunk, "Lose something?"

"Yep, my wallet."

"O.K. I'll help you find it."

After several minutes of diligent but unsuccessful searching around the lamppost, the policeman asked, "Are you *sure* you lost it here?"

"Who shed anything 'bout here? I losht it up the street."

"Then why in hell are we looking for it here?"

The drunk assumed a weaving posture of dignity and, with haughty condescension, replied: "More light!"

The issue for us is not one of "more light," but rather of "More light on what?" Technique as technique is not enough; we persistently must ask whether whatever technique we use is, indeed, applicable to the research task in hand.

I do not want to disparage the value of technique; I would like to see only that it be kept in perspective. The student should not be introduced to technique prematurely; instead, he should be made to understand that observation does come first. The student should discover how to observe events and experience and learn how to report these events free from verbal stereotypes. Alfred North Whitehead has stated the issue succinctly:

> My point is that a block in the assimilation of ideas inevitably arises when a discipline of precision is imposed before a stage of romance has run its course in the growing mind. There is no comprehension apart from romance.[12]

To help our students freshen their observations, we had better rid ourselves of some illusions. We must quit thinking of research as research with a capital R. Instead, we should seek to encourage creative and critical inquiry without being concerned obsessively with a form of empiricism that is ridden with what Whitehead has called the error of "misplaced concreteness."[13] Let me offer two examples of perspicacious observation. In the first example the observer is a distinguished historian; in the second, a great novelist.

Raymond Aron, professor in the Faculty of Letters at the University of Paris has recently published an exquisite study on "The Situation of Democracy," in which he compares the history of Western political institutions in the twentieth century.[14] He reports not a blessed standard deviation or Pearsonian correlation, not even a mean! Yet here I find a rich mine of concepts that can be extrapolated from nations to formal organizations. Why, Aron asks, do some nations provide a stable base for the development of a democracy, whereas others do not? Why, for example, do we discover in the Latin American nations a history which shifts between populist democracies and military dictatorships? Aron gives us a host of provocative cues for new concepts in the study of administration, for new ways of conceptualizing the dimensions of organizations.

He reports, in particular, new dimensions by which we can more accurately describe a democracy. With the guide of Aron's reasoning, it requires no wild leap of the imagination to see why many organizations—school systems, and even universities—reveal a history of organizational policy characterized by wide and repetitive swings from one extreme to another similar to those found in Latin American countries. Aron's skill, in short, is his skill in observing, in not being blinded by the filter of words which obfuscates the vision of so many of us.

The second example of clear-sighted observation is that of the Irish novelist, Lawrence Durrell, whose brilliance is vividly displayed in his tetralogy, *The Alexandria Quartet*.[15] His topic is love in our times—actually, love in any time.

In the first book of the tetralogy, *Justine,* Durrell tells the story of the infatuation of Darley, a young teacher, with Justine, the wife of a wealthy and politically influential Egyptian. At the end of the first volume, Darley gives his manuscript—that is, *Justine*—to one of the characters in the story, Balthazar.

In the second volume, *Balthazar,* Durrell has Balthazar return the manuscript to Darley, with corrections. In effect Balthazar says, "You are all wrong. It wasn't that way at all. Justine was not in love with you. You were only a 'cover' for her affair with somebody else." So the second volume deals with the same material as the first, but with the events seen through the eyes of a different character.

In the third volume, *Mountolive,* Durrell relates the life of Mountolive, a British diplomat. Darley, Justine, and the major characters of the first two volumes do not enter the story until about half way through the book. The same events are then viewed through a third pair of eyes. The first three volumes end at about the same point in time; only in the fourth and final volume, *Clea,* does the story move forward in time. Yet even at the conclusion of the tetralogy the reader is not certain which version of events is "true"—in a sense, they all are.

I urge students to read Durrell if only to shatter many of their verbal and perceptual stereotypes, to let them watch Durrell demonstrate the complete "as if" quality of every man's perception of his own experience.

At this point, a few colleagues must be wondering, "But what about objectivity?" To them I reply, "Let us quit deceiving ourselves." No scientist is nearly as objective as he pretends to be or would like to believe that he is. Note, for example, recent studies by Rosenthal and his colleagues at the University of North Dakota.[16] These investigators have shown how, even in simple laboratory experiments, experimenters are able to obtain from their human or their animal subjects precisely the data the experimenter wants, needs, or expects to get. Indeed, I respect objectivity, but I resent the blind, compulsive pursuit of it, especially if, in this pursuit, we deceive ourselves. It is past time for us to ask why some of our colleagues persist in doing meticulous, "objective" research on arid topics.

Consider the instance of a professor who enjoys a national reputation in the field of educational research—a man who does excellent research on learning. Yet, when one of his ablest graduate students proposed to him a Master's thesis in which she sought to study certain attributes of a national sample of elementary school principals, he courageously said, "If you find what you think you will, do you really think it is a good idea for you to do a thesis that may reflect against the teaching profession?" The student demurred and naïvely declared that she thought science was dedicated to a disinterested search for truth. He replied: "You do plan to take your Ph.D. in this department, don't you?"

I propose that we bring fresh observation to the entire issue of objectivity. I endorse objectivity, but I deplore the fraud of insisting upon objectivity in dealing with trivia while we slyly smuggle into the system errant subjectivity in respect to the central issue of what topics we do study. The subjectivity that enters into our choice of what topics we study is the most dangerous form of subjectivity, for it involves not a picayune question—for example, that of inter-rater reliability—but a question of far greater import: the morality of the investigator. Does he have the courage to study what is really worth studying? This aspect of subjectivity—the morality of the investigator—is one that should worry us all.

But when we move to the question of subjectivity in respect to technique, the scene changes. I grant that dependable (that is, reliable) measures are desirable, yet I refuse to get frightened by the introduction of subjective elements in research. I fear that much of the effort made to reduce subjectivity is futile. On this score, I believe that more of us need to follow the sweep of the exciting argument presented by Michael Polyani, originally a physical chemist and now a social scientist and philosopher. In his monumental book *Personal Knowledge,*[17] Polyani rejects completely the ideal of scientific detachment. He declares that knowing as an act of comprehension involves a change in the person carrying out the comprehension. Accordingly, comprehension must remain non-critical in that there exists no permanently fixed framework within which a critical testing of that comprehension can take place.

In science as well as in other areas of living, there are times when we must have the courage to take a gambler's risk. At certain junctures I would be willing to risk slightly less objectivity, were I to see a chance to gain richer human insight and fresher observation. Of course I would not have us resort solely to feelings, and certainly not at the expense of intellectual rigor. A scientist cannot afford to adopt the stand of Iphigenia in Goethe's play: "Ich untersuche nicht, ich fühle nur."[18]

No, I would not have us become Iphigenias. But I will wager that it is a touch of Iphigenia—a controlled touch, perhaps, yet a touch of Iphigenia—that gives Ross Mooney his creative insight into the nature of research. Anyone who has been privileged to read the opening chapter of the book Ross Mooney is now writing[19] will sense immediately that here is a warm, sensitive human being, attuned to man's aesthetic impulse. Nor do I consider it accidental that a research scholar as distinguished as Jacob W. Getzels should have done his early graduate work in comparative literature and should possess a discriminating taste in art. Yet I suppose I should remember, too, that Iphigenia was sacrificed to Artemis, the goddess of wildlife and hunting, and that even today the Iphigenias are placed at the mercy of hunters: faculty committees.

Conversely, I look at the work of other research investigators—men who are industrious and exacting but whose inquiries are mundane and whose findings are passionless. Let me return to the learning-experiment professor I referred to earlier. One day he drew himself up to his full height of high dudgeon to declare to me: "I have never read a novel." Men who take such pride in their cultural illiteracy have turned the art of science into a business. I pity them.

Over and over again I find that the scientists whose work I admire most are men who are at home not alone in the sciences, but in the arts and the humanities as well. Why? Because the essential human quality that enables a man to engage in creative inquiry is sensibility. Accordingly, I quote the conclusion of Harold Taylor:

> It is for this reason that the arts, since they have most directly to do with the development of sensibility, are an essential component of all learning, including scientific learning.[20]

The temper of the scientist must become more and more akin to that of the artist, not to that of the businessman and the production engineer. No longer can we, as civilized human beings, afford what C. P. Snow, the physicist and novelist, has referred to as the tragedy of *The Two Cultures*.[21]

How long, I wonder, will it take us to learn that the model of the physical and biological sciences may be the wrong one for us in education to ape? Since the events with which educators must deal are human events, they have closest affinity to the spheres of the philosopher, the poet, and the novelist. Too many orthodox psychologists are rigid; they are quick to treat with disdain any knowledge other than that which is empirical. But consider the relevance of the insightful analysis of the logic and language of teaching that recently has been reported by Bob Gowin at the University of Chicago.[22] Also, study *Language and Concepts of Education,* edited by Smith and Ennis, and read especially the chapter by Smith entitled, "A Concept of Teaching."[23] In these instances we discover compelling evidence of the unique contribution that logical and philosophical inquiry can make to educational research.

Yet we cannot rely upon the final stability of logical analysis any more than we can trust a naked empiricism. The mathematician Gödel, in his startling theorem,[24] has demonstrated wholly unsuspected and staggering imperfections in any system of deductive logic. He has shown that it is theoretically impossible to prove the consistency of any set of postulates which is, so to speak, rich enough in content to be interesting. The question, "Is there an inner flaw in this system?" is simply unanswerable.

Let me reiterate now in a slightly contrapuntal way, the themes that I have been seeking to develop. In short, let me suggest four specific, yet broad ways by which we can improve the quality of educational research.

First, we must enlarge the pool from which we draw trainees; I would secure young men and women who have a broad, liberal arts training and who, therefore, are likely to be more sensitive to the nuances of the human condition. Part of our difficulty is that the present system is rigged so that we discourage from research careers in education some of our ablest undergraduates. There is nothing to be gained by belaboring the point that most of us already know: many of our brightest undergraduates get discouraged by the banality of courses in education; they flee from our ranks. To attract to our profession bright young men and women who will make creative contributions to educational research, we must improve our undergraduate program. Not the least task in this respect is to rid our colleges of education of their surplus of "old maid" professors—of both sexes.

The second job is to improve the morality of those professors responsible for the training of research workers. Young people seek to emulate men whom they can respect. But I fear that the image of morality created by many professors is not one we would like our students to copy. For example, the amusement with which a professor refers to graduate students as a supply of cheap "slave labor" does not change the intrinsic, exploitative attitude that prompts him to make such a remark. On my first research job, the senior investigator blandly told me, "I'm exploiting you, Halpin. Of course. I know it. But that's all right; later on you'll get your chance. You'll have some graduate students of your own, and you'll get your chance to exploit them." This attitude sets up a shabby example of morality. We had better realize that a professor's responsibility is to liberate the creative capacity of the young research people who work with him. And we had better police our ranks to eliminate those men who use their positions not to liberate the young, but to exploit them.

Third, we need to examine the institutional arrangements within which research is conducted. Research in our universities has become Big Business. The universities are eager to have professors secure "outside" money. Nor is it without significance that when a contract has been negotiated the university's comptroller *immediately* deducts from the allotment the university's own "cut" for the project. In the case of "cooperative" contracts where the institution is supposed to make a matching contribution, it certainly is no secret that much of the "matching" money is, in effect, only "money on paper," and that the amount does not represent actual funds set aside in a separate account for this purpose. The investigator and the contracting agency are forced to engage in a conspiracy of silence about these shenanigans. Here again we encounter a procedure of dubious morality. How do we overcome it? I suggest that in some way the universities, themselves, need to be coerced into assuming greater responsibility for providing research funds on their own. Perhaps one criterion for deciding whether funds should be granted to a university by an outside agency would be an index of the amount of research funds that the university provides, entirely on its own, for its own research personnel. For example, personnel on research projects, particularly those people who do not hold faculty rank, frequently are viewed by the university as peripheral, if not indeed, expendable employees. What happens, for example, when a gap in time occurs between two research projects? Does the university itself pay the personnel so that competent people can be kept on the campus until a new contract is negotiated? I expect we know what usually happens.

The young people who work within institutional arrangements such as we now have quickly learn that research is a "dog-eat-dog" affair. Because the university itself is loath to assume full social responsibility to these young people as human beings, they, in turn, tend to become cynical and at times, I regret, even predatory. I doubt that this is a healthy atmosphere for developing creative scientists.

Fourth and last, we need to examine the sponsorship for educational research. The Cooperative Research Program of the United States Office of Education has been a boon to all of us. Yet, I am disturbed that we in educational research are forced to rely—for the most part—upon a single, major source of research support. The "portfolio" is not diversified enough.

Furthermore, we should examine another central danger in the entire project-proposal activity. Hans Selye, perhaps the most eminent endocrinologist alive today, remarked at a recent conference, "The research studies that you can put into proposal form for a government contract are probably the ones that are not worth doing in the first place." Perhaps Selye exaggerates, but, nonetheless, there is a vital point in his riposte: too much of our research endeavor encourages *activity* at the cost of creativity. It seems that we are afraid to support a man simply to give him a chance to think. I would like to see a few government agencies and foundations show enough courage to underwrite researchers without restricting them by any form of contractual commitment. An outstanding exception to the indictment I have made is the Center for Advanced Study in the Behavioral Sciences. Another research agency that shows a sophisticated respect for the "care and feeding of researchers" is the Office of Naval Research.

The man with a business outlook usually is aghast at the suggestion of giving anyone such a blank, signed check. His first rejoinder is, "How can we be sure that the man will work? If we pay him this way, maybe he'll simply take a vacation or retire." To this I can respond best with a comment made by Andrew Wyeth, one of our most gifted, contemporary American artists: "If I can't paint, I die." Likewise, creative research investigators are, indeed, "driven"; they can no more refrain from doing research than can a nightingale refuse to sing.

To those who think that my suggestion is impractical I would say that probably the price of a single B-70, placed instead into an endowment fund, could pay the salaries of a solid core of capable research workers for the rest of their lives. But here again the decision of how we, as Americans, spend our resources is a moral one. Do we want to spend the bulk of our resources with the tacit assumption that war is inevitable?[25] Or are we willing to devote a moiety of these funds to a few human beings who embrace a more hopeful view for mankind?

In making these proposals for the training of research workers, I know that I invite criticism for emphasizing so strongly the importance of feeling, as well as that of intellect. I do not intend to disparage intellect. A competent research worker requires skill in conceptual thinking. Indeed, I do not care to accept as an advanced graduate student an applicant who scores below a reasonably high critical level on the Miller Analogies Test. But intellect is not enough, especially if it is rooted in an arid personality. We have inducted into our graduate training programs too many young men and women who are so dedicated to intellectualism and objectivity that they deny their own emotional impulses and also shut off from themselves a whole range of aesthetic experience. Literally, such people are *deformed*. I prefer to encourage into scientific careers men and women who are at least whole human beings.

NOTES FOR CHAPTER 7

1. Presented at two seminars on research sponsored by the University Council for Educational Administration—May 10, 1961, at the University of Chicago; and August 30, 1961, at the University of California at Berkeley. Published as Ch. 19 in Jack A. Culbertson and Stephen P. Hencley (eds.), *Educational Research: New Perspectives* (Danville, Ill.: Interstate Printers & Publishers, Inc., 1963), pp. 311-324. Reprinted by permission of the publisher and with concurrence from the University Council for Educational Administration.
2. James K. Feibleman, "The Psychology of the Scientists," *Synthese*, 12, No. 1 March 1960), p. 90.
3. John Z. Young, *Doubt and Certainty in Science* (Oxford: Clarendon Press, 1953), p. 102.
4. In face-to-face situations we must also deal with a wide range of "muted language." See, for example, Ch. 5.
5. Benjamin Lee Whorf, *Language, Thought and Reality* (Cambridge, Mass.: The Massachusetts Institute of Technology Press, 1956).
6. Wendell Johnson, *People in Quandaries* (New York: Harper & Brothers, 1946).
7. Ernst Cassirer, *An Essay on Man* (New Haven, Conn.: Yale University Press, 1944), pp. 208-209.
8. Alfred Korzybski, *Science and Sanity*, 3rd ed. (Lakeville, Conn.: The International Non-Aristotelian Library Publishing Co., 1948).

9. Percy Bridgman, *The Way Things Are* (Cambridge, Mass.: Harvard University Press, 1959).

10. Percy Bridgman, *The Logic of Modern Physics* (New York: The Macmillan Company, 1927), pp. 3-9.

11. Harold Taylor, *Art and the Intellect* (New York: The Museum of Modern Art, 1960. Distributed by Doubleday & Company, Garden City, N.Y.), pp. 20-21. Reprinted by permission of The Museum of Modern Art.

12. Alfred North Whitehead, *The Aims of Education* (New York: The Macmillan Company, 1929), p. 52.

13. Alfred North Whitehead, *Science and the Modern World* (New York: The New American Library, Mentor Books, 1949), p. 52.

14. Raymond Aron, "The Situation of Democracy," *Daedalus,* **90**, No. 2 (Spring 1961), pp. 350-370.

15. Lawrence Durrell, *The Alexandria Quartet: Justine* (1957), *Balthazar* (1958), *Mountolive* (1959), and *Clea* (1960) (New York: E. P. Dutton Company).

16. Robert Rosenthal, Kermit L. Fode, C. Jack Friedman, and Linda L. Vikan, "Subjects' Perception of Their Experimenter Under Conditions of Experimenter Bias," *Perceptual and Motor Skills,* **11** (1960), pp. 325-331.

17. Michael Polyani, *Personal Knowledge* (Chicago: University of Chicago Press, 1958).

18. Johann W. von Goethe, *Iphigenie auf Tauris,* ed. by Philip Schuyler Allen (New York: Ginn and Company, 1906), Act. IV, Sc. 1, line 1650.

19. This book, as yet untitled, will deal with the nature of creative inquiry. See also Ross Mooney, "Training for Research in Educational Administration: A Rationale," Ch. 20 in Culbertson and Hencley (eds.), *Educational Research.*

20. Taylor, *Art and the Intellect.*

21. Charles Percy Snow, *The Two Cultures* (London: Cambridge University Press, 1959).

22. Bob D. Gowin, "Teaching—Its Logic and Its Language," *Elementary School Journal,* **61**, No. 4 (1961), pp. 179-190.

23. Othanel B. Smith and Robert H. Ennis (eds), *Language and Concepts of Education* (Chicago: Rand McNally and Company, 1961).

24. Ernest Nagel and James R. Newman, *Gödel's Proof* (New York: New York University Press, 1958).

25. One of the few men who has challenged this assumption is Henry A. Murray, distinguished professor of psychology at Harvard. See Henry A. Murray, "Unprecedented Evolution," *Daedalus*, **90**, No. 3 (Summer 1961), pp. 547-569.

8

The Dissemination of Research
Findings in Education[1]

To plead for the greater dissemination of research findings in education is to enjoy cozy harborage beneath the wings of angels because everybody applauds such a plea even as everybody cheers for God, Country, and Mother. The slogan—"the dissemination of research findings in education"—is unbeatable. We in America may not always be sure what education should be; some of us, indeed, may conspire to degrade the college degree into little more than a passport to suburbia. Yet we are "all for education." And pity the parent, the legislator, or the admiral who dares to question our budgets, our competence, or our motives.

No Brahma cow is more slavishly hallowed than is our "idea" of research. Yet, as Woodruff has noted, the role of research in education is still only foggily conceived:

> Educational research is a phrase that currently stands for everything from the use of reference books by elementary-school pupils to the most rigorous and systematic experimentation by trained personnel. A great deal of what passes as educational research is of extremely doubtful validity. Although a subjective version of research literally runs wild among administrative and teaching personnel, the role of good research in education is still undefined.[2]

Of course, many weird activities get designated by the name of "research," for in contemporary America we delight in "upgrading" everything. Every cramped, jerry-built ranch-house in the brash, new suburban development of Futility Acres is described as an "estate." The regular-sized box of detergent on the super-market shelf is described as the "SUPER" size, while the slightly larger size is identified as the "EXTRA GIANT SIZE." You will have noticed that the detergent is purchased not in a market, but in a "super"-market. Similarly, an art teacher's anecdotal report—biased and scarcely literate—of how he has enriched his students' experience by teaching them cartooning is upgraded and "dignified" by the name of research.[3]

In education we have become proficient in justifying the debasement of research. We console ourselves with the notion that "not all research has to be statistical; some of it can be simply 'descriptive'."[4] And we always have recourse to that seductive formula, "action research." As I observe what occurs in our colleges of education in the name of research, I am repeatedly amazed at our capacity for self-deception.

Finally, who would be foolhardy enough to question the value of "disseminating" information? In a society that fosters "communication engineers" and that, at every turn, assaults our eyes and our ears with vulgar commercials, it is sacrilegious to suggest that communication, per se, is not a sacrosanct end. It is therefore not surprising that we encounter in education the naïve assumption that if only we could disseminate research findings effectively enough, and could disseminate them to a wide enough audience, rapid and constructive changes would promptly take place in our schools. I fear that much of this effort proves to be a case of artificial dissemination.

If we are to progress at all in making research more viable, we must recognize slogans for what they are and we must rid ourselves of them. Often, when we seek to identify the realities which the slogans presumably represent, we find ourselves beleaguered by amorphous concepts.

At this point I cannot get too excited about the failure to disseminate research findings in education. We suffer less from a poverty of findings than from the lack of sufficient courage to act upon those findings that we do possess. For example, our state colleges and universities are plagued by a high incidence of student failure during the freshman year. This rate fluctuates little from year to year and we have at hand, even now, reasonably accurate means for predicting which students will fail. Yet, for political reasons, university administrators persistently maintain that every graduate of a state high school has the right and the privilege of attending a state university.[5] This privilege includes, of course, the privilege of foredoomed failure at the cost not alone of heartbreak for the student, but also of the pointless expenditure of scarce tax funds.

Likewise, at the national level we currently hear vociferous laments about the teaching of English. Indeed, the United States Office of Education is currently sponsoring a broad research program in this area: Project English. Here again, I believe that the issue is less a need for more research than it is a need for courage to act upon our present knowledge. If we want to raise the students' standards of English, then there is one obvious way to do it: raise the standards and raise them immediately. But we must *really* mean it, and the students must know that we mean it. The blunt fact, then, is that students who fall short of the standards will be failed and, if necessary, failed repeatedly, irrespective of whether their parents can, or cannot, exert pressure on the Board.

But who shall help us enforce these standards? Here we discover a situation so embarrassing that some professors of education would prefer to deny or repress available information; it reflects too unfavorably upon the teaching profession itself. The information is stark and simple: a significant proportion of the teachers in our public schools and universities mangle the English language.

Let me give a specific example of "standards" in English, as displayed by a group of school administrators. Marcella Miller has analyzed the written compositions of a national sample of 232 elementary school principals.[6] In each 100 written words the men made 4.8 grammatical errors; the women, 3.6. Several principals wrote 250-word compositions that contained only two or three genuine sentences; the remainder of each composition was jammed with sentence fragments. Roughly 78 per cent of the words that the principals used were among the first 1000 most frequently used words in the language. On a measure of linguistic flexibility[7] these principals scored lower than a sample of college freshmen and lower, indeed, than a sample of schizophrenics. On an index of the use of subordination in sentence structure (the use of dependent predicates and other forms of complex sentences), the principals scored below the level reported elsewhere for a sample of students in grades four through eight.

Here is our plight. If our students are to respect standards in English and to achieve effective communication, we must train personnel—administrators, teachers, and professors—to recognize such standards. It is no accident that our colleagues in the colleges of liberal arts refer to the jargon of educators as "pedagese." Nor will I accept the counterargument of those of my colleagues in education who say, "I have read some papers in the liberal arts college and they, too, are bad." The point is that we are teachers and, as such, we have accepted responsibility for setting high standards for ourselves and for others. The time is past for seeking to justify relativistic and elastic standards. We must admit the fact that our society will continue to produce generations of high school and college students who use sloppy English just as long as we continue to graduate and hire teachers who themselves use sloppy English.

I have dealt at length with these two examples—that of drop-outs among college freshmen and that of poor standards in the teaching of English—in order to emphasize that what we need is not more research or even a wider dissemination of present findings. We need only the courage to act on what we already know.

Whenever we reach such a schism between knowledge and action, it is fascinating to observe the regularity with which some professor or superintendent introduces an all too familiar ploy designed to immobilize any constructive effort for action. The ploy is this: "But after all, we *really* don't have enough information yet. We need more research on the subject." This technique uses the plea for "further research" as a delaying tactic in the same way that a wily administrator assigns a sticky problem to a committee "for study and action," knowing full well that the problem will get buried in committee, and that he thus will be relieved of responsibility for acting upon it.

Furthermore, I suspect that our drive to disseminate more and more information has an anxiety-relieving function; constant pressure to disseminate helps us to feel that we are *doing* something, and thus relieves us of the responsibility of facing up to our failure to act—a failure due not at all to a lack of research evidence, but solely to our own obeisance to political expediency.

There is another reason why I cannot get excited about the failure to disseminate research findings in education: many of the so-called findings are not worth disseminating. Indeed, the general quality of research in education is so inferior that I feel we had better attack the question of research standards before we worry too much about disseminating findings that possess only dubious dependability.

This is a good juncture at which to clarify a point that might otherwise be misconstrued as a contradiction. I have declared, first, that in education we do not suffer from a dearth of research findings but lack the courage to act on those findings which we do have. I also have said that I cannot be too concerned about the failure to disseminate research findings because many of the alleged findings we seek to disseminate are not worth disseminating. Paradoxically enough, both statements are true. To explicate this paradox we must examine the difference between the training of professors of education in the 1920's and 1930's, as compared with the training of present professors.

Our major legacy of findings in educational research comes to us from the period of the 1920's and the 1930's. Men of the caliber of Thorndike, Gates, Buswell, Symonds, and Pressey—to mention only a few names and to make no attempt at ranking them—enjoyed the advantage in their own graduate work of rigorous, "tight," and uncompromising research training. Also, they secured this training outside of colleges of education. In turn, these men introduced their own students to the same research tradition. Many students of this first generation, after they received their Ph.D.'s, were fortunate in being able to work in settings that made it possible for them to maintain the tradition. (Lorge, a direct heir of Thorndike, was a superb example.) But more than this, they had the courage to demand high research standards of their own students, no matter how disgracefully their colleagues in other parts of the college might allow standards to sag. But there were others of this same generation, especially during the depression years, who had to settle for jobs at Catatonic State Teachers' College. Here they found that few of their colleagues understood, let alone respected, a tradition of research. Because jobs were scarce, these new members of the Catatonic faculty decided that it was expedient for them to adjust to the local mores. And gradually, as they ceased to do research themselves and let poorer and poorer students slide by, they found themselves in the position where, piously as they might prattle about research, their own behavior made it starkly clear to their students that research was to be construed as merely an exercise.

Meanwhile, enrollments in colleges of education across the country increased as more and more teachers and administrators felt that they *must* get an M.A., an Ed.D. or a Ph.D. But at the same time that the demand for the degrees increased, the supply of professors who themselves had been trained in a solid research tradition decreased at an infernal rate. By now we have reached a point where the majority of our present professors of education simply are not competent in research. Whatever they do teach about research can be described best as derivative; it is not intrinsic to their own experience and knowledge. In colloquial language, what these professors do in the name of research is not "for real."

The entire picture is not dismal, for certainly there are men today whose competence equals or exceeds that of any of their predecessors, and who can more than hold their own in any group of social scientists. For example, one thinks of men such as Cronbach, Getzels, Ryans, Thelen, Robert Thorndike, and Torrance—to mention a few names and, again, with no intention of ranking. One must also take into account men not affiliated with colleges of education, whose research findings are of extreme importance for education: Hemphill and Calvin Taylor are cases in point. Even today we can find departments, colleges, or schools of education in which a great tradition of research is respected and lived up to in every way. Certainly anyone who spends even a few hours in Judd Hall at the University of Chicago quickly senses the central and viable role of research at that institution. The entire picture is not dismal, but neither is the prospect for the future encouraging. The pathetic point is that one finds few other colleges of education that maintain a research tradition like that found at the University of Chicago. Similarly, when one looks at university bureaus of educational research, institutions such as the University of Indiana, the University of Illinois, The Ohio State University, and the University of Minnesota stand out prominently. But whether we look at the men who are producing top-quality research, at the universities which support a strong research tradition, or at those bureaus of educational research that operate constructive programs, we encounter the same situation: a few highly visible names at the top of each group are prominent, but then the list diminishes rapidly. Nor do we find a smooth, continuous distribution of quality; rather, we are faced by a chasm between the great and the mediocre.[8]

A research tradition in a university can never be made viable unless it is supported by a majority of the senior members of the faculty. A common and a serious mistake made by many deans is to appoint a professor who is charged with the responsibility for upgrading research standards in a department or a college of education. The faculty usually concurs in the man's appointment at the time because, to a man, they are, at least verbally, in favor both of research and of high standards. But when the new professor does indeed try to do what he has been charged to do, he quickly finds himself viewed merely as a gatekeeper. And then, both the graduate students and the other professors devise ingenious stratagems for getting the students past the gatekeeper. Those professors who have never done a respectable piece of research in their lives and who incur violent psychosomatic symptoms at the very thought of bringing their own knowledge of research up to date by reading a few books, suffer embarrassment in their classes at questions raised by able students who have learned, from the research professor, modern ways of conceptualizing and attacking research tasks. Nagged by their own embarrassment, these professors next seek to punish the research professor, either by isolating him or by extruding him from their midst.

Let me illustrate this deplorable situation by three examples chosen from different parts of the country. About a decade ago, the school of education of a major western university appointed a professor who was assigned to teach courses in research methods and statistics required of all graduate students. The professor is a well-trained man who has exacted high standards. Because the first letter of his name happens to be "C.," the Ed.D. alumni now categorize themselves as having taken their degrees either B.C.— that is, "Before C.," or A.C.—"After C." The excruciating point in this instance is that the professors in one of the departments actually jest with the students about this "A.C." versus "B.C." joke. The jest is highly symptomatic; these professors fail to give "C." full support in that they become party to the students' game of how to devise a dissertation that will most painlessly get them past Professor "C."

The second illustration comes from another university, on the east coast. The professor concerned, who also gives a research methods class required of all graduate students in the school of education, has stated to me in a personal letter:

> You might be interested to know that I made a resolution this summer not to write any more articles critical of education. They take time and effort, and their effect is not worth the time and effort; few people seem to pay any attention to articles that are critical of education and that are, at the same time, written within the profession. . . .
>
> I'm trying to avoid being any more discouraged than I have been in the past by the utter lack of understanding by educators of what might be called an intellectual revolution. Last year I even wrote an appeal to our faculty . . . on the cultural or academic lag which we should do something about. It got almost nowhere. It made a slight impression, but very slight, I'm afraid. So, I'm viewed with a bit of hostile or affectionate suspicion, depending on the personal feelings of the particular colleague involved.[9]

The third illustration is taken from a state university situated between the two coasts. A professor was appointed a few years ago to give a research methods course required of all graduate students, and to upgrade the research standards within the college of education. It did not take too long for his colleagues to denounce him for trying to exact standards that were "too high" and for failing to "adjust to the local mores." Several graduate students who dread a tight course of any kind have now for two years delayed taking the research methods course that this professor offers, hoping that he will leave. The department chairman recently solved the students' problem: this quarter the course is being taught by another man—a man who has published nothing in any research journal but who does "understand the local mores."

Incidents such as these are being repeated in all parts of the country. They are relevant in the present context for an obvious reason: it is pointless for us to try to disseminate research findings in education unless we first equip people to understand the meaning of research and to comprehend research findings. If members of the teaching profession fail to secure a solid foundation in research or fail to gain a modicum of respect for it during their graduate training, I do not know where or how we can expect them to secure such an understanding once they have left the university.

I repeat that if we are to disseminate research findings in education we first must produce a wide audience that understands the structure of scientific thought. With rare exceptions we do not possess such an audience in education today; in their training and experience, our teachers and administrators have been shielded from solid instruction in the philosophy and the language of science. How many men are there, indeed, to teach them? As I listen to many professors of education, I am shocked at their ignorance of the nature of scientific thought, of what constitutes competent research. Yet men who themselves have never published a creditable study in a respectable research journal, guilelessly teach courses on research methods in education and have the audacity to direct master's theses and doctoral dissertations. This is tantamount to having a man teach art who has himself never painted a canvas, or who, indeed, cannot discriminate between "calendar" art and the work of a Matisse or a Wyeth. The result of this procedure is to sanction mediocrity and to inculcate in students the belief that research is just a necessary hurdle that one must jump to secure the degree that will put one up a further notch on the salary scale.

Many professors reinforce these negative attitudes through their own conspiracy of silence that fails to damn as shoddy much of the material that their students and colleagues perpetrate in the name of research. A great portion of that material does not deserve to be disseminated, and the students know this. For the most part, training in research in our colleges of education has become a farce. And even if an occasional student does manage, in spite of the system, to learn how to do competent research, what reward does he find in a school system? He receives scant encouragement. Indeed, if he insists that educational decisions be based upon research findings, he may even imperil his job. Why?

I suggest that there are two major factors which contribute to this impasse. The first is that the objectives of education are unclear and that its avowed purposes, even to such extent that they are clear, fail to receive unequivocal support from our society. The second reason for the impasse is that public education is a virtual monopoly in most American communities. Let us examine each of these points in turn.

The objectives of education are not clear because we have tried to make the school mean all things to all people. To the parent who insists upon high standards of scholarship for his children we say that we *are* maintaining high standards; conversely, to the parent who is concerned mainly with the social and personal adjustment of his children we say that this *adjustment* is our primary concern. To one parent we say that we are selective; to another, that we are, indeed, "democratic" in "meeting the needs" of every child at whatever level. We insist that we are dedicated to quality *and* quantity and seldom do we recognize the utter absurdity of this claim.

In America's status-obsessed society the school has become the individual's foremost social escalator for "getting ahead." Whether a person becomes "educated" or not is irrelevant. What he seeks is a seal of approval that presumably will allow him to compete more effectively in the job market. This situation has reached such a stage of travesty that some employers advertise in the newspaper for a "college-type man." This does not mean that the applicant even needs to have attended college, but he must look the part and dress conservatively for the part.

In our graduate schools of education, for example, we declaim publicly that we maintain high standards. But because a professor's effectiveness is too frequently measured by the number of people that attend his class to be exposed to his dubious wisdom, most professors lack the courage to extirpate from their midst those students who are intellectually unfit and who grace—or disgrace—the campuses for reasons that have nothing whatsoever to do with the purpose of a university.

Indeed, it is instructive to compare the research situation in education with what we find in medicine or in the defense establishment.

In medicine the purpose of the physician is clear: to improve the health and prolong the life of his patient. If the physician fails consistently, he soon finds himself without patients. If he is too grossly incompetent, or if he violates the ethics of his profession, his colleagues may restrain him. To stay in business he must keep abreast of new research developments in his field and he must be able to deal directly with new research evidence—without the aid of an interpreter or a middleman. The physician's purpose, of course, receives unequivocal endorsement from society.

The defense establishment too has a clear purpose: to protect our nation against a potential enemy. Here again, our society gives unequivocal support to this mandate; moreover, the role of research in this effort—as in the space and missile programs, for example—is abundantly evident to all Americans. The industries that support the nation's defense programs vie with each other to produce better and more efficient equipment. The competition for research "brains" is vigorous and, at times, almost piratical.

There is an obvious difference between the reliance placed on research in medicine and defense, as compared to the cavalier treatment it receives in education.

This brings us to the second reason for the impasse we face: education is a virtual monopoly in most American communities. In respect to this monopoly, we need only note the difference between a school and any private industry. For example, if I should open a small factory producing a new household gadget, it behooves me to make my product, at its price, as good, if not better, than the product of my competitors. Furthermore, it is quite possible that I shall encounter competition on a national, rather than a strictly local, basis. If, as president of the company, I should fail to show sufficient profit to meet my payroll and to declare dividends, I probably would have to resign. If my handling of the business is too sloppy, the organization will go bankrupt, and I will lose whatever capital I have invested in it.

Not so in education!

Whether an administrator and a staff operate a good school or an inadequate one, the school still stays in business. Win, lose, or draw, the superintendent will undoubtedly keep his job. Superintendents do get fired, but usually for political reasons—that is, for failing to please the "right" powers in the community, rather than for failing to provide the children with an educational program of high quality. Moreover, whereas competition in industry is based upon a national market, such competition as we have in education is based, at best, upon a highly provincial, local market. It is only in such instances as the national drafting of men for the armed services or in the awarding of merit scholarships on a national basis that we get a glimpse of the glaring way in which schools across the country differ in their academic accomplishments. In short, we in education do not have the same incentive to improve our operations as do men in industry.

Carlson has nicely described school systems as "domesticated" organizations:

> School systems belong to a class of organizations that can be called "domesticated"; that is, they are not compelled to attend to all of their needs. A steady flow of clients is assured, and although they do compete for resources, support is not closely tied to quality of performance. The business firm as a competitive industry, on the other hand, can be seen as existing in a "wild" setting. It is not protected at vulnerable points as is the school system.[10]

Furthermore, I am inclined to suspect that school executives enjoy their "domesticated" status, and by devious means seek to become more and more "domesticated." For example, I surmise that in education we deliberately keep our objectives muddy so as to minimize the possibility of an open and objective comparison between one school system and another. In short, I think we go out of our way to avoid an objective appraisal of what our schools are accomplishing—or failing to accomplish. For this reason, although we may give lip service to the importance of research, we do not want to use it in a real situation because we are afraid that it will reveal, both to ourselves and to the public, many flagrant flaws in American education.

It would be intriguing to speculate on some of the dynamics of personal choice that produce this situation. One wonders to what extent our dilemma is due to the kinds of people who enter education.[11] Our profession is composed, for the most part, of gentle people, many of whom have entered teaching in the first place because they dislike the rough and bruising competitiveness of business. And these gentle people abhor the idea of seeing their organizations become more "wild" than "domesticated." This reluctance might be justifiable were it not that the stakes in the game have now been radically changed by the present international situation.

Now, one salient characteristic of the "wild" environment is that its denizens, either through personal predilection or through coercion from the environment itself, place greater emphasis upon what McClelland and his associates[12] have identified as Need-Achievement, in contrast to Need-Affiliation. The scientist or research man is marked by a high degree of Need-Achievement.[13] Conversely, teachers and school administrators are marked by a high degree of Need-Affiliation. Indeed, one recent unpublished study of the biographical characteristics of a sample of 232 elementary school principals[14] shows that the principals fit neatly into the pattern of what has been described clinically as the "good child"; they are more preoccupied with conformity to group mores and with being liked than with a strong drive to achieve. To achieve, one must excel over others and must risk not being liked by those over whom one excels; the person with high Need-Affiliation is loath to take this risk.

This brings us to what I consider the crux of the entire educational research issue, of which the dissemination question is merely a facet. The problem is the collision between two "cultural systems." View, for a moment, American education from pre-school classes through the graduate school as one cultural system. Likewise, view the world of the scientist as another cultural system. Historically, the cultural system of education has developed in one way; that of science, in another. Each has attracted to its fold different kinds of members, and each has crystallized for its members different customs, rules of the game, and myths. There are some educators who would like to pretend that there is no real difference between the two cultures; I cannot subscribe to this belief. Furthermore, I contend that, if an accommodation is to be achieved between the members of both cultures, we must first quit denying that differences exist and must next boldly delineate both the focuses of these differences and their inexorable implications.

Because education operates within a political milieu, much of what we do in our schools reflects the consumer-orientation of American society. Guided by the slogan that "the customer is always right," we have tended to tailor our action to the "needs"— or rather, the "wants"—of the customer. The result is an effort to make everything as palatable as possible to the customer. The classics are watered down to the comic strip level to make for "easier" reading, and we indulge in even such atrocious simplifications as the caption used to introduce a recent movie version of *Hamlet:* "This is a story about a man who couldn't make up his mind." To appease the customer, our courses throughout the school system are marketed in terms of their painlessness. Bradbury has made a pertinent and perspicacious observation about the British schools, and it is one equally applicable to our own:

> Consider, for instance, the change in the meaning of the word educational. Once it meant "enriching, elevating, enlarging"; it now means "of little or no entertainment value; fuddy-duddy; square." One of our current problems is to divorce our school and university system from the smear of being educational; our Minister of Education has pointed out that some forms of education are congenitally dreary, and if they can't project a new image, they had better go.[15]

Not content with Instant Coffee and Instant Soup, we are determined that we now must have Instant Learning—drip-dry, crease-resistant, and effortless. Also synthetic!

In the aspiration for painless Instant Learning, many educators believe that were we only to find the "right" formula we could then translate all educational research knowledge into the language of everyday life. Both the search for this formula and those who pursue it are doomed to failure for a simple but fundamental reason: the language of science is different from the language of everyday life. This difference is not merely a difference of vocabulary; the very structure of scientific thought is radically different from the structure of thought that governs our daily life. The language of everyday thought can be described in one respect as the language of metaphor; in another, as the language of politics. The language of science, however, is concerned with the precise description of events and experience. It is based upon a "probability" view of the universe, and it seeks to purge itself of value-commitments and exhortations to action: the evidence must speak for itself. Conversely, the language of politics, as George Orwell has nicely demonstrated,[16] trades upon ambiguity, double-talk, and escape clauses. It is patterned upon an Aristotelian rather than a Galilean view of the universe,[17] and it is designed to persuade, to exhort, and to incite listeners to action—an action often so partisan that it violates every scientific rule of evidence. A chasm exists between those of us who think primarily in the language of science and those who think principally in the language of politics. Of course, to some extent we all use both languages, but, since phylogenetically the language of politics is the older of the two, it is the more common and the more entrenched.

The similarities and the differences between these two languages, then, cannot be treated as analogous to the similarities and differences between, for example, English and French. One cannot indiscriminately translate the language of science into the language of politics because the structure and purpose of each language is totally different from that of the other. If one is to understand the words of science he must also understand the structure of scientific thought; there is no short cut.

The scientific method is a way of thinking. The meaning of every concept in science can be understood only in terms of the complete set of operations which constitute its definition. Thus such concepts as "common variance," "degrees of freedom," and "level of statistical significance" each represent shorthand expressions for a long and complex set of operations. Not one of these concepts is comprehensible without a precise understanding of a basic course in statistics. Similarly, the meaning of the "authoritarian personality" cannot be understood apart from the long and complex set of operations reported by Adorno, Frenkel-Brunswik,[18] and others on the development of the "F Scale."

As an example of the scientific method in the field of educational administration, consider a recent study by Hemphill, Griffiths, and Fredericksen[19] of the administrative performance of a national sample of elementary school principals. This cogent study, which has dramatic implications for the selection and training of administrators, employs an elaborate factor-analytic procedure. One cannot reduce a report of such findings to the level of "You, Tarzan—me, Jane." Indeed, the administrator who would capitalize upon the findings of this study must be sufficiently knowledgeable to understand the concept of factorial dimensions.

The attitude taken toward such a study by different groups of administrators starkly illustrates the core of the dissemination issue in education. The majority of administrators is loath to expend the effort necessary to read and fully appreciate this study. These executives will complain that the study is too "technical" and too "deep," and that it contains a "lot of statistics." They will insist that in order to reach a broader public the same findings should be rewritten in "easier" language. The abiding faith nurtured by the proponents of this strategy is that it *must* be possible to translate the concepts of every research investigation into a form that approximates primer-talk. Had this same strategy been applied to the field of physics, Albert Einstein would have undoubtedly remained an unknown and the application of his findings to nuclear power would have been stillborn. He never knew enough to "meet the needs" of the lay reader. (He did once propose, however, that his theory of relativity could be "explained" to laymen in the form of the innocent question, "When does Zürich stop at this train?")

There is a minor group of educators, composed mainly of those who actually engage in research, who respond quite differently to the dissemination issue. They recognize that a slogan approach may be effective for stimulating impulse buying in a supermarket. They also recognize that, since the dissemination of research findings entails more than memorizing a new brand name, this advertising gimmick is inappropriate to our purpose. The real dissemination task is to increase the "literacy" of the consumer. But in education we seem to have preferred to dilute information in an attempt to "meet the needs" of the consumer rather than to raise his skills, so that he may "meet the requirements" of the situation. I am reminded of the exquisite remark made by Edith Wharton while she was working with the American Red Cross in Paris during World War I: "America is the only country in the world where, when two people meet and the first uses a word which the second doesn't understand, it is the first person who is embarrassed."

The difference between meeting the requirements of the situation and meeting the needs of people illuminates the differences between the culture of the scientist and the culture of the educator. The scientist, confronted by the host of complex phenomena presented by the universe, seeks to wrest from Nature her secrets. The phenomena he seeks to understand often are intractable, for Nature is sometimes unwilling to surrender her secrets to the first cavalier who flirts with her; the suitor must measure up to her requirements. The scientist must carve meaning from the phenomena with which he deals even as a Rodin or a Calder must carve from marble or metal whatever figure he gives to the world as his creation. Nature "meets the needs" of neither the scientist nor the artist; instead, she defies them both to meet her demands. Alberto Giacometti gives us beautiful insight into the creative drive:

> "Why does one paint or sculpt?" he said. "It's the need to dominate things, and one can only dominate by understanding. I make a head to understand what I see, not to make a work of art."[20]

Nor is the creative artist's motivation dissimilar to that of the scientist.[21] For this reason, only those men and women who possess a strong achievement-motivation are attracted to careers in science and the creative arts, and only those whose achievement motivation is strong enough and persistent enough survive beyond the point of dilettantism.

There was a time in American education when the requirements for graduation from either the elementary school or the high school were stringent and unequivocal; a time when a doctoral degree from a university attested to its bearer's scholarship and research competence. In this era each child was given the opportunity to receive as much education as his demonstrated achievement warranted. But beginning roughly with the post-World War I period, as rapid industrialization and urbanization took place in America, and as installment buying increased and the Advertising Age flourished, we witnessed new and tumultuous pressures for greater social mobility. Even as the traditional anchorages of society gave way under pressures, so did the schools succumb to the demands of a consumer-oriented society. The teachings of Freud and the doctrines of those anthropologists who stressed cultural relativism provided convenient rationalizations for a shift in the American character from inner-directedness to other-directedness.[22] During this process, what originally was conceived as an *opportunity* to receive an education became converted into the *right* to receive an education.

During those days when Teachers College was the Mecca for American teachers, the Jeffersonian idea of American democracy was prostituted into a cheap and sentimental equation between "democracy" and "equality."[23] Yet this was, after all, only one of the specious political slogans nurtured by the national temper during the years of the great depression.[24] Egregious misinterpretations of John Dewey's doctrines, cocktail party versions of Freud, and a desperate and obsessive urge to meet the needs of all students combined to produce new generations of teachers who were only too willing to reflect in their classrooms the most meretricious features of a consumer-oriented society.[25] Candidates attracted to the education profession increasingly became characterized by a high motivation for affiliation in contrast to a high motivation for achievement. Further impetus was given to this change by the group dynamics movement which was ardently embraced by many colleges of education; professors happily pitched the tone of their classrooms to a new note of "togetherness" and "group-think." In short, the culture of the school system came to emphasize among its personnel human qualities and motivations that are antithetical to the motivations of the scientist and the research man.

A recent incident that occurred at a meeting of educational administration professors pungently illustrates the difference between the dominant values of educators and scientists. I had met for the first time a highly competent psychologist who had been conducting important research in education. While he and I were chatting informally, along with a coterie of his graduate students, he asked my opinion about a colleague whose publications he had read but whom he had never met. I hesitated a moment and then replied, "He's a very nice person." The graduate students smiled knowingly. The psychologist's eyes twinkled with amusement, and he commented laconically, "That's what I thought." (And the next tumbrel lumbered up to the guillotine.)

If one teacher were to make this identical remark about another —"He's a very nice person"—it would be interpreted as high praise; for a scientist, such a judgment is the embrace of death. Why? Because for a scientist the salient criteria are a man's knowledgeability, competence, and productivity. His products must stand on their own merit, and their worth is not to be judged either by their own popularity or by the personal popularity of the investigator. Contrariwise, in teaching, the major criteria are a man's social skills: How well does he get along with other people? Is he pleasant and affable? Does he "adjust" to the local mores?

Yet, at the same time that our society and our schools were promoting togetherness, other-directedness, and ethical relativism, other forces were stimulating a tremendous growth in technology, with the result that the research man suddenly found himself invested with a new and Messianic aura. For the schools to fail to jump on the bandwagon of scientific research was unthinkable; research was made into a shibboleth, even though the concept of research was hideously diluted in the process. And this is where we stand today. In education we are seeking to merge the culture of education and the culture of science; we want to combine the flabbiness of a consumer-orientation with the intellectual rigor demanded by scientific research. One is reminded of a current TV commercial for an American, compact car. The announcer, greasy with affability, discourses at length upon the "compactness" and "economy" of the car. Then, without pausing for fresh breath and with the smile of a complacent camel, he adds, "But it is a BIG car, too," and extols its bigness. In a society that accepts, with no ravage to its sensibilities, the claim that a car is both a small car and a big car too, is there any wonder that we also accept the claim that our schools provide for both quality *and* quantity?

It is not surprising that educators naïvely expect teachers, selected and trained in the consumer-orientation of education, also to perform effectively as productive members within the achievement-oriented culture of science. But here I surmise that we are asking for the impossible. And the sooner we recognize the irreconcilables within our demands, the better off will we all be. The crux of the issue is that in a consumer society most of us are reluctant to admit that we must inevitably lose something in every choice we make.

As Griffith has noted, our society fosters the superficial and discourages the original and the thorough:

> Considering the nature of their work, most people feel rushed. Creativity itself in such a climate must account for its time, and often cannot wait on inspiration but must adapt what is close to hand. We thus tend to take a decorator's interest in other cultures—ransacking museums or far-off places for combinations of colors or design motifs we can borrow from them—and no wonder that we "use up" these other cultures so fast and move on to something new. Fashion can never stay long enough to discover what a culture was really about, but moves on restlessly like one of those crop-picking machines that whooshes across an entire field, gathering in its claws all that it can profitably pick up and leaving behind what would have been uneconomic to pause over. This year a Polynesian theme; next year the Etruscans. The present temper of the arts, to satisfy people's longing for something more than the bleak and efficient functionalism of our uncrafted homes and offices, runs toward diluted borrowings (simplified Victorian, etc.). The designer's task, in adapting a past elegance, is to see that what is intricate be made simple, or capable of easy reproduction, for we no longer have time to be original or thorough: we adapt, we imitate and we multiply, and are becoming a society of tomb robbers.

And in a footnote to this passage, Griffith adds:

> And since our pace is what it is, we then have soda fountains, which are another form of profitable approximation: we must have speed and therefore accept clutter; we demand economy and must tolerate crowding and rapidity of turnover. Drugstore counters are a hurried substitute for restaurants, and the American, understanding their function, puts up with their annoyances. While a counterman slops an egg into a pan and whips up some ready-made tuna mash, an adman—at a low unit cost—has been at work on the menus, spreading his crispy crunchy promises that have no relation to what will be delivered; for it is the American custom never to acknowledge a lowering of standards in service or product, but to deny stoutly that anything has been lost along with what has been gained.[26]

We Americans persist in suppressing from our consciousness the discrepancy between the glowing advertisement and the product itself, between the promise and the fulfillment. Even as the ready-made tuna mash served at the drugstore fountain belies its savory image on the menu card, so do our devout statements about what we are doing in education give the lie to our accomplishments. Thus within the citadel we devise mouth-watering descriptions for our educational menu-card: "The Pursuit of Excellence," "Education for Creativity," "Special Programs for the Gifted," "Guidance," "Teaching Geared to Individual Differences," "Education for the Space-Age." But any correlation between the slogans and the mash served to the students is purely coincidental. And even as the decorators pursue a Polynesian theme one year, and an Etruscan one the next, so do our preschool faculty conferences establish a new, enticing theme—with slogans to match—for each new school year.[27] At the start of the school year the administrative staff whips up a new froth of enthusiasm, appetizing enough to make the teachers forget—at least, for the moment—that last year's froth provided no nutrition.

But in a society where words have been ripped loose from their semantic moorings, it is easy to become anesthetized to the fraud of our empty, verbal litanies. Indeed, it is an anesthesia of this very kind that makes us fail to see how inevitable the collision must be between the culture of education and the culture of research.[28]

Nor are we going to solve the dissemination problem by trying to force the culture of research into meeting the needs of the culture of education. If an accommodation is to be achieved between these two cultures, I submit that the change will have to be made the other way around; the culture of education will have to be modified to meet the requirements of the culture of research. And I am not sure that we in education are at present prepared, or even willing, to accomplish this.

These remarks about the dissemination of research findings in education would not be complete without comment about a popular suggestion that has been offered as a solution to our dilemma: we develop "middlemen" who will function between the scientist and the practitioner and who will "translate" the findings of the scientist into a form more comprehensible to the practitioner. This is, indeed, a tempting idea. There is only one thing wrong with it: it will not work.

The advocates of this idea gloss over the fact that nothing remotely similar exists in other professions. The physician, in his training, must learn to read and understand medical research; he is trained to draw upon primary sources. Popular opinion notwithstanding, I must denounce as a canard the suggestion that the *Readers' Digest* functions as the middleman for the medical profession. The lawyer, too, must deal with the precedents of prior cases and must be equipped to function without an interlocutory middleman. Likewise, the engineer must have sufficient knowledge of physics and structural mechanics to apply new research findings to the practical tasks with which he deals from day to day. Indeed, in proposing that educational middlemen be trained to function between the scientist and the practitioner we admit to a failing that—at least, in this respect—disqualifies education as a profession. The core of this failing is not hard to find: we need only look at our undergraduate programs (and, sadly, even at our graduate programs) for teachers to see how seldom our students are required to deal with primary sources. This is in marked contrast to what takes place in such disciplines as psychology and biology. To spare our students from effort and boredom, the material in education textbooks is presented to them in the form of predigested pap. Indeed, some of the textbooks seem to be so removed from primary sources that one surmises that they have been "written" by applying scissors, Scotch tape, and a table of random numbers to the ten most popular books previously published on the same subject.

The notion of the educational middleman is based upon another fallacy: the ideas of the research man can, or even need to be, translated into another language. To some extent, the scientist himself is at fault in failing to communicate effectively, and I do not intend to exculpate him for this. When his jargon blocks communication he must be condemned. But here I believe that we must take into account the often-disregarded point that there are two kinds of jargon—sacred and profane. Let me deal with these in reverse order.

Profane jargon is composed of clichés, half-formulated concepts, slogans, loaded words, and parades of abstract terms for which there are no clear referents. Jargon of this kind usually results from the infrangible fact that the author's ideas are not clear. Because his ideas are not clear he covers his bed of imprecise ideas with a blanket to match—a patchwork quilt of fuzzy language. This jargon is marked by a dearth of concrete images, by an array of inert, passive verbs, and by nouns that have been converted into new, grotesque verbs. In these instances, the scientist is inclined to invent new words simply because the poverty of his own language and his cursory acquaintance with literature prevent him from recognizing that most of his ideas could be expressed in simple, and often vigorous, English. This type of vocabulary must be condemned because it fails to communicate even what few clear ideas it may contain. But even more, profane jargon must be denounced on aesthetic grounds: it is ugly.

Jargon may also mean the technical language of a science. Because science must be conceived, in large part, as a special language, and *because the syntax of science is as important as its content*, we cannot eliminate the use of special language and special concepts in scientific writing.[29] This jargon results not from fuzzily conceived ideas but from ideas that have been defined operationally and usually with devastating clarity. This is sacred jargon, and it is not to be defiled for the blandishments of the popularizers.

Here is where we run into a refractory problem. The scientist's critic feels uncomfortable in the presence of new concepts and concludes that the author's technical terms are just new words for old ideas; he then summarily condemns as jargon not only the words but the concepts themslves. This allegation misses the point: the scientist has created, in fact, not just new words, but new ideas. In creating new ideas the scientist classifies phenomena into fresh categories—boxes that do not always coincide with the categories presented by naïve experience. These new categories cannot always be described in orthodox, everyday language. Faced with this contradiction, the critic, speaking to the scientist, resorts to the gambit, "Can't you use ordinary words to say what you mean? Don't you *really* mean . . .?" In short, the critic tries to force the scientist's concepts into the structure of his own verbal categories. The only answer the honest scientist can give is, "No, I don't *really* mean that at all. I mean precisely what I have said." The critic bristles, for he considers his own categories inviolate. To understand what the scientist is saying, the critic must now relinquish his preconceived categories. In order to understand any single concept in the scientist's language, the critic must first understand the total theoretical context within which each concept is imbedded. This requires greater effort than the critic is willing to expend; it is easier for him to ridicule the scientist's legitimate use of jargon than for him to exert the energy necessary to understand it. The scientist's own abusive use of profane jargon allows the critic to justify his own unfounded attack upon the scientist's use of sacred jargon. Unfortunately, many scientists make themselves easy victims for such attacks.

Misunderstanding on both sides arises out of inertia or sheer laziness. Profane jargon impedes communication, and the blame must be placed on the scientist's slothful attitude toward clear writing. The critic's resistance to sacred jargon equally hinders communication, and the blame rests with the critic's failure to differentiate between the language of science and the language of everyday life.

These obstacles to the success of the middleman proposal are formidable enough, but typical attempts to follow through on this proposal are quickly grounded by another starkly practical problem: where do we find competent middlemen? Certainly, the fatuous and condescending attitude of both the scientist and the educational practitioner toward prospective middlemen is less than decent. Even the advocates of the middleman plan imply that the middleman should serve as a type of editorial assistant, at a status level only slightly above that of the average secretary and certainly below that of the research technician. The men who hold to this view become chagrined when they discover that they cannot locate a suitable candidate for the job. I have known only two or three people who could qualify. Although these people were interested in this work and had been interviewed for such jobs, in each instance they could only reject with contempt the niggardly salary offered. Nor were they willing to be treated as subprofessional lackeys. I think that we must recognize an uncomfortable truth: a competent middleman must possess skills of a different, and possibly higher order, than those of either the scientist or the practitioner. The middleman jobs are top-level positions that should command salaries commensurate with the skills demanded. But I know of no college of education, and certainly of no school system, that has budgeted enough funds for a skilled middleman. Further, I do not believe that the ego of either the scientist or the practitioner will permit him to be gracious in granting a middleman the status he deserves. I repeat: this is not a job for a young manuscript editor or a part-time employee from the English department; and it is not a job for an indigent but well-intentioned doctorate student in education. If the middleman proposal is to work at all—and I am not sure that it will—then we would have to create a new occupation. We would have to budget ample funds for the men and women to fill this role and would have to devise a rich program for training a new professional breed. If this were done, and were done with sufficient support, perhaps the effort would pay off. But we should realize at the outset how enormous a task this would be.

Yet, even if we should be able to persuade legions of top-quality middlemen to devote themselves to the dissemination task in educational research, their work would be futile unless we can simultaneously accomplish four objectives:

1. Raise the standards of research so as to produce a profes-

sional corps which can understand, respect, and act upon research findings.

2. Recruit for the profession, *and retain in it*, young men and women who possess strong achievement-motivations, conjoined with the intellectual and creative capacities required for research careers.

3. Strengthen teachers' motivation to do research by rewarding such efforts and by developing within our schools an organizational climate that encourages creative inquiry.

4. Incite competition among the schools and ruthlessly publicize not alone those schools that are doing exemplary work, but also those that are not.

My views can be construed as being gloomy, but I could not be so scathing in my indictment of the present situation in educational research did I not trust in the ultimate victory of rationality and possess deep faith in the future of American education. To save the patient, a surgeon sometimes must cut deep. Yet a responsible physician will not even bother to operate unless he believes that there are greater than chance possibilities that the patient will survive, and unless he knows, too, that the risk of the operation is a lesser evil than are the imminent and certain ravages of the disease itself. Analogously, in the surgical role that I have taken toward the "culture" of education, I, too, take risks. But I take these risks not because I despise the patient, but because I love and respect him and because I am gravely worried about his welfare.

NOTES FOR CHAPTER 8

1. Prepared for the Phi Delta Kappa symposium held at the University of Oregon, July 11, 1961. Published under the title "Problems in the Use of Communication Media in the Dissemination and Implementation of Educational Research," Ch. 6 in Stanley Elam and Keith Goldhammer (eds.), *Dissemination and Implementation. Third*

Annual Phi Delta Kappa Symposium on Educational Research (Bloomington, Ind.: Phi Delta Kappa, 1962), pp. 171-200. The last section of this chapter was also published separately under the title "Jargon— Sacred and Profane," *Phi Delta Kappan,* **43**, No. 6 (March 1962), pp. 237-239. Reprinted here by permission of the publishers. However, I must disclaim responsibility for the title under which this chapter appeared in the book edited by Elam and Goldhammer; that title is an excruciating example of the very "profane jargon" that I have condemned in this chapter.

2. Asahel D. Woodruff, "Educational Research and the Curriculum," *The School Review,* **66**, No. 4 (Winter 1958), p. 402. Copyright 1958 by the University of Chicago.

3. If the teacher's graduate committee chairman were not to concede that the disjointed set of lesson plans which the candidate submits as a thesis actually does constitute research, the poor teacher would not get his M.A. degree and hence would not obtain his increment on the local salary schedule. And after all, what else is the purpose of a Master's degree?

4. I, too, agree that good research is not confined to the statistical. See, for example, Chs. 6 and 7. The pivotal issue is whether the investigator uses a method appropriate for the type of study he conducts, and whether he chooses other than the statistical method not solely because he is unable to cope with the precision required by this method.

5. I recently heard one university president sententiously deny that this was the case in his state. He declared that only those high school graduates were admitted to the university who, on the basis of certain high school grades and college freshmen tests, secured a "predicted" grade point average of 1.7 (on a scale from zero to four this represents a grade level between D and C). With "standards" such as these, it might be easier, and certainly no less exclusive, to admit every candidate who has a body temperature of 98.6.

6. Marcella M. Miller, "A Psychological Analysis of Written Compositions of Elementary-School Principals" (Master's Thesis, Department of Educational Psychology, University of Utah, 1961).

7. The type-token ratio devised by Wendell Johnson. See Wendell Johnson, *People in Quandaries* (New York: Harper & Brothers, 1946), pp. 500-502.

8. I fear, too, that with the passage of time the great institutions will become greater while the mediocre ones will become poorer. The administrators of the latter group will, of course, make pompous,

public statements about the high standards they maintain in both faculty and students. I surmise that these administrators repeat such statements as much to convince themselves as to convince a gullible public.

9. Used with the writer's permission, but naturally no point is to be gained by disclosing his identity.

10. Richard O. Carlson, "Succession and Performance Among School Superintendents," *Administrative Science Quarterly*, 6, No. 2 (September 1961), p. 227. A more detailed report of this study, by the same author, has been published under the title *Executive Succession and Organizational Change* (Chicago: Midwest Administration Center, University of Chicago, 1961).

11. See, for example, Egon G. Guba, Charles Bidwell, and Phillip Jackson, "Occupational Choice and the Teaching Career," *Educational Research Bulletin*, 38, No. 1 (January 14, 1959), pp. 1-12, 27-28. Note also Jack N. Elton's study, "A Comparison of Personal Value-Patterns: Elementary Teachers, Elementary Teacher-Trainees, and Art-Trainees" (Master's Thesis, Department of Educational Administration, University of Utah, 1961).

12. David McClelland *et al., The Achievement Motive* (New York: Appleton-Century-Crofts, 1953).

13. Ann Roe, *The Making of a Scientist* (New York: Dodd-Mead, 1953).

14. Andrew W. Halpin and Don B. Croft, "The Biographical Characteristics of Elementary-School Principals," Unpublished report to the Cooperative Research Branch, United States Office of Education (Bureau of Educational Research, University of Utah, 1960).

15. Malcolm Bradbury, Extracts from "All Dressed Up and Nowhere to Go," © *Punch*, London, 1961, No. 6314, p. 433.

16. George Orwell, "Politics and the English Language," in *A Collection of Essays* (Garden City, N. Y.: Doubleday Anchor Books, Doubleday & Company, Inc., 1954), pp. 162-177.

17. See Kurt Lewin, *A Dynamic Theory of Personality* (New York: McGraw-Hill Book Co., Inc., 1935), Ch. 1.

18. Theodor W. Adorno *et al., The Authoritarian Personality* (New York: Harper & Brothers, 1950).

19. John K. Hemphill *et al., Administrative Performance and Personality* (New York: Teachers College, Bureau of Publications, Columbia University, 1962).

20. As quoted by Alexander Liberman in *The Artist in His Studio* (New York: The Viking Press, 1960), p. 69.

21. See Harold Taylor, *Art and the Intellect* (New York: The Museum of Modern Art, 1960); also, Lawrence K. Frank, *The School as Agent for Cultural Renewal* (Cambridge, Mass.: Harvard University Press, 1959), p. 32.

22. For a brilliant analysis of the social impact of Freud, see Richard LaPiere, *The Freudian Ethic* (New York: Duell, Sloan and Pearce, 1959). The shift in the American character toward other-directedness is reported, of course, in David Riesman *et al.*, *The Lonely Crowd* (New Haven, Conn.: Yale University Press, 1950).

23. There are two democratic traditions: the Anglo-American with its emphasis upon liberty, and the French or Continental with its emphasis upon equality. George H. Sabine ("The Two Democratic Traditions," *The Philosophical Review,* **61**, No. 4 [October 1952], pp. 451-474) has analyzed the incompatibilities between these two traditions. It is amusing to note that demagogues and vulgarians, intent upon using "democracy" for their own purposes, unfailingly favor the tradition of Rousseau over that of John Locke. See, too, Gerald Johnson, "Overloaded Democracy," *Harper's Magazine,* **199**, No. 1192 (September 1949), pp. 83-87.

24. Out of this same temper emerged America's uncritical acceptance of Keynesian economics.

25. Malcolm Bradbury's comment on consumer society ("All Dressed Up and Nowhere to Go," © *Punch,* London, 1961, No. 6317, p. 536) is apposite: "Let me not give the impression that the consumer society which I have described in these articles is a grim, anonymous world, a world harsh to live in; it is clear that if this were so few of us would wish to live in it. As it is, most of us do; most of us have, indeed, never had it so good, and since both of our political parties are dedicated to enlarging its style and its scope we may assume that it is what we all want. It is a pleasant world, a world that softens the harsh realities, a world that doesn't strain us too hard. It is a world that is dedicated to happiness; it tells us what happiness is (happiness is buying things) and then provides the opportunity for it. It is a world in which human decency and respect still have their place; thus Dr. Ernest Dichter tells us in his book *The Strategy of Desire* that he has discovered by motivation research that undertakers will improve trade if instead of going to a house of mourning and asking 'Where's the body?' they say 'Where's Mr. Smith?' So things which were once done because humanity was considered a value are being done again; they are good for business. Friendliness has not gone; thus if you omit to renew your subscription to *Reader's Digest* you will receive a letter

from a most amiable girl saying that she is your friend and can scarcely sleep at night until you renew. Public relations takes over the equipment of private relations—and the pleasantnesses and decencies of life are not lost, just used differently. The consumer society is a pleasant and lulling experience, like stepping into a warm bath, and it would be churlish to deny the pleasures of it."

26. Thomas Griffith, *The Waist-High Culture* (New York: Harper & Brothers, 1959), pp. 205-206, and footnote on p. 205.

27. In our culture, the desperation to be different in ways that do not really matter becomes pathetic. One Salt Lake City realtor currently is advertising Oriental ranch houses. In a similar vein, a Los Angeles realtor is advertising Hawaiian bungalows, with Roman bath. In a correspondingly frantic attempt to titillate the consumer's fancy, an enterprising gift shop in a Los Angeles suburb is now selling genuine Russian ikons; if the buyer wishes, he can have a "custom" ikon made to order in his own image. In the merchant's frenzy to incite his customers to keep ahead of the Joneses, I can't understand how he ever overlooked the obvious but perfect sales pitch: "If I kon, you kon, too." In the idea of having ikons made to order, I find a poetic irony for a civilization that finally has reached the point where man literally makes his God in his own image.

28. This collision presents a problem similar to what Charles P. Snow has discussed in *The Two Cultures and the Scientific Revolution* (New York: Cambridge University Press, 1959). But I think that Snow has oversimplified the issue; there are three cultures in conflict, not two. In addition to the clash between the humanities and the sciences, there rages a further struggle between both of these traditions and the tradition of politics and the market-place. Although Snow has touched upon this third struggle in *Science and Government* (Cambridge, Mass.: Harvard University Press, 1960), the ramifications of this complex, three-way conflict deserve a far more critical analysis than they have yet received.

29. Ernst Cassirer, *An Essay on Man* (New Haven, Conn.: Yale University Press, 1944), Ch. 11.

All I say is by way of discourse, and nothing by way of advice. I should not speak so boldly if it were my due to be believed.

Montaigne

INDEX

Superscript note reference numbers—e.g., [25]—follow those text pages listed in which authors have not been identified by name.